W9-CGL-089

manufacturing
Desire

Arthur Asa Berger

manufacturing
Desire

Media, Popular Culture, and Everyday Life

Transaction Publishers
New Brunswick (U.S.A.) and London (U.K.)

First paperback printing 2008
Copyright © 1996 by Transaction Publishers, New Brunswick, New Jersey.

All rights reserved under International and Pan-American Copyright Conventions. No part of this book may be reproduced or transmitted in any form or by any means, electronic or mechanical, including photocopy, recording, or any information storage and retrieval system, without prior permission in writing from the publisher. All inquiries should be addressed to Transaction Publishers, Rutgers—The State University of New Jersey, 35 Berrue Circle, Piscataway, New Jersey 08854-8042. www.transactionpub.com

This book is printed on acid-free paper that meets the American National Standard for Permanence of Paper for Printed Library Materials.

Library of Congress Catalog Number: 95-37827
ISBN: 978-1-56000-226-0 (cloth); 978-1-4128-0765-4 (paper)
Printed in the United States of America

Library of Congress Cataloging-in-Publication Data

Berger, Arthur Asa, 1933-
    Manufacturing desire : media, popular culture, and everyday life / Arthur Asa Berger.
        p. cm.
    Includes bibliographical references and index.
    ISBN 1-56000-226-3 (alk. paper)
    1. Mass media and culture—United States. 2. Popular culture—United States. I. Title.

P94.6.B47   1995
302.230973—dc20   95-37827
                                                                      CIP

For David W. Noble

Contents

VII Everyday Life: Introduction

VIII Comparative Perspectives: Introduction

Acknowledgments

I would like to thank Mary Curtis, who suggested I do this book, and all the people at Transaction Publishers, who have done such a professional job of publishing it. I've had a long and happy relationship with Irving Louis Horowitz and Mary Curtis and their colleagues at Transaction Publishers, and have appreciated their friendship and encouragement over the past twenty years.

I've benefitted from the work (and in some cases the friendship and support) of a number of people and would like to acknowledge my appreciation by naming some of them: Aaron and Mary Wildavsky, David Noble, Mulford Q. Sibley, Ralph Ross, Sigmund Freud, Karl Marx, Groucho Marx, Stan Lee, Umberto Eco, Roland Barthes, Claude Lévi-Strauss, George Gerbner, Michael Real, Vladimir Propp, Ferdinand de Saussure, Victor and Leoni Rosonoer, Stanley Milgram, Marshall McLuhan, Jean-Marie Benoist, Isaac and Roz Silberman, Peter Clarke, Mike Noll, Daniel Dayan, Elihu Katz, Chaim Eyal, Ron Compesi, Stuart Hyde, Herbert Zettl, Howard and Barbara Ginsberg, Maxwell Henry Goldberg, Kim Schroder, Karl Erik Rosengren, Steen Sauerberg, Klaus Bruhn Jensen, Bo Reimer, Giusseppe Gadda Conti, Mary Douglas, David Manning White, Richard Hoggart, Johan Huizinga, Bronislaw Malinowski, Margin Grotjahn, Vyacheslav Ivanov, Mircea Eliade, Agostino Lombardo, M. M. Bakhtin, Fustel de Coulanges, and Yuri Lotman.

I am grateful to the following publishers for allowing me to reprint a number of articles that appeared earlier (I have revised most of them for this book): the Haworth Press for "Of Mice and Men"; The International Society for General Semantics for "Eleven Ways of Looking at the Gulf War"; and Longman Publishers for my article "The Manufacture of Desire." My article "Comics and Popular Culture: Not Just Kids Stuff" appeared in the July, 1990 issue of *The World & I,* and my article "Funnies are Good for Us" appeared in the May, 1992 issue of *The World & I,* and are reprinted with permission of *The World & I,* a publication of *The Washington Times Corporation*, copyright © 1990, 1992. My article "Texts in Contexts" appeared in F. Korzenny and S. Ting Toomey, *Mass Media Effects Across Cultures*, 1992 and is reprinted by permission of Sage Publications. My articles "1984: The Commercial," "The Terminator," and "Popular Culture and The Public Arts," (originally published at the introduction to the recent Transaction edition of Gilbert Seldes, *The Public Arts*) are published with permission of Transaction Publishers. My article "What's in a Joke?" appeared in *Elementa: Journal of Slavic Studies & Comparative Cultural Semiotics* (vol. 1, no. 3, 1994) and is reprinted by permission of Harwood Academic Publishers. My article "The Semiotics of Public and Private Space" appeared in *Media Development* (vol. 37, March 1990). The other chapters were written specifically for this book.

Introduction: Terror, Media, Popular Culture, and Everyday Life in America

When I published *Television as an Instrument of Terror* in 1980, I was ambivalent about the term *terror*. I used it, first of all, as a "grabber," as something to attract people's attention, but also because I thought television had revolutionary and subversive powers that people, as a rule, didn't recognize. I had used the title once before, in the first of a number of columns I wrote for *Focus* magazine, published by public television station KQED in San Francisco.

Television as a Mindless Medium

For most people then (and perhaps now) television was seen as a rather mindless medium of entertainment and, therefore, not terribly important in the scheme of things. The idea of connecting television and terror seemed rather preposterous. Television called to mind situation comedies, variety shows, sports shows, news programs, and commercials; silly stuff, for the most part. Where do you find the terror?

I found terror in the hidden compulsions that television spread, in the bodies of the actresses and models in commercials that gave men a ridiculous view of what women were supposed to look like and made ordinary women feel that there was something wrong with them, and in the upper-middle-class visions of the good life that television portrayed as normal, thereby suggesting that all who did not have the so-called good things in life were somehow deficient. That was before little children had been taught by television to be conscious of brand names and before adolescents started killing one another for $150 sneakers.

I saw television (and other media as well as the popular art works carried on them) as inflicting a reign of terror on people, which was all the worse since people didn't not recognize what was happening to them.

1

All they knew is that they were uneasy about what they had achieved and what they could expect and seemed trapped, all too often, in a vicious cycle of insatiable consumer lust, endless debt, and a corrosive sense of envy (or, in sociological terms, *relative deprivation*).

I suggested that television was an instrument of terror, the primary instrument of terror, because it was the dominant medium of the day. It still is. Recent figures suggest the average person in America watches four hours of television per day and spends the equivalent of nine years of his or her life in front of the television set. Television, as an audio-visual medium, has the greatest impact on individuals of all the daily media; only film, shown in movie houses with relatively huge images and high-fidelity sound, has a more powerful visceral effect.

As I wrote in my column, "The Last Word" (in August, 1976):

> The measure of television's power is that hardly anyone is aware of it—though they may watch it five or six hours a day—and young people, even adolescents, cannot imagine what life was like before television. (What did people *do?*) Young people are subjected to an estimated 650,000 commercials while they are growing up, each of which pressures them to buy this or that. Is there no terror there?

> And what about all the people who do not "measure up" to the images and life-style television projects? What about those who are not middle class, what about women who do not have the "correct" bodies, what about those who cannot afford the products hawked and feel anxiety and even self-hatred? What about all of us who are no longer, God forbid, young?

That article was published in 1976. That was before television had played a major role in changing, perhaps revolutionizing (some would say destroying) our society as we knew it; before television had changed, perhaps corrupted, the political process.

Television and Terror in Contemporary American Society

Now, in a society that seems, in many areas, to be in advanced stages of disorganization, in a society where students bring guns to school, where eleven-year-old children are "hit men" ("rubbed out" by fourteen-year-old killers), where televised news reports of killings have become an everyday, routine experience (the televised equivalent of a standing head in print media), the idea that television might be an instrument of terror does not seem quite so absurd. Television is full of gratuitous violence and what can best be described as soft-core pornography. Violence and sex rule the airways and often come together in perverse combinations of violence as sexual gratification and at other times as violent sexual gratification.

The medium itself has certain structural characteristics, which I discuss in this book, that lead to disorientation and a kind of moral numbness. But there is also the content to be considered. Television can bring us great plays, operas, music, exciting sporting events, and all kinds of other wonderful things. There is nothing in the medium itself that necessitates the violence and hypersexuality we find in it. But television is a mass medium and economic and commercial considerations tend to (but not always, fortunately) drive the programming decisions, so what we get, all too often, is a cultural "wasteland."

We cannot say that television—the medium everyone loves to hate— is the sole cause of our numerous social problems, only that it is a contributing factor; maybe even a major contributing factor. But that is enough, I would suggest, for us to start thinking about what we should do—before the terror grows more ubiquitous, before our social institutions fall into greater disarray, or those that are in trouble fall apart.

The tragedy, I believe, is that a medium that could do so much does so little, that could be a means of enlightenment has become an instrument of terror.

Screens and Violence

I realize that statistics show that most kinds of crime are "down" in 1994, but most people perceive our society as a violent and dangerous one, a so-called "cruel world," and we know that people's perceptions affect their behavior. This perception is shaped, in large measure, by local and network television news programs, which are full of stories about drug related killings, drive-by shootings, drug busts, and various other crime stories, disasters, and so on. Large numbers of people don't read newspapers or magazines but get their news only from television. In this respect, with its focus only on certain areas of life, television news is most decidedly a perverted mirror of society. We can generalize things and say that most of the screens we watch—in movie houses, on television, and in our video game players—are permeated with violence.

On Media-Culture

This book is about the mass media, popular culture (sometimes called the popular arts or the public arts), and everyday life. As I use the term, the *mass media* carry or spread or broadcast various popular arts and the *media* and the *popular arts* play a major role in shaping our everyday lives. The media and the popular arts have become, for many people, the content of our leisure hours: we watch television four hours a day, listen to the radio driving to and from work, listen to recorded music, read comics and other magazines, perhaps read the newspapers, and play video games. We can tie the mass media and popular culture together into something called media-culture, which covers both the media and the art works or texts they carry.

Education and Instruction

All of these experiences help "educate" people; we learn from our experiences and media-culture is the content of our experiences. We can make a distinction between education and instruction. I use the term *education* to cover all of our experiences and suggest that we learn from our experiences, even though we may not be aware that this process of education is going on. *Instruction,* on the other hand, involves formal teaching by professors or others, who usually are certificated, and who presumably have the best interests of their students in mind.

If we recognize that all the television shows we watch, all the movies we see, all the comic strips we read, all the video games we play, are "educating" us, are giving us ideas about what is good and bad, about how to solve problems, about how to relate to other people in society, about what our responsibilities are to others, then the way we think about our media-culture will be different from the way we would think about it if we see our media-culture as little more than mindless entertainments.

It is the "education" we are getting from our media-culture that is the subject of this book. I examine commercials, television shows, comics, film, humor, and everyday life in terms of what beliefs and values are found in them, what attitudes toward ourselves and our societies are contained in them, how they achieve their effects, and what they reflect about American culture and society. In this Introduction I introduce a number of topics and ideas and methods of analysis dealt with and exemplified in more detail in various chapters in the book.

The Problem of Consciousness

I don't believe that the creators of mass-mediated texts consciously try to educate us; writers create stories and teleplays and screenplays that they think will entertain people, though sometimes they deal overtly with social and political themes in these texts. I don't think people who read or see or listen to these texts are aware, generally speaking, of the extent to which these texts are educating them, giving them ideas about the nature of love and life and society.

We are, after all, dealing with works of art—of varying degrees of quality, admittedly, but nevertheless, creative works that have to be interpreted as such. The problem with the way scholars deal with popular culture, as I have pointed out in various writings, is that the humanists look at the aesthetic qualities of these texts and neglect their social and political significance and that social scientists look at the social and political significance of these texts and neglect their aesthetic aspects.

With the development of cultural studies, things are changing, and we now have scholars from a number of different disciplines examining mass-mediated texts and trying to make sense of them, using essentially a multidisciplinary perspective. That is the approach I have taken and you will find I use a number of disciplines or approaches in analyzing the media, popular culture, and everyday life. My method is to use whichever disciplines offer, in combination, the best reading and understanding of the text or topic under consideration.

One paradox we face is that relatively simple texts, or to be more accurate, ones that seem to be relatively simple, often require rather complicated efforts of analysis and interpretation. This is due to the fact that texts and works of art (even ones that are not elevated or sophisticated) are, by nature, complex phenomena and don't yield themselves easily to explication. Meaning always has to be elicited from works; they don't volunteer very much. When you have texts that rely on sound and visual images, like television and film and video games, things become even more difficult and problematical.

Areas of Concern in Dealing with Media-Culture

This book, let me point out, is not a revision of *Television as an Instrument of Terror* but an entirely new book, though it deals with the same topics: the media, popular culture, and everyday life. In the original *Television as an Instrument of Terror*, I suggested that there were four focal points that one could examine in dealing with popular culture, all of which were connected to one another:

1. the work of art (or text),
2. America (the society in which the text is found),
3. the artist (author), and
4. the audience.

What I left out was the medium through which the art work is made available to audiences. If we put the medium in the center of things we arrive at the following diagram:

Focal Points in Analysis of Media Culture

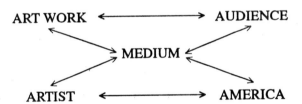

In analyzing popular culture, we can focus on any one of the above topics or several of them at the same time, depending upon our interests.

If we focus on the art work or text, for example, and examine a movie or television narrative, we can use media aesthetics to see how the text achieves its effects, or semiotics to see how it generates meaning. Or we can look at the roles of women, the socioeconomic background of the characters, the use of stereotyping, and similar sociological concerns. In addition, we can consider the value system and beliefs of the main characters and the way the text relates to different political cultures in our society. Or we can use literary theory and deal with topics such as theme, point of view, and stylistic aspects. We can also use psychoanalytic thought to investigate topics such as the motivations of the characters and the way symbols and other phenomena might affect the psyches of the audiences of a given text.

The various disciplines and intellectual domains that can be brought to bear on a text are shown in the diagram below:

Modes of Textual Analysis

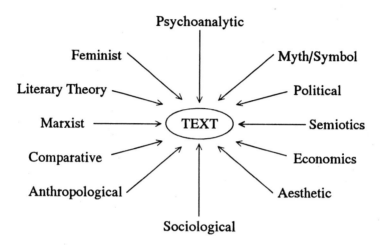

We can add other methodologies to this chart as well, though I have suggested a number of the most important ones. What is important to recognize is that there are many different disciplines that can be used in examining texts. (I have shown how different disciplines deal with humor in my *Blind Men and Elephants: Perspectives on Humor,* 1995, and have also discussed methodological considerations in more detail in my *Essentials of Mass Communication Theory,* 1995.)

We can do the same kind of thing for the other focal points in the chart or, in some cases, deal with several concerns—such as the relation between the artist and the audience or the relation between the artist and the media. There are, then, a number of different areas we can investigate, each of which can be investigated using different disciplines, depending upon what we are interested in and what we want to find out.

We should also recognize that criticism doesn't appear "out of the blue." Critics, media analysts, whatever you want to call them, always have some discipline or methodology or concern that they consider to be paramount, behind their work. What this means is that critics usually are attached to some approach or "school" and this attachment colors their work. Some critics are Marxists, because they believe that Marxist theory best explains how texts and media function in society, while other critics might believe that semiotic theory, psychoanalytical theory, or ethical theory is the best approach to use.

The mass media and popular culture are best thought of as battle-grounds, where armies of critics fight with one another about method-ological matters and the applications of various approaches and methodologies to the focal points mentioned above. When dealing with texts, for example, the question is not who is right and who is wrong, but who offers the most profound, interesting, and illuminating analysis and what methodologies do they use to do so.

Many critics use a combination of approaches, because they believe more than one approach is necessary to interpret texts. You will find, for example, that I use semiotics and psychoanalytic theory in my analysis of the famous Mackintosh "1984" commercial and offer an example of eight different critical perspectives in my article "Eight Scholars in Search of an Interpretation," which shows how eight different disciplines or approaches can be used to analyze a joke. Given the complexity of texts and the many different ways of analyzing them, it is not unusual, then, to be able to find a number of different interpretations of a given text.

In addition, although individuals make their own choices when they decide what to watch on television at a given hour on a given night (or, to be more exact, what to select from what is available), when they make their choices they become members of that text's audience. We can segment or classify audiences according to age, gender, income, race, socioeconomic class, values and life-styles, and other similar de-mographic and psychographic categories.

This is done by organizations that sell this information to local sta-tions and networks and this information is used to set rates for commer-cials. Television stations and networks, we should recognize, sell audiences to advertisers and the nature of these audiences is very im-portant. A large audience of people who have little discretionary in-come is not worth much to many advertisers. An audience composed of people with a great deal of money is of considerable interest to the mak-ers of expensive cars and other luxury items. So the relation between a text and its audience is of interest not only to media critics and analysts but also to advertisers and, of course, to the writers and directors and others who create texts and want them to be read or watched, by as many people as possible, also—by the largest common denominator, which is not the same thing as the lowest common denominator.

We are now in a position to consider a theoretical topic that has been argued about by critics of different persuasions for many years—the mass culture argument. Are audiences full of alienated individuals who are best described as "vidiots" and swallow everything the television set "feeds" them, as many critics have suggested? Or is that characterization of audiences mean-spirited and simplistic?

The Mass Culture Argument

Social scientists have been arguing about mass culture for many years. In 1953, more than forty years ago, in an article entitled "Communication Research and the Concept of the Mass" (published in the *American Sociological Review*), sociologist Eliot Friedson wrote:

> In the dictionary the mass is defined as the great body of the people of a nation, as contrasted to some special body like a particular social class. Lazarsfeld and Kendall use such a definition when they write "The term 'mass' then, is truly applicable to the medium of radio, for it more than the other media, reaches all groups of the population uniformly." This notion of the mass merely implies that a mass communication may be distinguished from other kinds of communication by the fact that it is addressed to a large cross-section of a population rather than only one or a few individuals or a special part of the population. It also makes the implicit assumption of some technical means of transmitting the communication in order that the communication may reach at the same time all the people forming the cross-section of the population. (vol. 18, June, 1953)

Friedson argues that this definition is inadequate and moves on to a second interpretation of the term *mass* that lists its four basic characteristics : it is heterogeneous, the individuals in the mass society are separated, they do not know one another, and there is no leadership to this mass.

He then quotes sociologist Herbert Blumer, who wrote (in an article "The Molding of Mass Behavior Through the Motion Picture" [from *Publications of the American Sociological Society,* 1936]) a number of criticisms that were typically made in those days about "the mass(es)":

> [the mass] has no social organization, no body of customs and tradition, no established set of rules or rituals, no organized group of sentiments, no structure or

status roles, and no established leadership. It merely consists of an aggregation of individuals who are separate, detached, anonymous.

These characteristics of the mass were also used to describe "mass culture," and contemporary critics have used it when dealing with the mass media and popular culture.

Friedson points out that these notions are all derived from theoretical presuppositions and that they are not factual. He mentions movie-going, which is often a group-based activity. He reminds us that "word of mouth advertising" is considered to be the most effective kind of advertising there is, which suggests that members of audiences are not as separated or estranged from one another as "mass" theorists claim they are.

He also mentions opinion leaders. Opinion-leader theory argues that there is a "two-step flow," that people belong to small groups and are exposed to opinion leaders and often are affected by them. All of these matters suggest that people are not as separated from one another or alienated from one another and society in general as Blumer and other mass society theorists have suggested. Blumer's article was written in 1936, so we can see that the argument about mass society and mass culture goes back a long way—and even before then, social scientists were speculating about "the masses" and "The Popular Mind" as we will see in chapter 1, where I quote Gustav Le Bon on the subject.

Some social scientists would, in fact, argue that we do not live in a "mass society," but in a society full of subcultures, and the danger we face is not from overorganization but from various degrees of disorganization and anarchy, especially when it comes to the media and cultural phenomena. There are now thousands of magazines that deal with every subject imaginable as well as innumerable "zines," made possible by the desktop publishing revolution, that deal with everything under the sun, including some subjects that are unimaginable.

There is one other subject that I would like to consider that is relevant to our concerns. It is one I have alluded to already, when I discussed the different disciplines and domains that can be used to interpret texts and deal with the other focal points. The subject I will conclude with involves the way individuals read, interpret, deconstruct (what you will) texts.

Reception Theory and the Mass Media

Reception theory has been developed by theorists such as Hans Robert Jauss and Wolfgang Iser, professors at the University of Constance in Germany. Reception theorists focus their attention on the role that audiences (that is, readers or decoders of texts) play in the scheme of things, and not on the actual texts themselves.

As Wolfgang Iser put it in his essay "The Reading Process: a Phenomenological Approach" (which appeared in *New Literary History* 3, 1972),

> the phenomenological theory of art lays full stress on the idea that, in considering a literary work, one must take into account not only the actual text but also, and in equal measure, the actions involved in responding to that text. Thus Roman Ingarden confronts the structure of the literary text with the ways in which it can be *konkretisiert* (realized). The text as such offers different "schematized views" through which the subject matter of the work can come to light, but the actual bringing to light is an action of *Konkretisation*.

What Iser suggests here is that audiences play a major role in what can be called the "realization" or "actualization" of a text.

Iser distinguishes between two oppositions: the artistic, which refers to the work created by the author and the aesthetic, which refers to the act of realization, which is done by the reader. He describes this as follows:

> If this is so, then the literary work has two poles, which we might call the artistic, and the aesthetic: the artistic refers to the text created by the author and the aesthetic to the aesthetic realization accomplished by the reader. From this polarity it follows that the literary work cannot be completely identical with the text, or with the realization of the text, but in fact must lie halfway between the two. The work is more than the text, for the text only takes on life when it is realized, and furthermore the realization is by no means independent of the individual disposition of the reader—though this in turn is acted upon by the different patterns of the text.

In a sense, then, literary works don't exist until they are "realized" by a reader. Texts do have a virtual or immanent reality, but it is not actualized until someone (a reader) reads, sees, or hears the text.

Ingarten suggests, also, that the reader has an importance in realizing texts that is equal to the importance the author has in creating texts. Thus, the world is turned upside down, as far as our ideas about the importance of authorship are concerned—for artistic works no longer exist on their own, and those who create texts can no longer claim "sole possession," so to speak, of their works. In communication theory terms it means that the receiver of messages now has become equal to the sender of messages. These ideas can be shown in the chart that follows:

TEXT	WORK	READER
Author		Audience
Artistic plane		Aesthetic plane
Sender		Receiver
Creates a text		Realizes the text
Text a system of signs		Text a site for creation of meanings

According to reception theory, we must not privilege the text and must take into account "the role of the reader" (to quote the title of one of Umberto Eco's books) and the way different readers (or listeners and viewers, in the case of audio-visual media) interpret texts. Texts, it can be argued, don't exist on their own, but rather are entities that need to be brought into being by readers. Many authors might find it repugnant to think that their works, like Cinderella, can only be awakened when they are kissed by a reader/Prince Charming, but Iser and other reception theorists do have a point.

A Final Note

I have cast a wide net in this book. I deconstruct the classic American breakfast, analyze television commercials in detail, show how *Star Wars* is a modernized fairy tale, tell and interpret a funny joke eight different ways, and compare Mickey Mouse with the remarkable Ignatz Mouse, the hero of *Krazy Kat*. I analyze Teva sandals, *The Terminator*, Russian jokes, the O. J. Simpson trial, the semiotics of space, and pop culture in Thailand. I also deal with the evolution of the study of popular culture and with different methodologies that can be used in studying it.

I hope you will find this book useful and entertaining and that it will contribute to your having a better understanding of what popular culture is, how it can be studied, and what impact it may be having on our culture and society.

I
Theoretical Concerns: Introduction

When dealing with the media and popular arts (what is sometimes called mass culture, mass-mediated culture, or media culture) a methodological question always arises: how do we analyze them? What techniques and methods can we use to do justice to the aesthetic dimensions of works of popular art (or texts, as they care called by critics) and to their social and political dimensions? What is needed, I suggest, is a multidisciplinary approach, one that does justice to the aesthetic complexity of mass-mediated popular art texts and, at the same time, does not neglect their impact on our social and political institutions and culture in general.

Chapter 1 deals with the work of Gilbert Seldes, who wrote many books on the popular arts, including one called *The Public Arts,* published in 1924. Seldes was a pioneer who recognized the importance of popular culture, refused to dismiss it as nothing but "junk," and offered a number of important methodological insights about how we should analyze it.

He argued, for example, that the popular arts provided models for behavior and pointed out, as an example, that when Clark Gable was shown in a movie without an undershirt, the sales of undershirts plummeted. Seldes also championed the notion of using a multidisciplinary approach when dealing with the public arts, suggesting it would need a "team of researchers" from the various social sciences to find out why people feel the way they do about the movies.

In this chapter I point out that the study of popular culture, traditionally done by sociologists and an occasional American Studies or literature professor, has evolved into cultural criticism and cultural studies. As Seldes's hero Jimmy Durante used to put it, "Everyone wants to get into the act!" What happened was that scholars came to recognize that culture of all kinds was important, and so people from many disciplines started studying popular culture as well as elite culture. The post-modernist movement also helped, since it argued that there was no significant difference between popular and elite culture.

The chapter on critical communication theory (chapter 2) deals with that school of media criticism, which tends to be, I suggest, somewhat doctrinaire and formulaic. Critical theorists are not necessarily Marxists, but they use many of Marx's concepts in analyzing the mass media and popular culture in American society. I find many of their positions reasonable, and think of myself as, in many respects, a critical theorist. But there is something about the predictable nature of their criticisms that I find troubling.

There is a hermetic quality to much of their writing, as critical scholars quote one another, use one another's articles in their readers, and so on. Is there the functional equivalent of a "mutual admiration society" at work here?

I wonder, also, at the impact critical theory has on our students. Do they find our arguments compelling and write papers based on a sincere belief in the ideas of the theorists they read? Or do they parodize us and give us the kind of papers we want to see? Or that they think we want to see?

There are all kinds of problems associated with critical theory, but the same applies to all the other methodologies, as well. There is no royal road to interpreting popular culture and the mass media. What we have to do is use whichever combination of techniques and methods seems most appropriate to the subject being dealt with and to what we want to find out. In popular culture and media studies, as in other fields, the problem being studied (read the text being analyzed) dictates the methodologies that are to be used.

1

New Perspectives on Popular Culture and the Public Arts

In the early sixties, when I first started working on popular culture—writing about comic strips, fast foods, televised wrestling, advertising, and so on—the subject was considered, at best, a marginal one by most academics. If hundreds of millions of people did something, such as read the comics or watch television, many scholars, for a variety of reasons, considered these matters unimportant or irrelevant.

How can you take the reading the comics in the morning newspaper seriously, they suggested, when you use the comic pages (and maybe the editorial pages?) to wrap garbage in the evening? (Ironically, we now take garbage seriously and urban archaeologists, who call themselves "garbageologists," collect it, study it, and use it to help gain information on everyday life in America and other countries as well.)

Our attitudes about the media and popular culture have changed, radically, in the past couple of decades and the study of what was once called "mass culture" (but now is known as popular culture or public culture), the mass media, contemporary culture, or as Seldes put it, "the public arts," has become a central concern, if not a preoccupation, for academics in areas (and departments) as varied as philosophy, literature, history, communications, political science, and sociology.

That is because we now recognize that culture, in the anthropological sense of the term, has consequences and popular culture is, whatever else it may be, a kind or form of culture. In recent years, as a result of the spread of postmodernist thought, the distinction between popular culture and other kinds of culture, "elite" culture, or as I would suggest (facetiously) it might be described, "unpopular" culture, has been attacked. Except at the extremes, such as professional wrestling on television and *Finnegan's Wake,* I would argue, it is difficult to distinguish between popular culture and elite culture.

We study popular culture because we think it has aesthetic significance and because we believe it has a great deal to tell us about the values and beliefs of members of society, as a whole, and of the numerous subcultures that exist in any given society.

Seldes as a Pioneer

It is remarkable, then, that as early as 1924, in *The Seven Lively Arts,* Gilbert Seldes was writing about popular culture and taking it seriously. He did not dismiss it as subliterary, ephemeral, junk—though much of it is, of course. A good deal of so-called "serious" art, he points out, is second or third rate, if not worse. As Seldes wrote in "A Personal Preface" to *The Seven Lively Arts:*

> My theme was to be that entertainment of a high order existed in places not usually associated with Art, that the place where an object was to be seen or heard had no bearing on its merits, that some of Jerome Kern's songs in the *Princess* shows were lovelier than any number of operatic airs and that a comic strip printed on newspulp which would tatter and rumple in a day might be as worthy of a second look as a considerable number of canvasses at most of our museums. (1924, 3)

He adds that more or less unwittingly he was setting up "a sort of rivalry between the arts" (1924, 3) and that "the very thing I was to protest against—the grading of the arts and placing some of them forever at the lower table—was taking place" (1924, 3). These lively arts became, he adds, the mass media. I would suggest that we think of the media as carrying and affecting various popular art forms.

As he put it, after a description of his work at Paramount, he suddenly recognized that "the lively arts had turned into the mass media" (1924, 10). He adds:

> They had become part of our daily lives and the pivot on which this revolution turned was the radio receiver, the box in the home which, as far back as 1915, David Sarnoff had predicted—and described as a "domestic utility." (1924, 10)

This revolution was, it turns out, relatively minor when compared to the impact that television was to have on the lively arts and on society, but that is another matter—and one which has occupied the attention of many researchers.

But the approach of most social scientists working on television (until the relatively recent development of culture criticism, and a particular aspect of it, cultural studies) was essentially a social-psychological one. These researchers were not interested in works from the public arts and in television programs as interesting texts but in their effects on audiences and society. Since there is a significant relationship between aesthetic aspects of a text and its impact on individuals and effects on society, in neglecting texts the social-psychologists were getting distorted results—or so I would argue.

At the end of *The Seven Lively Arts,* Seldes makes an important point:

> It happens that what we call folk music, folk dance, and the folk arts in general have only a precarious existence among us... And the popular substitutes for these arts are so much under our eyes and in our ears that we fail to recognize them as decent contributions to the richness and intensity of our lives. The result, strange as it may appear to devotees of culture, is that our major arts suffer. The poets, painters, composers who withdraw equally from the main stream of European tradition and from the untraditional natural expressions of America, have no sources of strength, no material to work with, no background against which they can see their shadows; they feel themselves disinherited of the future as well as the past. (1924, 298-99)

This notion is a significant one, for popular culture has traditionally been attacked as being inimical to the elite arts, as lowering the general level of taste, of appealing to the "lowest common denominator." It seems, if we take a historical approach, that Seldes was correct on this issue and that the popular arts have not destroyed the elite arts, but energized them. Think, for example, of the use that classical composers have made of folk music in various "serious" orchestral works.

In 1950 Seldes published *The Great Audience* in which, as he puts it, "my misgivings about our popular entertainments were recorded." It was, he says, a "glum book." Then, in 1956, he wrote a book in which he tried to deal with his ambivalence about popular culture and the mass media. As he explains it, "I tried to balance my two themes—the delight I take and the fears I experience—in *The Public Arts*" (1924, 10).

This ambivalence that Seldes felt about the public arts informs much of the thinking of analysts of the popular arts and the mass media. We are fascinated by them, we often find them pleasurable, intriguing, and interesting, but we can't help wonder whether or not they are, in ways that we may not recognize or understand, harmful and destructive of our well-being.

The Public Arts

Seldes starts *The Public Arts* with a letter to Jimmy Durante and Edward R. Murrow, to whom he dedicated the book in admiration and affection. In this letter he suggests, prophetically, that news and entertainment "are parts of one field" and that "the lively arts and the mass media are two aspects of the same phenomenon, which I now call 'the public arts.'" Seldes uses the term because, as he explains, nobody can be, completely, a private person anymore, in that our existence depends on others and their existence depends on us.

Durante, Seldes suggests, makes life more enjoyable and Murrow, he adds, makes it more understandable. He continues this line of thinking as follows:

> For the comedian creates an audience and hands it over to the news analyst, and when that audience has met statesmen and philosophers and demagogues and poets it returns to the comedian, living more fully, using more of its faculties. (1956, 6–7)

Seldes adds that his great fear is that we may end up with two audiences—a large one for the comedian (and by extension the mass media) and a small one for the communicators (that is, those who broadcast the news and, in addition, so-called "serious" works of art).

This great divide will not happen, Seldes believes, because nothing is final about the public arts; they are always changing, always looking for something new, different, exciting. They may degrade themselves, from time to time, as they compete for public favor and a large audience, but this is part of the process of continual change that leads to progress, which is the reason Seldes is hopeful.

What strikes you as you read *The Public Arts* is how thoughtful Seldes is, how he anticipates many of the topics that media scholars and culture critics now debate. He does not write in a scholarly manner, using academic jargon, but his book is solidly argued and not, by any means, mindlessly celebratory or simplistically appreciative. He suggests, for instance, that the movies provide "models of behavior." He mentions that when Clark Gable took off a shirt in one of his movies and revealed that he wasn't wearing an undershirt, the sales of these garments plummeted and that when two stars toasted one another with pink champagne, the drink became very popular.

This "model of behavior" hypothesis, when applied to the matter of violence in the media, a central concern of media scholars, social scientists of various persuasions, and many others, is one that is still being debated. He is alert, also, to the possibility of people becoming addicted to special kinds of fiction, to genres such as the mystery story (and in contemporary times, romance novels). People have also become addicted to the media, themselves. Many people, who would not think of themselves as such, are now television "addicts" who watch it for many hours each day, regardless of whether or not anything that interests them is being broadcast.

People, he continues, develop a special kind of emotional relationship, something akin to passionate love, for film (what we used to call *the movies*). This passion, he adds, is stronger than the one people feel for the radio or television but it is too complicated for him to figure out, though he does have some ideas that explain why this special relationship exists. In discussing this passion, he suggests, it would take an interdisciplinary team of researchers to find out why people feel the way they do about the movies:

> I shall not try to do the work, which would require a team of researchers: a psychologist, an aesthetician, a sociologist, and a banker, for instance. I make my guess after observing the variations in the visual art as practiced first by the silent movies, then by movies with sound, and finally by television. I would like to think that the movies are so universally loved precisely because they are a subtle and complex form of art, but I cannot prove this, so I settle for another explanation: the movies are loved because they are the first form of fiction presented visually in which the way of telling the story anticipates all the needs of the spectator before he is aware of them—in a sense, the way the story is told does all the work for the spectator and gives him the highly satisfactory sense of exercising a divine power. (1956, 7)

Seldes recognized, at a very early date, that movies are a complex medium and require a great deal of effort to understand. He may have underestimated the relationship many people have with characters in television shows, especially soap operas or serial television shows such as *Dallas*.

The study of film has become a very important subject in the academic world and has moved from analyzing the themes, values, and beliefs found in the film to a study of how the films generate meaning. Film theory is now very deep (sometimes so deep that it is opaque), integrating semiotics, psychoanalytic theory, aesthetics, political theory, and a number of other disciplines. Film theorist draw upon the theories of a number of philosophers and scholars, many from the continent, whose writings are extremely complex—if not unintelligible—to make their analyses.

It is the French who are given credit for having discovered film and recognizing that it was not just a simple medium of entertainment. (It is the French, also, who lionize the work of Jerry Lewis, a subject of considerable amusement to many people in America.) But Seldes recognized this in the early 1920s. The first two chapters in *The Seven Lively Arts* are about Charlie Chaplin and film comedy, as a matter of fact. In a chapter at the end of the book he explains to the people making films that, in reality, they are dealing with "*movement governed by light,*" and must be aware of the significance of the visual aspects of the medium.

Movement, he adds, involves everything dealing with pace and light, anything that can be made visible to the eye, even things like emotions. He continues:

> It will occur to you that the cut-back, the alternating exposition of two concurrent actions, the vision, the dream, all are good; and that the close-up, dearest of all your finds, usually dissociates a face or an object from its moving background and is the most dangerous of expedients. (1924, 276–77)

Seldes shows a very sophisticated understanding of the importance of media aesthetics—camera work and editing—and anticipates much of the theoretical work done on film in recent years.

Seldes also has a fine chapter on animated film, "The Lovely Art: Magic" in *The Public Arts* that focuses on Disney's work, though it mentions other animators. Seldes writes:

> I would say that the animated cartoon is one of the three supreme examples of the multiple or diversified nature of these [popular] arts, in many respects more typical, purer, and consequently more of a test case than the two others, jazz and the feature picture. (1956, 35)

He adds that Disney's work had a cruel streak to it and is critical of much of Disney's later work. It was his successors, such as the animators at United Productions of America (UPA), who went on to develop the animated cartoon while Disney created a number of new careers for himself. Seldes's insights into Disney's cruelty and what might be described as the "dark" side of Disney, were picked up later on by writers such as Richard Schickel, whose book *The Disney Version* dealt with

Disney from a psychoanalytic perspective and suggested that, among other things, Disney had anal traits.

Seldes concludes this chapter with a reaffirmation of one of his basic ideas. The development of the animated cartoon, which started off superbly, became somewhat debased, and then returned to its former brilliance, shows something important. As Seldes writes,

> all the stale equations in which good and bad and popular and highbrow figures were exploded by Disney first and by UPA later...The whole progression is a warning to us never to despair and equally a warning never to be satisfied with the second-rate, for the first-rate can be at least as popular. (1956, 45)

This notion is contrary to the argument of many critics of popular culture. They argue that in the world of art and culture there is a Gresham's law in operation and that the poor inevitably drives out the good. Thus, we end up, inevitably, with works that appeal to the lowest common denominator in their attempt to appeal to the largest number of people. (This is necessary since the networks and advertising agencies, in effect, sell audiences to companies advertising products and services.)

Is it not possible, Seldes counters, that one can appeal to the largest common denominator by creating works of genuine merit? He cites work by Disney and the UPA animators in a medium that was generally seen as only for children to suggest that the public arts can create works of artistic merit and sophistication, no matter what the medium. In the last thirty years or so we have come to realize that animation is not a trivial medium and that works of compelling value can be created in this medium. Disney's *Fantasia* is an example.

Academic Interest in the Arts and Creative Activity

We seldom think about it, but a considerable amount of attention is devoted to understanding and interpreting the arts and creativity in universities. Obviously, art departments are involved with the study of the arts and the creation of works of art, in a variety of media—everything from oil painting and sculptures to textiles and prints. The same could be said of music, dance, and theater departments, which are devoted to the performing arts.

But communications departments and film departments also deal with the arts. These departments generally are involved with them in a number of ways: works are created (films, television shows); important texts are analyzed; and research is done on topics such as the way films generate meaning, the work of auteurs, performance matters, and the impact of the media and their most important texts on society and culture. In the same light, English departments, literature departments, comparative literature departments, and rhetoric departments study literature, in the broadest sense of term (and this often involves the public arts and popular genres, such as science fiction, detective stories and romances as well as media, such as film and television). The same applies to foreign language departments; they teach people how to read and speak languages, but most of the effort is generally devoted to studying the culture and, in particular, the literary and artistic expressions in a given country or language group.

In short, scholars from many disciplines are interested in the arts, lively and dull, popular and elite, public and private. They are interested in how works are created (in what might be called the creative process, in the broadest sense of the term) and what effects texts and media might be having on their audiences. Seldes was correct, then, when he suggested that it would take a team of scholars, from many different disciplines, to understand the appeal of movies—and, we might add, the appeal and significance of all of the other public arts.

What's in a Term?

What Seldes called *The Public Arts* have been described by other terms, such as popular culture, the popular arts, mass culture, the mass arts, mass-mediated culture, and more recently, public culture. Each of these terms conveys something slightly different. They are used to describe arts that are contrasted with works often described as part of elite culture, the elite arts, or high culture.

Popular culture refers to the world of situation comedies, comic strips, MTV, radio and television talk shows, football games, stand-up comedians, mystery stories, popular romance novels, and so on. Elite culture refers to operas, ballets, classical music (symphonies, chamber music, etc.), masterworks of painting and sculpture, serious novels and plays, and other art forms that require, generally speaking, relatively sophisticated sensibilities. As I pointed out earlier, many critics now argue that it is spurious to argue that popular culture and elite culture are different in significant ways. I will return to this matter shortly, in my discussion of postmodernism.

Seldes explains why he uses the term *public arts*. In his letter to Edward R. Murrow and Jimmy Durante he says:

> Our dependence, for our pleasures and for ideas on the popular arts, on the movies and radio and television particularly, gives another significance to the word "public." You represent institutions as powerful in shaping our lives as our schools, our politics, our system of government—and anything that affects the entire public is by nature compelled to serve the public. (1956, vi)

The term *public* has different connotations than the term *popular*. Public suggests something involving the community as a whole, something that has social and political implications. It is something involving all the people, in contrast to something that is private, and involving only limited numbers of people.

Popular, on the other hand, refers to taste. We describe something as popular if it has immediate and widespread appeal, if it is something that ordinary people can understood and appreciate. There is a difference between the terms: one suggests something pertaining to the social and political world and has, connected to it, the notion of responsibility—something done, for example, in the public interest or for the public good. Popular doesn't convey this sense; it deals with the size and nature of the audience of a work of art or medium. There is an implication, as I have suggested, that if something is popular it is because there has been a kind of leveling, a lowering of taste.

Mass Culture and the Mass Society

When we get to the term *mass*, we find a word that is somewhat pejorative. Mass conveys a group of people lumped together in some kind of a formless entity; people in a mass are held to lack individuality and personal identity. The term *mass man* or *mass woman* is used, for instance, to suggest someone who is part of a so-called mass society, a person without a distinct identity, without his or her own values, and without a sense of personal responsibility who can, as a result of his situation, be easily be manipulated by the mass media.

There is a classic and rather extreme description of this mass man in Gustav Le Bon's *The Crowd*, subtitled, interestingly, "A Study of the

Popular Mind." In his chapter on "General Characteristics of Crowds" Le Bon writes:

> We see, then, that the disappearance of the conscious personality, the predominance of unconscious personality, the turning by means of suggestion and contagion of feelings and ideas in an identical direction, the tendency immediately to transform the suggested ideas into acts; these we see, are the principle characteristics of the individual forming part of a crowd. He is no longer himself, but has become an automaton who has ceased to be guided by his will. (1960, 32)

These crowds, Le Bon points out later, can only think in images and are only affected by images. That is why what he calls "theatrical representations" (and what we would call the public arts) are so important and so powerful. He writes, "The entire audience experiences at the same time the same emotions, and if these emotions are not at once transformed into acts, it is because the most unconscious spectator cannot ignore that he is the victim of illusions" (1960, 32).

This notion is very similar to the "hypodermic needle" theory of the mass media, which argued that everyone in an audience was affected the same way by his or her exposure to the media—a theory that is no longer accepted by most media scholars. In the same light, the notion that the media have "massified" us and can brainwash everyone is generally discredited, as we discover that individuals interpret or decode the texts they are exposed to in a variety of ways.

It makes a big difference, then, whether we describe a television program such as a production of a play (perhaps by a "serious author") as a work of public art, an work of popular culture, an example of mass art, or a text (the term critics conventionally use now for specific works) brought to us by the mass media. Or is it an elite art text that is broadcast on a mass medium?

In 1957, one of the more important books on popular culture, edited by David Manning White and Bernard Rosenberg, was published. It was called *Mass Culture: The Popular Arts in America*, and contained a number of articles by scholars, many of whom were critical and negative about mass culture and, by implication, American culture. *Mass Culture Revisited*, a sequel to the book, edited by the same authors, appeared in 1971. There have been numerous other collections of essays and books about popular culture over the past forty years. In the sequel David Manning White speculates about the differences between popular culture and high culture and why the general public does not seem to appreciate high culture. One reason, he suggests, is that high art "demands, of both creators and audiences, motivation and years of dedicated interest." But he defends the public arts, and argues that Rosenberg's attack on them (Rosenberg described television as "a cancerous growth that systematically unfits a person for art and vice versa") is simplistic and that the cultural level in the United States is, in fact, rising.

The Problem of *Largo Desolato*

Let me discuss something now that relates to this argument. Recently I saw a brilliant production of Vaclav Havel's comedy *Largo Desolato* on public television. The production probably was seen (and has been seen, in the course of its various broadcasts) by huge numbers of people, perhaps in the millions. Was *Largo Desolato* an example of public art, popular culture, elite culture, mass culture, or something else—such as mass-mediated culture? Because of the confusions and complications that the broadcast of so-called elite works of art cause (Is it art? Is it popular culture? Is it mass media?) many critics now argue that it is a waste of time to make these distinctions. There are what we call the arts. Some works of art are well done and others are not, and it is the function of the critic to explain why a given work is good or bad, what effects it might be having on society, and so on. We shouldn't waste our time trying to classify every text and put it in its "correct" box or make apodictic statements about what texts carried in a certain medium "must" be.

In other writings I have has asked, why is popular culture so "unpopular"? The answer I gave is that popular culture is not unpopular with the ordinary man and woman, but with certain critics who use it to snub their noses, so to speak, at the hoi polloi. It is no longer acceptable to attack people directly, so some elitists attack the general public's taste and culture. Critics are always coming up with classification systems, "high brow" and "low brow," U and Non-U, to put people down.

Popular Culture Moves from the Periphery to the Center

It was in the middle of the 1980s, approximately, that the study of the public arts or, as what we more commonly call popular culture, moved from being a marginal concern to being a central one in the universities. If you add up the time most people devote to popular culture—the time they spend listening to news shows and talk shows on the radio, the time they spend watching news shows, situation comedies, action-adventure dramas, soap operas, sports programs and other kinds of shows (and movies) on television, and the time they spend reading comics, news articles, the sports section, feature articles and entertainment features in the newspapers and, perhaps, listening to music on their stereos—you discover that most people spend a great deal of time with popular culture, which is, in large measure, their culture.

The average person, for example, watches close to four hours of television each day, listens to the radio two or three hours a day, and spends some time reading newspapers and magazines. People fill up their leisure hours with popular culture and this popular culture, there is reason to believe, has profound effects on individuals and on societies, in general.

The study of popular culture has, itself, been changed from one that sees popular culture as an investigation of our entertainments and something "separate" from culture, per se, to being central to culture. Popular culture has been incorporated into a larger, more "serious" (one might say) undertaking, what is often called cultural studies.

Cultural studies erases the distinctions between popular culture and elite culture. There is culture, and it is culture, in all its themes and variations, whether high or low, popular or unpopular, that is the subject of interest. Defining culture is extremely difficult, but most critics in cultural studies understand it in broadly anthropological terms, as involving the belief systems and values that are passed on from generation to generation and the meanings people find in artistic texts, objects, events, and practices. Culture, from the perspective of modern cultural studies critics, is not an epiphenomenon, a kind of residue of the economic system, but is something that has an impact that is more or less co-equal to the economic system.

Stuart Hall, in an influential article, "Cultural Studies: Two Paradigms" (reprinted in Richard Collins, et, al, *Media, Culture & Society*), explains what is probably the dominant perspective in cultural studies. This perspective

stands opposed to the residual and merely reflective role assigned to "the cultural". In its different ways, it conceptualizes culture as interwoven with all social practices; and those practices, in turn, as a common form of human activity: sensuous human praxis, the activity through which men and women make history. It is opposed to the base-superstructure way of formulating the relationship between ideal and material forces, especially where the "base" is defined as determination by "the economic" in any simple sense.... It defines "culture" as *both* the meanings and values which arise amongst distinctive social groups and classes, on the basis of their given historical conditions and relationships, through which they "handle" and respond to the conditions of existence; *and* as the lived traditions and practices through which those "understandings" are expressed and in which they are embodied. (Collins et. al, 1986, 39)

The economic system, in this paradigm for cultural studies, is no longer privileged and is no longer seen as fundamental.

There has been an evolution in the way culture critics have analyzed the relation that exists between the economic relations that pertain in a society, the "base" in Marxist terms, and a given society's social institutions and culture, the "superstructure." So-called vulgar Marxists argued that the base determines the superstructure. Next, it was asserted that the base did not determine the superstructure, a position difficult to defend, but "shaped" it in varying ways. Now, with the development of cultural criticism, many critics argue that the economic system and the culture found in a given society are, more or less, co-equal.

The second paradigm in cultural studies is that of what Hall calls the "structuralisms," and focuses on the concept of ideology more than on culture, per se. He discusses the work of the great French anthropologist Claude Lévi-Strauss and others, who he suggests were influenced by the work of Ferdinand de Saussure and linguistics. The structuralists attempted, broadly speaking, to read culture as a text and concerned themselves with the classifications, categories, and codes, which people were unaware of, generally speaking, but which shaped their behavior. Culture, in certain respects, can be seen as a collection of codes and one of the duties of the culture analyst is to discover these codes and explain how they have affected individuals and shaped a society's institutions.

Neither culturalism, the first paradigm, nor structuralism, the second paradigm, are adequate in Hall's view to deal with culture but, he suggests, a synthesis of the two, a focus on linguistics and social structure or, to put it another way, attention to the core concepts of culture and ideology, holds the best promise for cultural studies. Hall's article was written in 1980. Since then, cultural studies has spread from Great Britain, where it developed, to many other countries, and from communications and media departments to many other departments in universities. It has also evolved, considerably, as linguistics scholars, literary theorists, media analysts, and philosophers have focused their attention on the subject.

In this respect, it is worth taking note of some of the books involving popular culture and cultural studies that have appeared in recent years.

A Bibliographical Interlude

I will list, and use selections from catalogue descriptions, to characterize some of the more important books that have been published in this general area.

Cultural Studies, edited by Lawrence Grossberg, Cary Nelson, and Paula Treichler. "Their essays address race and minority discourses; ethnicity and postcolonialism; postmodernism; feminism; cultural policy; the politics of representation; aesthetics; ethics; and technology. At the same time, *Cultural Studies* explores the specific cultural work performed by rock music, Chicano art, detective novels, African-American writing, the AIDS epidemic, architecture, reproductive freedom... *Star Trek* fandom, and New Age technology."

Patricia Mellencamp, *High Anxiety: Catastrophe, Scandal, Age, and Comedy.* "Operation Desert Storm, *I Love Lucy*, Anita Hill, *Twin Peaks*, Jim and Tammy Faye Bakker, *Murder, She Wrote*, Oprah, Geraldo, and Phil: these and other subjects come together to form an "anxious" mosaic in Patricia Mellencamp's *High Anxiety*."

Marjorie Garber, *Vested Interests.* "*Vested Interests* is a tour de force of cultural criticism: its investigations range across history, literature, film, photography, and popular and mass culture, from Shakespeare to Mark Twain, from Oscar Wilde to Peter Pan, from transsexual surgery and transvestite 'sororities' to Madonna, Flip Wilson, Rudolph Valentino and Elvis Presley."

Hilary Radner, *Shopping Around: Feminine Culture and the Pursuit of Pleasure.* "*Shopping Around* investigates issues of contemporary popular narrative, feminine pleasure, and consumer culture, viewing the permutations of the feminine subject as a textual construction evolved through everyday life. A wide spectrum of texts are examined, including *The Taming of the Shrew, Moonlighting, Vogue, Jane Fonda's Workout Book*, and Harlequin romances, exposing the fact that women 'read' within a complex and conflicted arena."

Andrew Wernick, *Promotional Culture.* "Through a detailed analysis of advertisement as promotional text, Wernick critically assesses—both culturally and sociologically—the impact of advertising on shaping contemporary culture. He traces the impact on promotion from selling consumer goods to the spheres of electoral politics and the university, and he poses fundamental, thought-provoking questions about how the individual acts as a communicating subject."

Orrin Klapp, *Inflation of Symbols: Loss of Values in American Culture*. "Klapp defines what inflation of symbols means, and how it affects values in social relations, popular culture, mass contagions, fads and fashions, even smiles and kisses."

These books are only a small sampling of the books being published on popular culture, the mass media, cultural studies, and related concerns. Many publishers have series devoted to one or more of these topics. For example, in a recent catalogue, Routledge devotes five pages to cultural studies, but the whole catalogue, on culture, media, and film, is really about the topic. Sage Publications has series on popular culture and another on "Theory, Culture and Society," which focuses on cultural theory, in general, and postmodernism, in particular. Transaction Publishers reprints important books in communications and the mass media in a series, "Classics in Communications," and also publishes a number of new works on popular culture, media, and communications. Many other publishers put out books that deal with the public arts and cultural studies.

We are now prepared to investigate our final topic, a much-talked about and little understood one, postmodernism. What the postmodernist thinkers tell us, and I am simplifying things someone here, I admit, is that American culture, which is dominated by popular culture, is the most representative postmodernist culture. We have evolved, in America, without recognizing what we've done, the pre-eminent postmodernist society, for better or worse.

America as a Postmodernist Society

It's hard to be precise about postmodernism because people use the term in so many different ways. There's no official, standard, universally accepted definition of the term—but, of course, the same can be said about most terms. We have seen, for example, that culture is a rather slippery concept. Despite the difficulties of pinning postmodernism down, there are a number of ideas generally associated with it.

The term *postmodernism* suggests that we have moved *past* or beyond modernism; postmodernism gets its identity, one might say, by being an "un-cola." We know what postmodernism isn't; it isn't modernism. Modernism is associated with writers such as Kafka, Proust, Pirandello, Faulkner, Eliot, and Calvino; with visual artists such as Picasso, Matisse, and Braque; with composers such as Bela Bartok, Stravinsky, and Schoenberg. Modernists reject narrative linearity for simultaneity and montage, they are interested in paradox and ambiguity, and see reality as open-ended and uncertain.

But what is postmodernism? It has been described by Mike Featherstone in his essay "In Pursuit of the Postmodern: An Introduction" as having the following features:

> the effacement of the boundary between art and everyday life; the collapse of the hierarchical distinction between high and mass/popular culture; a stylistic promiscuity favouring eclecticism and the mixing of codes; parody, pastiche, irony, playfulness and the celebration of the surface "depthlessness" of culture; the decline of the originality/genius of the artistic producer and the assumption that art can only be repetitious. (*Theory, Culture and Society,* vol. 5, nos. 2 & 3 [June 1988], 203)

Todd Gitlin has offered a list of examples of postmodernism in American culture that shows the degree to which American culture might be seen as a quintessential example of a postmodernist culture. He writes, in an essay "Postmodernism Defined, at Last!" (published in *Dissent* and reprinted in the *Utne* reader, July/August 1989, 52–53):

> One postmodernist trope is the list, as if culture were a garage sale, so it is appropriate to evoke postmodernism by offering a list of examples, for better and for worse: Michael Graves' Portland Building, Philip Johnson's AT&T, and hundreds of more or less skillful derivatives; Robert Rauschenberg's silk screens; Andy Warhol's multiple-image paintings, photo-realism, Larry Rivers erasures and pseudo-pageantry, Sherrie Levine's photographs of "classic" photographs; Disneyland, Las Vegas, suburban strips, shopping malls, mirror-glass office building facades, William Burroughs, Tom Wolfe, Donald Barthelme, Monty Python, Don Delillo, Joe Isuzu "He's Lying" commercials, Philip Glass, *Star Wars*...Max Headroom, David Byrne, Twyla Tharp (choreographing Beach Boys and Frank Sinatra songs), Italo Calvino....

This list defines by exemplification and suggests the extent to which it can be argued that American culture is postmodern.

We have travelled a long way. We started with Gilbert Seldes and the public arts, with comic strips and animated films, and with Jimmy Durante. (How ironic. He used to sing a song with the lyrics "everybody wants to get into the act." That is what has happened.) The public arts (or popular culture, which is somewhat more inclusive) were seen as trivial, ephemeral, and insignificant. We then discovered that the subject was taken seriously because it was held to reflect important values and beliefs found in societies and was, therefore, valuable as a tool to uncover aspects of society that other modes of analysis bypassed. As scholars started paying more and more attention to popular culture, a number of theorists started getting worried and theorized that we were becoming "mass men and women" living in a mass society and being indoctrinated by the mass arts.

Then came the development of cultural studies, which argued that cultural phenomena were not epiphenomena, not derivatives of the economic system, but existed as co-equal, so to speak, with the economic system. Cultural studies is now, I would argue, the dominant approach to dealing with the public arts, the mass media, popular culture—whatever you wish to call this area of interest.

Cultural studies, I might point out, is dominated by European theorists such as Barthes, Baudrillard, Lévi-Strauss, Foucault, Lyotard, Lacan, Althusser, Bourdieu, Kristeva, Lefebvre, and Saussure (to list some of the major luminaries from the French language contingent), plus others from Germany, Russia, Italy, and Great Britain.

We find the same names in the reference lists at the end of most articles by cultural critics. They tend to cite these theorists and one another and to publish articles by their friends (who, in turn, publish articles they wrote) and so it goes, spinning merrily on. I mention this because there is a tendency for these critics to focus their attention on some areas and neglect others, due to their paradigms, their preoccupation (one might say) with only certain points of view. This does not mean that they are doing important and interesting work, but it has the danger, I feel, of becoming too self-referential and too ideological.

Now, with the development of postmodernist theory, we find that popular culture and so-called elite culture are one and the same and that American society, with its shopping malls, its mirror-faced buildings, its pop artists, its fast food joints (and I could go on and on here) is, for better or worse, a postmodernist society and quite likely the pre-eminent one. (We were, without being aware of what we were doing, expressing our "incredulity toward metanarratives," as the postmodernist theorist, Lyotard put it.)

We didn't realize it before, because we didn't have Baudrillard and Lyotard to tell us, but when we thought we were wasting time reading the comics and watching situation comedies on "the boob tube," we were really being postmodern. That makes a great deal of difference.

2

Teaching Critical Media Analysis
for Pleasure and Profit

I've taught media analysis, critical and uncritical, for a number of
years and wonder, every once in a while, whether what I'm doing, ultimately, is "shovelling the moral equivalent of chataquas against the tide,"
so to speak. Let me offer some speculations about the problems we face
when we try to get students—especially undergraduates—to take critical media analysis seriously. (Graduate students in communications and
various social science and humanities departments, who are often re-
ceiving scholarships [that is, their way is being paid for by others] are,
so it seems, much more receptive to the critical studies point of view
than students in other fields.)

We all like to bite the hands that feed us and there's nothing like
being tenured and well paid at a respectable university to make one
want to bring the whole decadent bourgeois system crashing down.
Nothing better, that is, except getting a grant to do research and show
how the media conglomerates are destroying or are a threat to our democratic institutions. If we get some grant money from the media conglomerates, all the better.

Problem 1: Students Don't Understand What We're Talking About

One of the problems is that many students who may, in some cases,
be taking courses in communications, radio and television, media arts
and similar departments, to fulfill requirements (and would be much
happier dollying in and out in some television studio) don't understand
what we are talking about. I've found that sometimes students can grasp
the concepts we teach, but can't apply them on their own. You can ask

them to define the terms and they can do that tolerably well, in some cases. But using the concepts is a different matter. There's a kind of gap between understanding concepts and applying them. Then, when they read critical texts or journals we might assign, that deconstruct texts or analyze media corporations, they claim they find the readings opaque. Or if not opaque, far out and ridiculous. It's tough challenging the invincible ignorance or closed minds of some undergraduates, and some graduate students as well.

Problem 2: Formulaic Aspects of Critical Theory

Students complain that critical theorists are always talking about the same stuff, over and over again. It's very much a case of "round up the usual conceptualizers" and use them to *épater* the bourgeoisie. There is, one must admit, a certain recipe-like, doctrinaire aspect to much critical communications thought and writing.

It's as if we have a list of people: Baudrillard, Barthes, Foucault, Marx, Althusser, Bakhtin, and the likes and we keep cycling everything through the grid of their concepts. Are critical communications scholars prisoners of their categories? If we are, how can they hope to reach our students?

Problem 3: Wannabes Don't Wanna *Epater* Themselves

The students, many of whom are, thanks to well-to-do parents, members of the bourgeoisie or petty bourgeoisie—or who desperately want to become members of these socioeconomic groups—don't want to *épater* themselves. Large numbers of students think things are pretty fine, except, of course, for "boring" lectures, tuition, the cost of books, and the parking problems they face. They will put up with courses on critical communication and maybe even parody their teachers (consciously or unconsciously) and write the kind of term papers we ask of them, but ultimately their hearts belong to Daddy Warbucks and the assorted hypermillionaires and billionaires they read about or see on television. As one of my students put it to me, "I wanna make a lot of money."

Maybe, when these students graduate and face the problem of not being able to find jobs, or the kinds of jobs they thought they'd be getting, the seeds of critical theory will start to grow, and they'll, at least, vote for an occasional Democrat? But who knows? And is this progress?

Problem 4: What's Right? Who's Left?
And What About Decentered Totalities?

A look at writing by critical theorists shows that there are any number of groups with different critical perspectives, leading to what we might call "critical or ideological clutter." The writings of feminists, gays and lesbians, Native Americans, African-Americans, Latinos and Latinas, Physically Challenged, and various other groups, often in combination (such as Physically Challenged Feminist Latinas) tend to get in the way of one another, generating a culture of complaint that tends to weaken the messages of each and tends to confuse students.

All of these groups want to challenge the status quo, of course, and have, often, legitimate complaints to make, but just as in consumer culture, where there are too many commercials, too many complaints lead to confusion and paralysis. People can fall victim to complaint fatigue in the same way that many are falling victim to donor fatigue.

Problem 5: A Theoretical Dilemma Caused by
Wanting to Have Your Cake and Eat It

When we teach communications from a critical point of view, we assume that one of our tasks involves exposing the ideological content of many of the texts broadcast by the mass media. We attempt to give the students concepts that they can use to see through the illusions generated by the media and informing much of our consumer culture.

There is an implicit assumption that texts such as advertisements and commercials, soap operas, comic strips and books, and novels (popular and otherwise) have an ideological dimension to them that should be exposed and also generate images and beliefs that are held to be destructive. These messages, we assume, are communicated to people and affect audiences, whether the people in these audiences recognize this or not. The audiences must, more or less, get the same message.

But many of my students raise an interesting problem: they don't "see" the ideological messages, even when I point them out. They have lots of theory behind them. After all, as the semioticians have pointed out, people "decode" texts differently, based on their education, social class, culture, religion, ethnicity, gender, region, and so on. Let me quote a joke that shows this.

> A drunken salesman is in a bar in western Montana, and sees a news report on the television about President Richard Nixon. The man yells "Nixon's a horse's ass." A cowboy sidles up to the salesman and says "Better watch what you say around here, pardner." "Oh, I'm sorry. I didn't realize this was Nixon territory," he says. "It ain't," says the cowboy. "It's horse territory."

The point is, we can't be sure how people will interpret a message, or as the students would say, "understand where they're (the people who write the scripts) coming from."

Another "take" on the matter of aberrant decoding comes from the reader response theorists, such as Wolfgang Iser, who argue that it takes the "reader" to bring a text into being and that different readers makes sense of a given text in different ways because these texts are indeterminate, full of gaps, that the reader fills in.

It's one thing to argue, as some critical thinkers tend to do, that people may not realize they are being subjected to hegemonial, ideological domination and manipulation and to point out the hegemonic ideological aspects of various texts which, it is assumed, shape, or at least profoundly affect their behavior. But this position takes a leap of faith that many students cannot make. It assumes that unconscious messages, unrecognized by audiences or those who receive the messages, shape their (and maybe even our?) behavior and society and, most importantly, that we all get, more or less, the same message. (This matter of different ways of reading, decoding, making sense of mass-mediated texts and culture in general is, you will find, a common theme running through this book.)

Is this the hypodermic theory or magic bullet theory of media we are dealing with—cast off long ago as simplistic, but now reborn and in camouflaged form trying to sneak into favor?

Problem 6: Assumption of a Powerful Media?

Critical media theorists must assume that the media are powerful; otherwise, why bother? But media scholars have pointed out that our attitudes about the strength of the media alternate with our notions that the media are weak. Over the past fifty years, various strong and weak theories of the media have been elaborated, but we've not been able to demonstrate that one or the other theories of the media are correct. In the 1990s I would say that most of the media theorists see it as strong. But there are problems with this position.

As a case in point, consider Eastern Europe. Many of the countries behind the Iron Curtain were subjected to decades of ideological newspapers, radio programs, television shows, and films, yet they cast off the Communists with hardly a second thought as soon as it was clear that the Russian army wasn't going to invade them.

In recent years critical theorists have been emphasizing the way people can resist media indoctrination and can subvert texts in their own interests. If the media are weak, why get so hot and bothered about the media's alleged hegemonial ideological domination which, it can now be argued, often doesn't seem too dominating? Are critical theorists off base, spending too much of their time on the superstructure?

Problem 7: Hermetic Mutual Admiration Society Elites

As my students have pointed out (mostly graduate ones, here), if you look at the papers written by critical theorists, what you find, often, is that they spend a great deal of time quoting one another. That is, when they are not quoting the various continental thinkers from whom they draw their conceptual sustenance. There's a relatively small number of academics who are quoted over and over again and who quote and refer to one another endlessly.

Is this mutual citation "society" a functional alternative to a mutual admiration society, and is membership in the club tied to matters like critical-ideological purity? We found this abhorrent in Russian society, with its agitprop bureaus and cultural commissars. Is it now acceptable? It's hard enough to get students to read anything, but they complain they are, in essence, continually reading the same article, though the emphasis in each might be somewhat different, depending upon the ideology, values, position, and group affiliations of the writer.

Problem 8: Preaching to the Choir

There are, it must be said, large numbers of students who feel that the concepts they get from critical theorists, European and American (yes,

Americans do have some critical conceptualizers here and there) are important and valuable. That is, the ideas the students get from these theorists help them understand what is going on in American culture and society. These students write papers that are not parodies but are serious and heart-felt.

Are we, in essence, too often preaching to the choir—to the converted (or those who are easily reached) and are we wasting our time and energy trying to teach the other students, who may find some of our ideas interesting or amusing, but really want to figure out how to make big bucks so they can afford large houses, expensive cars, and lead the "good" life?

We all hope, I imagine, that somehow, with some students, at some time and in some place, by force of logic or circumstance (or both), what we have taught them will make a difference, and that they will use what they learn to help fashion a more just and more humane society. I am, here, parodying the well-known statement to the effect that all we can say about media effects is that some people who are exposed to some media are affected in some ways.

Final Thoughts

It's comforting to know that students in our classes spend a good percentage of their time thinking and daydreaming about sex. A study of audiences at lectures reveals that 20 percent of the class at any given moment is having sexual fantasies, 20 percent are reminiscing about something (maybe past sexual fantasies?), and large numbers of them are thinking about food and, surprisingly (8 percent), religion. Only 20 percent, according to a study I read, are paying attention to the lecture and of that 20 percent, only 12 percent are actively listening. The students aren't paying much attention to any of our colleagues, either, so we shouldn't get discouraged if many students don't seem too enthusiastic or terribly interested in what we are talking about. Their resistance to our efforts to de-indoctrinate them is not generally ideological, then (though from time to time we do often find ideological conservatives to do battle with) but physiological and, in particular, sexual and digestive. When physiology enters the room, in the form of a person about whom we are stricken with sexual fantasies, logic flies out the window. So does ideology, rationality, common sense, and most everything else.

Given these difficulties, fighting heroically against not only the bourgeoisie but against hormones and digestive juices, it's amazing that we who teach critical studies (or anything, for that matter) are as successful as we are.

II
Advertising: Introduction

The Macintosh "1984" television commercial, broadcast only once, during the 1984 Super Bowl, is one of the most celebrated commercials ever made. It is an extremely complicated text, which requires the use of a number of different disciplines to deal with adequately. In chapter 3 I interpret "1984" using techniques such as semiotic theory, psychoanalytic theory, political theory, and mythic analysis. I offer this analysis as a case study, to suggest some of the methods one can use in dealing with a text of such richness and complexity and to show how these methods can be applied to a text. It makes many demands on its viewers or, to use the contemporary jargon, "readers." For example, the title has intertextual significance, and alludes to George Orwell's famous dystopian novel *1984*. If one has never heard of the novel, the title of the commercial loses its resonance. The heroine of this little drama, who throws a sledge hammer at a video screen, can be seen as having mythic significance. She is a modern-day, feminized, David figure, who destroys a video "giant," Goliath.

In chapter 4, "The Manufacture of Desire," I discuss the significance of the advertising industry in America, with a focus on alcohol commercials directed toward young men and women. I offer a primer on how one should interpret television commercials, listing a number of different factors to consider.

It is best to think of commercials as short plays, as manufactured dreams, as micronarratives that are meant to persuade viewers to purchase a given product or service. We analyze these narratives the way we analyze any narrative, in terms of plot, characterization, and dialogue. We have to deal with rhetorical techniques of persuasion, and other matters such as the use of humor or attempts to generate anxiety in people.

We must consider the role of the television medium in these texts. We have to deal with the kinds of shots that are used and the way these shots are edited, along with the way music and sound effects, among other things, are used in making our analysis.

While this section focuses on advertising, it has methodological implications for many other areas of concern, relative to popular culture and the mass media. For the two chapters, between them, not only deal with some of the more important methods that can be used to analyze commercials (and other texts as well), they also show how these techniques can be utilized.

We can look upon this section as, among other things, operationalizing the suggestion made by Seldes about the need for interdisciplinary teams of experts to analyze popular culture texts. In this section, I use a number of disciplines and techniques to make sense of two commercials. In the section that follows, on humor, I continue in this vein. I take a joke and analyze it in great detail. Then I show how a number of different approaches can be used to make sense of a different joke. It is to the subject of advertising, and the way it can be analyzed, that we now turn.

3

1984: The Commercial

The commercial starts with the number 1984 appearing on the screen. We then cut to an extreme long shot of vaguely perceived figures marching through a tunnel joining gigantic structures. We cut then to a long shot of figures marching. They all have had their hair shaven and are wearing dull uniforms. They have no expression on their faces. There is a closeup of their heavy boots. A quick cut shows a blonde woman, with a white jersey and red shorts, running. We see her only for an instant. The next cut shows the figures again and then we cut to a shot of her being pursued by helmet clad storm-trooper figures. There is cutting back and forth in the commercial between the blonde woman and the troopers pursuing her. We see another extreme long shot of the inmates of this institution sitting in a huge room. They are watching a gigantic television set. A figure wearing glasses is addressing the inmates, who sit staring at the television image as if in a hypnotic trance. He is talking about their being free, united, and so on. The blonde woman, who is carrying a sledgehammer enters the room. She hurls the sledgehammer at the television screen and there is a gigantic explosion. The explosion creates an image that looks somewhat like that generated by an atomic bomb. The inmates stare, dazed and open-mouthed, at the screen. A message from Apple computers appears on the screen informing viewers that Apple will be introducing a new computer—The Macintosh—shortly.

The Background

This commercial, directed by Ridley Scott, was shown only once, during the 1984 Superbowl, though it (or parts of it) also has been aired, from time to time, in features on advertising and the computer industry by a number of news programs. The commercial was created by Apple's advertising agency, Chiat/Day, of Los Angeles. It cost $500,000 to make and $600,000 for air time. Apple was hesitant to use it and only decided to do so at the very last minute. An executive in the agency revealed that Apple actually called England to stop production of the commercial, but by the time they called the commercial had already been shot.

It is a remarkable text. The actors in the commercial were skinheads from England, who were recruited to play the roles of the prisoners. (Since 1984, when the commercial was made, the skinheads have emerged as a worldwide phenomenon of disaffected youth, who are attracted to right-wing, neo-nazi organizations.) The commercial has a much different look from the average commercial and takes a considerably different approach to the matter of marketing a product than we find with most commercials.

Ridley Scott, the director (or "auteur"), is a distinguished figure in the film world, (*Alien, Blade Runner*) and the commercial has his signature—its look, its narrative structure, its message all suggest an art film rather than a commercial. I believe that many "creative" people in the advertising industry could create aesthetically interesting and artistically pleasing works (and sometimes they do) were they not prevented from doing so by the companies whose products they are advertising. A great deal depends on the nature of the product being sold and the nature (that is, corporate culture) of the company selling the product.

In the remainder of this chapter I will examine some of the most important images from the text and speculate about how they generate meaning, what that meaning is, and how viewers might be affected by these images. I will also say something about the narrative itself. It is often held that there is no minimal unit in a television text to deal with (unlike film, which has the frame). I don't think this is a major issue, for one can always isolate important images and scenes to analyze, so that even if one doesn't have frames, one does have "shots" or images, which serve the same function.

Orwell's 1984 *and Ridley Scott's* "1984"

The title of this commercial brings to mind George Orwell's novel, *1984,* and the text of the commercial is based on the idea of totalitarian dystopias. The world of the 1984 commercial is that of a perverted utopian community, a total institution, in which every aspect of people's lives is controlled—and, in particular, their minds. We see 1984, the commercial, in terms of *1984,* the book. Here we have an example of what is known in semiotic literature as "intertextuality." We "read" one text in terms of another, or with another text in mind. The events in the commercial would have much less significance if we hadn't read or didn't know about Orwell's classic novel, *1984.*

The title also is connected to a great deal of speculation that occurred in America in the year 1984 about Orwell and his "dire" predictions. Thus, merely seeing the title generated ambivalent feelings. Would it be about the year 1984 or about the novel *1984?* (Many social commentators have argued that the year 1984 did not, by any means, bring the kind of society that Orwell imagined.) The title left people in suspense.

The Total Institution

The first shot resolved any questions that might have been generated by the title. We see an extreme long shot of gigantic structures, connected by a tubular tunnel, in which we can dimly perceive figures marching. The scale of the scene is terrifying. The figures are minute and seemingly irrelevant when contrasted with the huge buildings in which they are incarcerated. One almost thinks of blood flowing through veins.

Thus, the spatiality of this scene and the image of control and conformity generated by the columns of figures tells us immediately that the commercial, 1984, is indeed about an Orwellian world. This is reinforced in the next shot, which is a long shot of the prisoners, all with shaven heads and heavy, ill-fitting uniforms, marching sullenly in columns in the tunnel.

The Boots

There is an important shot that occurs shortly when there is a cut to a closeup of the prisoner's boots. The heavy, thick-soled boots, shown moving in unison, reflect the degree to which the inmates are under the control of their masters. (This is an example of metonomy, which confers meaning by association. In particular, it is an example of synecdoche, in which "a part can stand for a whole.")

The shot of the boots is meant to intensify the message. (We may even recall, as another example of intertextuality, the famous shot of the boots in *The Battleship Potemkin,* though the situation in that film was somewhat different.) Uniforms suggest lack of individuality and depersonalization and, in the content of the commercial, dehumanization. Thus, the shot of the boots, moving in common, strengthens this message by emphasizing one part of the human being and isolating it from the image of the whole human being.

The uniformity of the prisoners feet as they march, the rather sullen and lethargic nature of their marching—all these suggest that these inmates have been reduced to the status of automatons. It is the same kind of reductionism that occurs when we talk about young people being "college material" or football players as "horses," though it is much more exaggerated and intensified here.

The Blonde

Into this scene of marching zombies, of dehumanized and depersonalized bodies, there appears, for just an instant, an image of a beautiful blonde woman who is running down a corridor. She wears a white shirt and red shorts. We can see her breasts heaving as she runs. She runs directly at us, the viewers, on the Z-axis of the screen. The figure appears for perhaps a second or two, and then we return to the marching bodies and scenes of totalitarian control.

Who is she? We do not know, but the fact that she exists tells us that there must be forces of resistance in this totalitarian society, that not all are enslaved. We see, shortly, that she is being pursued, by a troop of burly policemen who look terribly menacing in their helmets with glass face masks. Her color, her animation, her freedom, even her sexuality, serve to make the situation of the inmates even more obvious and pathetic. Her image functions as a polar opposite to the enslaved men and even though we only see her, the first time, for a second or two, her existence creates drama and excitement.

The Brainwashing

In this scene we have a long shot of the inmates, sitting in rows, gazing at a gigantic television screen in the front of the auditorium, where a "big brother" figure is shown speaking to them. They are mute, expressionless, and seem to be almost hypnotized by the figure on the television screen. The message we get from this image is that mind control is an important element in the operation of this totalitarian society.

By implication, of course, control of the media (the gigantic television screen reflects this) is vital for control of the minds of the inmates—and perhaps everyone. Is this scene a metaphor for contemporary society, in which we, like the inmates, gaze in a hypnotic stupor, at figures who "brainwash" (or try to, at least) us? Is the distance between the world of the 1984 commercial and American society less that we might imagine? These questions are raised by this image.

Are we "like" these prisoners and are we "mind controlled" the way these prisoners are? We may not wear their uniforms, have shaved heads, or be prisoners (or recognize that we are prisoners, that is) in some kind of a total institution. But could it be because the control is more subtle, the indoctrination less apparent? There may be more control over us than we imagine. That is one of the questions raised by this image.

Big Brother

We see little of the Big Brother figure, only a few shots in which we see him spouting gobbledy-gook to the inmates. The choice of the actor to portray this character is very interesting. He looks like a clerk or minor bureaucrat from some organization. He is in his fifties or sixties, wears glasses, and is definitely bland, unanimated, and without much in the way of personality. He speaks in a low, rather monotonous voice. Indeed, for all we know, he may only be a minor functionary in whatever vast organization runs this society.

The message we get from a figure like this is that totalitarian institutions are essentially bureaucratic, held together not by charismatic individuals but by drab, conformist, rule-following bureaucratic types who do their jobs in a routine matter and do whatever they are told to do. They are not that different from the inmates in many respects, although the control exerted over these figures may be less overt.

The Message

Here is a transcript of the message that the Big Brother figure gives to the inmates. He speaks it, but it is also shown in captions running across the bottom of the screen.

Today we celebrate the first glorious anniversary of the information purification repentance. We who created from out of this time in all history a garden of pure ideology, where each worker may loom secure, from the test of purveying contradictory thoughts. Our communication is enormous. It is more powerful than any fleet or army on earth. We are one people with one will, one resolve, one cause. Our enemies shall talk themselves to death and we will bury them with their own confusion. We shall prevail…(At this point television screen is shattered.)

The first thing we notice is that this rhetoric is somewhat garbled and confusing. It talks about events we know nothing of, though we can imagine what might have transpired. The language has the ring of indoctrination—there is a "glorious revolution" being "celebrated." The language contrasts, starkly, with the scenario in which it is being used. There is talk in this futuristic, oppressive hyper-urban setting of a "garden of pure ideology" and the "security" that the workers should feel from all this.

It is *communication* that is given the major role here. It is a more powerful force than the military, it unites the workers/inmates/prisoners into a collectivity (or is it mass society) with "one will, one resolve, one cause." Then there is that wonderfully comic line about the enemies of this society "talking themselves to death." It is the rhetoric of persuasion, and we have the sense that the inmates of this society have been exposed to this kind of talk almost endlessly. That is, they have been brainwashed by this doubletalk.

The language, with phrases such as "information purification repentance," is that of mind control and psychic domination, and the commercial does a wonderful job of imitating it (and perhaps, in a sense, of parodying it). The goal preached is escape from "contradictory thoughts," which leads to "one will." In other words, the essentially human function of considering options and alternatives is to be obliterated—or has it been already?

The Explosion

There are several scenes in which we see the blonde woman twirling a sledgehammer (as she prepares to throw it at the screen) and the police racing toward her. She launches the sledgehammer and it smashes into the gigantic television screen. There is an explosion and we see, briefly, an image vaguely similar to that produced by an atomic bomb.

The explosion, which destroys the screen image—and by implication the domination by the mass media of the inmates—is the most significant act in the commercial. With this act a great blow is struck for freedom and we are led to imagine, in our own minds, what might follow. We are shown very little. Implicit in this scenario is the notion that once the control of people's minds by a totalitarian regime is broken, the destruction of that regime more or less follows automatically. This does not have to spelled out. It is like lancing a boil—when the system of pressure is punctured, healing can take place. The exploding screen signifies, then, the destruction of the totalitarian order that generates mind-controlling images on that screen.

The Response

After the explosion we cut to a scene in which the inmates are shown openmouthed, staring in disbelief at what has happened. They are, relatively speaking, emotionless and display no affect other than bewilderment. They have been so brainwashed, we are led to believe, that they are incapable of any kind of response. At least, in the immediate present. We hear a low hissing sound, as if air is escaping from the gigantic television apparatus in the front of the room. The camera pans the inmates as the announcement from Apple rolls onto the screen.

The Announcement

We see the following announcement:

On January 24th, Apple Computers will introduce Macintosh and you will see why 1984 won't be like "1984."

The brevity and simplicity of this announcement, which takes but a few seconds, contrasts with the excitement and visual richness of the commercial. In this situation the understatement serves to "shout" at us and to gain a great deal of interest. Apple Computers tells us that it is introducing a new computer, but also that this new computer has enormous political and social implications—for it will save us from ending up as victims of a totalitarian state.

There was a great deal of material about the Macintosh computer in the press and computer fanzines, so those interested in computers already knew about it. When the Macintosh computers went on sale, Apple sold approximately 17,000 the first day—a figure far beyond what they had anticipated. People from Chiat/Day talk about that as if it was the commercial that sold all those computers—an assumption that is very questionable.

The Heroine as Mythic Figure

The blonde heroine of this microdrama calls to mind several different heroic figures from our collective consciousness. First, there is something of the "David and Goliath" in this story—a small, seemingly weak, and in this case female, character brings down a Goliath figure by hurling a stone (sledgehammer) at it. In the commercial there are some close-ups of the Big-Brother/Goliath figure that simulate the size relationships between David and Goliath.

It is a missile to the head that does the job in both cases. With the destruction of the Goliath, of course, the forces of good can prevail. So the blonde represents a female version of David, and I would imagine many people might see some kind of a resemblance between the David and Goliath story and the events in this commercial. Here we find how intertextual readings can enrich an event and give an image a great deal of cultural resonance.

In addition, the woman can be interpreted to be an Eve figure. The fact that the Apple corporation's symbol is an apple with a bite out of it tells us that. But the blonde heroine also functions like Eve, for ultimately what she does is lead to knowledge of good and evil in a reverse garden of Eden. Before she shattered the image, the inmates were brainwashed and had but "one will, one resolve, one cause." What information these poor souls had was "purified." Their state is vaguely analogous to that of Adam before he ate of the apple. It is the tasting of the fruit that leads to Adam and Eve's "eyes being opened" and that is the beginning of human history, one might argue.

Thus, the blonde heroine is an Eve who brings knowledge of good and evil, and by implication, knowledge of reality, to the inmates. We do not see their transformation after the destruction of the Big Brother figure—indeed, their immediate reaction is of awe and stupefaction—but ultimately we cannot help but assume that something important will happen.

It is quite possible that this beautiful blonde figure may also represent, in our psyches, the Apple corporation. We know that corporations have different images in people's minds—often based on symbolic figures in advertisements and commercials. On the basis of this commercial one might guess that the corporate image we have of Apple is that of a beautiful blonde woman (who liberates men from political and psychological domination and ignorance). Much of this would be at the unconscious level, of course.

In any case, it's probably a good image for a computer company to have, since one of the biggest problems computer manufacturers have is fighting anxiety about the difficulties of operating computers— Macintosh's very reason for being, as a matter of fact. If people see Apple computers as beautiful blondes, so much the better for the corporation.

Psychoanalytic Aspects

From a psychoanalytic standpoint, the heroine is an ego figure who mediates between a monstrous and perverted superego figure, Big Brother, and the de-energized and devastated ids of the inmates. The id, as it is commonly defined, involves impulses and desires; the superego involves guilt; and the ego mediates between the two, trying to maintain an element of equilibrium. Ids are needed to give us energy and superegos are needed to prevent us from becoming creatures of impulse. Both can, I suggest, become perverted.

We see how the blonde is an ego figure in the chart that follows:

ID	EGO	SUPEREGO
inmates	blonde	Big Brother
perverted	normal	perverted
no energy	strong	no heart

As an ego figure, the heroine has to mediate between the inmates, whose ids have been weakened and drained of energy and the brainwasher, whose superego has become monstrous and distorted. One might see vague elements of an Oedipal conflict, in which a young female and an older, perhaps even "fatherly" figure have a very difficult relationship, to put it mildly.

The Mediator

One important function of the mythic hero or heroine is to mediate between opposing forces in an attempt to resolve some basic opposition.

The text of this commercial is very binary and the blonde heroine serves to identify and highlight the oppositions found in it. There are, in essence, three characters in this text. First, there are the inmates who function as one character. Then there is the Big Brother character (and the police who are part of him). Finally, there is the blonde heroine. Her function is to resolve the oppositions, one way or another—and she does this.

In the chart that follows I will contrast the inmates and the Big Brother figure. Here we are eliciting the paradigmatic structure of the text which, according to Lévi-Strauss, tells us its real but hidden meaning (as opposed to the surface meaning, which we get with a syntagmatic or linear narrative analysis).

INMATES	BIG BROTHER
obey	commands
uniforms	regular clothes
hairless	hair
listen	speaks
brainwashed	brainwasher
look at	is looked at
mindless	calculating
dehumanized	dehumanizing
alienated	alienating
emotionless	heartless

The blonde heroine, with her gorgeous hair, her vitality, her energy, her force, resolves the dialectic by destroying Big Brother and making it possible (we imagine) for the inmates eventually to regain their humanity. She also makes us aware of the depths to which the inmates have sunk, for unlike them she resists, she has a mind of her own and she accepts danger.

Thus she contrasts with both the inmates and with Big Brother, whom she destroys. The inmates and Big Brother are reverse images of one another—both drab, depersonalized, and locked into a slave-master relationship that defines each character and on which both may turn out to be dependent.

Alienated Proles

The inmates, workers, automatons—whatever you wish to call them—reflect with terrifying clarity the way modern bureaucratic states can destroy humanity and lead people into a state of radical alienation. We have here a classic case (even if somewhat oversimplified and parodied) of, in Marxist terms, a mindless proletariat being manipulated by a heartless bourgeoisie. This bourgeoisie rules by virtue of its control of the media and the manipulation of the consciousness of the proletariat. The situation in the commercial is one in which the horrors of a capitalist society are shown pushed to their logical conclusion, where workers are now enslaved and the society in which they live has become a totalitarian one.

The blonde heroine's actions symbolize revolution. She stands for the role of progressive forces (pushed underground in this society) in leading a stupefied proletariat out of its chains. Since this proletariat has been brainwashed, it is incapable of action and is, perhaps, even reactionary. Hence, it remains passive while the revolution takes place, and can only stare in open-mouthed wonder at the destruction of the power structure than enslaves it.

In this scenario, the power of the media is shown as central, and when it is put out of action, the rest is almost automatic. Interestingly enough, this message is not too far removed from the overt message of the Apple corporation—that access to user-friendly computers will prevent a totalitarian society from coming into being. Apple thus defines itself as a "revolutionary" force in the quasi-totalitarian world of hard-to-use computers where power will be held by those who know how to function in the information society.

The Macintosh will prevent society from splitting into two groups— those who have access to computers and are part of the information society and those who know nothing about computers and are condemned to menial jobs, and will form a class of workers that will have little economic power and little status. Apple is, in our imaginations, the beautiful blonde who will prevent a rigid information-based class system from evolving and, by implication, a "totalitarian" or totalitarianlike society. The Macintosh brings knowledge of good and evil to mankind and womankind and all it takes is a bite (or is it byte?).

The Big Blue

It is not too-far fetched, I would argue, to suggest that the totalitarian society shown in this commercial is an indirect representation of IBM, International Business Machines. Apple sees itself as a small, humanistic, open corporation battling a gigantic, super-powerful, and highly bureaucratic corporation, IBM. There are two readings to which this insight leads.

In the first, the whole story is about IBM. The Big Brother figure is the corporate leadership and the inmates are meant to symbolize the IBM workers who are controlled (white shirt and tie, etc.) by IBM. IBM has a reputation for being rather strict about the way its workers and sales people dress and this commercial may be alluding to the regimentation identified with IBM. The second reading suggests that IBM is the Big Brother and that the American public is the inmates—a public that has been duped and controlled by IBM, but which is about to be liberated by Apple and its Macintosh computer.

The battle resolves itself down to one between the beautiful blonde heroine fighting against the monolithic monster—a bureaucratic corporation full of faceless nobodies mindlessly following rules and regulations and "enslaving" the multitudes. The Macintosh is the sledgehammer that Apple has to throw against IBM—a user-friendly machine that will, democratically, make computing available to all. Apple is now trying to sell the Macintosh to business people, where IBM seems to have a lock on the market. How well it will succeed is questionable since there is not a great deal of business software available yet for the Macintosh and Apple's "blonde" image may, in fact, work against it.

Conclusions

Although the 1984 commercial cost a great deal of money to produce (perhaps three or four times as much as a typical high-budget commercial) and air, due to the notoriety it attracted, it ended up being a very good buy. We must remember that it only aired once, yet it was the subject of a great deal of media attention and it fascinated the huge audience that was watching the Superbowl, when it was shown.

As someone in the creative department at Chiat/Day explained to me, "good campaigns end up being relatively inexpensive." A good commercial (and campaign) may cost a great deal to produce and air, but if its impact is sufficiently strong, on attention per-thousand basis it might work out to be relatively cheap.

Chiat/Day (and Apple) took an unusual approach with this commercial. It was in the un-Cola genre and focused its attention *not* so much on the benefits to be derived from using a Macintosh but, instead, on the dangers inherent in not using one. The commercial wasn't selling a specific product in a direct manner. Instead, it used indirection and suggestion to build an image for Apple and Macintosh and, at the same time, cast aspersions on its main rival, IBM. In the course of sixty seconds it created a memorable microdrama (which is what many commercials are, actually) that worked subtly and indirectly. Like many commercials it was highly compressed, with neither a beginning nor an ending. (Many commercials don't have a beginning but do show a "happy" ending, with someone using the product or service advertised.)

The ending implied in the 1984 commercial focused on the avoidance of something hateful rather than the gaining of something desirable. In its own way, there is an element of conditioning involved here; we have a condensed form of aversion therapy. The argument, like the commercial, is very binary. If there are only two possibilities, Apple and IBM, and IBM (and all that it and its imitators stand for) is shown to be horrible, one is led to choose Apple. One acts not so much to gain pleasure (though that beautiful blonde attracts us) but to avert pain— Big Brother and the dystopian world (IBM) that he represents.

The 1984 commercial launched the Macintosh brilliantly. Apple continued to attack conformity—in the business world—in its 1985 commercial, which showed blindfolded businessmen jumping off a cliff, like lemmings. But this ad lacked the polish and aesthetic complexity found in 1984 and it was followed up by rather meager event—Apple announcing a few minor items in its campaign to get businessmen to purchase Macintoshes for their offices.

What will happen in the future remains to be seen. Some think that Apple is now fighting for its life and that if it doesn't penetrate the business market and make changes, it will become a minor player in the computer-sales wars. Others argue that Apple's penetration of the school market and the individual or nonoffice market is so great that it will remain IBM's major competitor. Whatever the case, its 1984 commercial was a fascinating and extremely rich text.

1994

Ten years after the 1984 commercial was shown, it still is mentioned and shorts from it are aired from time to time. Even though the Macintosh had a superior operating system, Apple still remains a relatively marginal player in the computer world. It has less than 15 percent of computer sales in a typical year.

In part, this marginality is because the Apple corporation made, so many people in the computer industry argue, a major strategic mistake. Instead of licensing its icon-based system, and preventing Microsoft from becoming the giant it became, Apple was content to make big margins on its computers, to have high profits on its computers but, relatively speaking, small sales.

Had Apple licensed its operating system, it would have cut Microsoft off at the pass, so to speak. Apple thought its enemy was IBM, but it was mistaken. Apple's real enemy was Bill Gates and Microsoft. By the time Apple recognized this, the battle was lost as Microsoft developed Windows software that imitated the MAC's operating system.

In recent years, Apple has found itself facing financial problems and has finally decided to let selected other manufacturers use its operating system. But Apple lost the chance it had to become the dominant force in the computer business that it quite likely could have become. It will take more than a beautiful blonde woman with a sledgehammer to rescue the beleaguered Apple corporation from its marginality.

4

Manufacturing Desire:
Alcohol Commercials and Society

Advertising is an enormous puzzlement. It is a multi-billion-dollar-a-year industry and employs some of the brightest and most creative people in American society (at very high salaries, to boot). Nevertheless, people who work in the industry have difficulty proving that it works, especially in the long term.

Item: an advertising executive told me "probably half of the money people spend on advertising is wasted...but nobody knows which half."

Item: advertising agencies are forced to talk out of both sides of their mouth at the same time. They must convince clients that advertising is effective—in generating sales, attracting new customers, or holding on to the customers a company already has. But when they are asked by governmental agencies or consumer groups about what they do, when it comes to advertising products such as cigarettes and alcohol, for instance, they argue that they have very little impact.

The situation seems to be that although nobody in the business world is certain how advertising works, there seems to be a consensus that it is necessary and that advertising campaigns are worth the enormous amount of money they often cost.

Item: commercials on the 1994 Superbowl cost approximately one million dollars for a minute.

Item: an advertising executive told me about a campaign for a soft drink. "Before we started advertising in Denver, only 12 percent of the people knew of the existence of the soft drink we were pushing. After the campaign, something like 80 percent of the people knew about it."

We are left with the conclusion, if we believe what advertising agencies tell us (and the companies they make advertisements and commercials for) that advertising works in mysterious and strange ways and that although nobody is sure precisely how it works, precisely, it does have an impact—though its power to shape John or Jane Q. Public's behavior is really quite minimal.

This may be true in the sense that we cannot be sure that a given commercial or campaign will shape a given individual's behavior—or will be the primary force in shaping that person's behavior—but collectively we can see that advertising has an impact; that is, it affects people "in general." Corporations aren't going to spend hundreds of billions of dollars a year because they are good samaritans. Nor are politicians, who spend millions of dollars on television campaigns, good samaritans either.

I would argue that advertising is a very powerful force that plays a major role in the economy (it motivates people to work so they can earn money and buy things) and, increasingly, in the political sphere. It has the power to influence and in some cases shape people's behavior, broadly speaking. In the campaign by forces opposed to the Clinton health care plan, in 1994, the "Harry and Louise" commercials are said to have eroded support for the plan by something like twenty percentage points. This is not to say that all campaigns work or that they work the way advertisers and advertising agencies imagine they will. But in the long run, taking a broad look at human behavior, it seems quite evident that advertising exists and is used because it "works" the way those paying for the advertising want it to work.

What is Advertising?

Advertising has the following characteristics:

A. Advertising agencies purchase time to broadcast commercials, made for companies selling products or services, on radio or television stations or space for print advertisements in newspapers, magazines, or other publications.

B. Advertisements are designed to attract the attention of a large number of people with suitable demographics and the proper psychographics to some product or service.

C. Advertising attempts to create the desire for the purchase of products and services advertised on the part of those reading print advertisements or listening to radio commercials or watching and listening to television commercials.

D. Advertisers hope to convince, to persuade, to motivate and, most importantly, to get people to act, to *do* something. This something generally involves moving from the desire for products and services to actually purchasing the products or services. There are, of course, many forms and genres of advertising—and it pervades the media and our lives—from the billboards on our highways to the print ads in the publications we read and the commercials on radio and television.

This chapter focuses on radio and television commercials (and on the latter more than the former) and the role they may play in stimulating the consumption of alcoholic beverages by young people.

It is worth noting some of the ideas mentioned in the most common definitions of advertising. We find such terms as *arouse* and *desire,* which suggest that there are very powerful "affective" and perhaps even unconscious or "irrational" elements at work in advertisements. (Traditionally we use the term *advertisements* for print advertising and *commercials* for radio or television advertising, and advertising for the industry. I will follow that custom.)

A Different Perspective on Commercials

The model that many social scientists have used in studies of the impact of advertising is a psychological one (or perhaps social-psychological one). People are tested to see whether they recall advertisements or whether their attitudes or opinions have been changed by having been exposed to advertisements. This approach, which often is quite sophisticated in terms of research design, frequently indicates that advertising has little or no effect on respondents. Or, to be more precise, none that can be detected or measured—or, in some cases, no long-term effects.

Psycho-Cultural Model

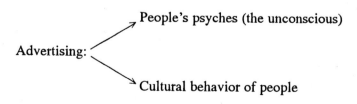

Advertising:
People's psyches (the unconscious)
Cultural behavior of people

I would suggest that a different model should be applied, one that focuses not on opinion or attitude change but, instead, on two different matters: one is people's psyches and the other is cultural behavior. Focusing on individuals or groups of individuals in test studies often suggests that advertising plays no significant role in decision making. Yet, an examination of advertising as a cultural phenomenon suggests something quite the opposite—a conclusion that might explain why revenues for advertising keep growing and why businesses continue to advertise. Advertisers are not irrational; they do not spend money "raising flags up flagpoles to see whether anyone will salute" because of idle curiosity. (Advertisers may not be irrational, but the companies that advertise assume that people are irrational. Or, more precisely, that people respond to messages that avoid ego-dominated "rational" decision making, that have an effect on unconscious elements in their psyches that often shape their behavior.)

The devaluation of the power of advertising by advertising agencies and by businesses that use advertising is generally an attempt to escape from regulation by governmental agencies and to escape from criticisms of being manipulative and, in some cases, antisocial, by consumer groups and other interested parties. Communications scholars, I might point out, have wavered in their assessments of the power of media. Thirty years ago scholars concluded that the media were powerful; then they changed their minds and concluded that they are weak. Now, it seems, the notion that the media are powerful is once again gaining acceptance.

Given this situation, when the media were seen as weak, advertisers could argue that advertising was relatively trivial—a service to inform or entertain the public, but little more than that. Yet, at the macro level, when we look at collective behavior, it seems that advertising does have power. *It is advertising's role as a cultural and political force that is significant.* We may lack the tools in the social sciences to show how advertising affects specific individuals or small groups of people in tests, but when we look at advertising as a cultural phenomenon, the situation is strikingly different.

One argument that advertising people use to defuse criticism is the "post hoc ergo propter hoc" argument. Just because something happens *after* something doesn't mean it was *caused* by it. That is, just because Y follows X does not mean that X caused Y. Thus, if John sees a beer commercial on television and then drinks a beer, it does not mean the commercial caused John to drink the beer. Nobody can argue with this. But when you move to the collective level, and have lots of people drinking beer after having seen lots of beer commercials, there is good reason to believe that the beer commercials might have some role to play in the behavior of the beer drinkers.

That is, commercials for alcoholic beverages may not be the sole causative factor responsible for people drinking, but they may play an important contributing role. Since the public airways are held "in trust," so to speak (and are supposed to broadcast "in the public interest") by television stations, the question we must ask is whether this "trust" is being abused.

Another reason that leads us to suspect that commercials play an important role in stimulating the consumption of alcohol stems from the fact that television viewers and radio listeners are exposed to so many commercials. It has been estimated that the typical television viewer, who watches approximately four hours per day, is exposed to between 500 (a conservative estimate) and 1000 television commercials *per week*. A relatively high percentage of these commercials (especially in programs that males tend to watch) are for alcoholic beverages and, in particular, beer. This redundancy, this continual repetition, must have a powerful impact on people—especially upon impressionable young people.

(One reason it is so difficult to establish, via experimental methods, a direct causal link between television commercials and alcohol consumption is that television is so ubiquitous that it is very difficult to find a "control" group, a group of people who are not exposed to television. That is why I think the anthropological "model" is more useful since it focuses on culture and on the role that alcohol plays in this culture. I will say more about this shortly.)

Television Commercials: How They Work

I will focus my attention here on television commercials since they are, it is generally held, the most powerful form of advertising. Commercials should be seen as works of art that have their own conventions; they might best be thought of as minidramas that employ all the techniques of the theater and the cinema to achieve their aims. At their best, they use language brilliantly, they are dramatic, they employ the most sophisticated techniques of lighting and editing, they have wonderful actors and actresses who use body language and facial expression to get their messages across, and they often cost enormous amounts of money, relatively speaking, to produce—many times the production costs (on a per-minute basis) or the programs in which they are shown.

The power of the human voice is well known. When this is added to strong narratives, music, sound effects, and superb writing, it is easy to see why the commercial is such an incredible means of persuasion. Let me list here some of the specific techniques that are used in alcohol commercials to add to their power.

A. *Sports Heroes.* Young people often identify when sports heroes and emulate their behavior.

B. *Sexuality.* Many of the commercials overtly connect alcohol consumption with sex. These commercials often use beautiful women in them; they are shown as an integral part of the drinking experience.

C. *Humor.* Many of the commercials are extremely funny. This humor generates feelings of well-being, which become attached to the commercials, and to the products they sell. They also suggest that drinking isn't "serious."

D. *Fun.* These commercials appeal to the "fun ethic" of young (and not-so-young) people, who are shown that drinking is fun, in itself, and connected to having fun, in general.

E. *Success.* Alcohol is often tied in commercials to people who are successful. Drinking, and perhaps knowing "how" (and *what* brand of beer or liquor) to drink, then becomes a sign of success.

F. *Reward.* Drinking is often shown as a "reward" for people who have worked hard and who, therefore, "deserve" their drinks. This appeal works at both the blue-collar level and at the white-collar level. The rewards one gets are fun, comradeship, pleasure, and sex. All of these matters are connected to the uses of alcohol by young people and that is the subject I would like to turn to at this point.

The Uses of Alcohol by Adolescents

Let me suggest here, some of the uses that young people make of drinking. We will find that many of these uses are reflected in alcohol commercials, which suggests that these commercials help socialize or enculturate young people. What I am talking about here is sometimes called "tacit enculturation." On the overt level, these commercials try to persuade everyone (including young people) to drink. On the covert level, they also teach them attitudes and values, suggest ways of behaving, and do many other things. One might even argue that often commercials have unintended consequences, ones the creators of the commercials do not and cannot anticipate.

Drinking, for many young people, is associated with being "grown up," adult, popular, perhaps even sophisticated. It is connected, in their minds, with sociability (being like others who are popular and "with it") and having lots of fun, especially with members of the opposite sex. There is often an element of adolescent "revolt" in drinking—in doing something forbidden, going against parental wishes (while imitating parental behavior, all too often) and asserting one's individuality and autonomy. One can show discrimination (via the selection of what brand of beer one drinks) and adopt various personae: hip, cool, wild, lunatic, and so on.

It is also seen, by many young people, as a means of escape from the pressures they feel. That is, drinking leads to inebriation, a state in which young people feel "free" of parental and cultural inhibitions and, somehow, more themselves. It is an escape response that is facilitated by the popular view of the drunk as a comic, at times even heroic, figure. The terms young people employ for drunkenness are connected to their rebellious spirits: one gets "smashed," "bashed," or "roaring drunk." There is, in our culture, a kind of happy, animalistic spirit given to all this and people are often kidded (and made into comic heroes) for their drunkenness and the things they do when drunk.

Obviously, the use of alcohol as a dis-inhibitor has a certain "payoff" for young people who wish to use alcohol as an excuse for whatever kind of wild or antisocial behavior they would like to indulge in—and escape judgement. Adolescents, we know, frequently experiment with all kinds of things when they are young and we should expect this. But we must also be mindful of the social cost of some of this experimenting and of the fact that in the case of alcohol, the consequences are often disastrous—both to the individuals involved and society at large.

Item: in 1983, "accidents involving young drunk drivers claimed 7,784 lives, according to an article in *The Los Angeles Times* (10 January 1985). "That means young people caused 40% of the nation's drunk-driving fatalities." Adolescence is generally considered to be a period of great change, often accompanied by considerable psychological turmoil and anxiety about identity and the future. In this state, young people are particularly susceptible to persuasion by commercials, which hold out the promise of various kinds of resolutions of the difficulties that they face.

There also may be a "rational" element to the use of commercials by young people. They may, quite consciously, decide to "accept" the persuasions of commercials so they can justify, to themselves, their desire to drink and experiment with alcohol. Unfortunately, too often, these experiments lead to tragedy, as *The Los Angeles Times* statistics demonstrate .

Teleculture

I use the term *teleculture* to emphasize the role that television plays in society. Television is not a simple entertainment that merely reflects the culture in which it is found. Television does, of course, reflect culture, but it also profoundly affects culture. It does this, in part, by focusing attention on certain aspects of culture and not paying attention to others; by creating certain kinds of heroes and heroines and neglecting other kinds.

Television is, I believe, the most powerful socializing and enculturating force in society. It entertains but it also instructs, even when it is not trying to do so. It has usurped the roles formerly played by other actors in the socialization process. Who used to be the basic socializing actors? Let me list them.

Parents. With the changes that have taken place in the family structure and the breakdown in parental authority in America, the role of the parents in socializing young people has greatly diminished.

Priests. The clergy also clearly has a diminished role, though some elements of the priesthood have discovered television and now use it for their own purposes. This use of television by the clergy, however, tends to be associated with fundamentalist sects (and, in some cases, charlatans), and not with "mainstream" religious organizations.

Professors. Teachers and other academics used to play a significant role in socializing young people and still do, but it also has been diminished. This is because teachers cannot compete with popular culture and, in fact, have to spend their time doing what they can to counter the power of the media.

Peers. We know that adolescents are particularly susceptible to peer pressure, and at various moments in the developmental cycle peer pressure is much more significant to young people than parental pressure. But who or what, may we ask, socializes peers? How do peers get their values and attitudes? They, too, like the "opinion leaders" who allegedly affect the beliefs of older generations of people, are socialized by the media.

Pop culture. It is, I believe, simplistic to argue that popular culture is the sole, only, single determinant of behavior, but it probably is correct to argue that it plays a major role (or, at least, an increasingly important role) in the socialization of young people. It is television that is of major significance here, for it is television that broadcasts (and affects, as well) much of our popular culture. The most important genre on commercial television is, of course, the commercial.

I might add that in some cases drinking is found in television programs (and films broadcast over television), which means that the content of the program serves to intensify the message of the commercials—that drinking is good, is a source of pleasure, and is "part" of life. One of the main functions of alcohol advertising is to "naturalize" this kind of behavior. That is, a cultural activity (drinking) is made "natural" and part of the scheme of things—something that "goes without saying," something we don't think about. This may be one of the most important functions of liquor advertising—to naturalize drinking and make it part of everyday life.

A Primer on Analyzing Television Commercials

Here I would like to consider some of the more important aspects of television commercials. We must remember that a television commercial is, as I pointed out earlier, a special kind of work of art—one which is created to persuade, to shape behavior in specific ways. But it still is a work of art and therefore can be analyzed much the same way a film or television program can be understood: in terms of its various components and the role they play in the production.

The narrative structure. What happens in the commercial and what significance do the various actions and events have? How might the actions and events affect viewers and what meaning do they have for people? In this area we focus on the story line of the commercial and its symbolic significance.

Dialogue and language. What do the characters say to one another and, in some cases, what are they saying to us? What devices do they use to gain our attention or affection and to persuade us? What rhetorical techniques, such as alliteration, metaphor, or metonymy, are used? What kind of language is used? What use is made of phenomena such as humor, comparisons, associations, exaggeration, praise, and logic?

Actors and actresses. Sometimes we forget that when we watch commercials we are seeing actors and actresses plying their trade. But rather than trying to convince us they are Hamlet or Ophelia, they try to convince us they are housewives who love this or that product or rugged he-men who love this or that brand of light beer. Do we feel attracted to them and empathize with them? What kinds of symbolic figures are used as characters in the commercial? What use do the performers make of facial expression, body language, and their voices? What about the clothes they wear? How old are they, and what significance do their ages have? What's interesting about the setting in which they are found?

Technical matters: lighting, color, editing, and music. Here we concern ourselves with how lighting, cutting, and shot selection impact upon viewers. For instance, close-ups lead to a different feeling about things than long shots, and shots from below convey different attitudes toward power than shots from above. Does the commercial have many quick cuts in it? If so, what impact does this have? How are things lighted and what kind of use is made of color? All of these matters are kinds of "messages" and must be included in any analysis of a television commercial.

Sound and music. We are profoundly affected by sound and music, which seem to have the power to work directly on our psyches. What use is made of sound effects? Is there music used? If so, what kind and for what purposes? How does it affect us?

Signs, symbols, and intertextual devices. Signs and symbols are phenomena that represent other things: a cross can represent Christianity, the sacred, religion, and so on. *Intertextuality* refers to the process by which we interpret one text in terms of another. Thus parody, for example, is based upon ridiculing a text (which must be known in order for the parody to work). The associative power of texts can be used to suggest things or ideas connected with the original text. This means that commercials can take advantage of what people already know—about history, literature, the arts, and popular culture—in getting their messages across.

In short, every aspect of a commercial—from the typefaces used in captioning to the hairstyles of the performers—can be considered as potentially important. Commercials are complex and "rich" works of art that demand a great deal of attention if one is to discover the mechanisms by which they achieve their aims.

Conclusions

Let me offer, here, a summary of the main points I have made and the conclusions that I draw from these points. First, *advertising is a huge industry that plays an important role in the socialization of people, young and old, in American society*. It provides what might be called "product knowledge," and research evidence suggests that even young children, at five or six years of age, know a great deal about many of the products advertising on television (and are often able to sing the jingles from commercials).

Second, *corporations advertise because it is effective in a number of different ways*. Advertising campaigns often have as the primary goal, we are told, holding market share but it is reasonable to suggest that these campaigns also attract new users. People who are exposed to commercial campaigns may not be able to recall the commercials they have seen or provide evidence that their opinions and attitudes have been affected, but advertising campaigns leave a certain kind of feeling with people, generate a certain kind of sensibility. In the case of beer commercials, it is that drinking beer is a natural part of everyday life (though we know that drinking beer is not a natural, but a cultural phenomenon). The beer industry once had a campaign something to the effect that "In this great land, beer belongs," which shows quite clearly what these campaigns are supposed to do. Drinking beer (and other liquors) becomes "naturalized" or validated.

In addition, I have suggested that *television commercials,* in particular, *are extremely complicated and powerful texts (or art works) that work in a number of different ways*. I offered a list of some of the factors to be considered in analyzing commercials. This complexity, the fact that works of art affect people in strange and complicated ways, makes it difficult to measure their effects. But the fact that corporations continue to advertise, and often increase their advertising budgets each year, leads us to conclude that advertising does "work." We have only to look around us, and observe the way people behave (in supermarkets, at work, at parties) to see the power of advertising.

Finally, I have suggested that *commercials are part of what I call "teleculture,"* which is now probably the most important enculturating and socializing force operating in society. *It is naive to think of television* (or any of the mass media) *as simply an entertainment,* which does not have a profound impact upon the people who watch it. For one thing, we know that the average person watches television about four hours per day. If television does generate "culture," as I've argued, that is a tremendous amount of time for it to enculturate people.

Television has usurped the place that used to be occupied by parents, the clergy, teachers, and other institutions as socializers of the young. We learn from all of our experiences, a phenomenon called "incidental learning" (though we may not be conscious of the fact that we are learning), so because television is such a large part of our experience, it must play an important role in "teaching" us about life.

It also happens that for a number of reasons, adolescents are particularly susceptible to the entreaties of alcohol commercials, which pose a particular threat to their well-being and happiness (and one might even add, considering the statistics about adolescents and drinking-related automobile accidents, their survival). The conclusion I draw from my analysis of alcohol advertising on television is that *alcohol commercials should not be allowed on television.*

The public owns the airwaves, which are leased to television stations and networks in "the public's interest." I do not believe this interest is being served by broadcasting commercials for alcoholic beverages. If, for some reason, it is not possible to take these commercials off the airwaves, counter-advertising should be allowed, which would alert people to the dangers caused by consuming alcohol. The consumption of alcohol is not a trivial matter, though beer commercials often make "light" of it, quite literally. The answer is not to place the responsibility on each individual, for many people, especially young people and adolescents, do not have the psychological resources to resist the blandishments of the advertisers. Alcohol is a social problem that demands a societal solution.

III
Humor: Introduction

The structure of this section on humor is similar in nature to that of the section on advertising that preceded it. Chapter 5 is a detailed semiotic analysis of an important genre of Russian joke, Radio Erevan jokes. Chapter 6 offers a multidisciplinary interpretation of a joke, showing how different approaches offer varying insights into the joke and related matters, such as who is involved in the joke and the society in which the joke is told.

The Radio Erevan jokes were told when the Russian Communist government was in power. The jokes are based upon people calling Radio Erevan and asking it questions. The answers Radio Erevan gives reveal how inept it is and, by implication, how inept the Russian Communist system that is behind Radio Erevan is, as well.

In this chapter I briefly discuss some of the more common theories about why people laugh: superiority theories, psychoanalytic theories, and incongruity theories. I also deal with a typology I developed on what makes people laugh—a list of forty-five techniques that are, I suggest, found in all humor. I elicited these techniques by making a content analysis of many different kinds of humor. This typology, along with chapters on various aspects of humor showing how it can be utilized, is discussed in considerably more detail in my book, *An Anatomy of Humor,* published by Transaction Publishers in 1993.

Chapter 6, "Eight Scholars in Search of an Interpretation," takes a joke about gay men at bar and offers eight different brief analyses of this joke. The chapter shows how rhetoricians, semioticians, communication theorists, psychoanalytic critics, sociologists, philosophers, and political scientists might interpret the joke.

In actuality, it is not unusual to find critics who utilize several methods of interpretation, combining two or three of the methods mentioned above. The reason for this is that texts of all kinds, even ones that seem as simple as jokes, are actually much more complicated than they seem and often have implications for a number of different areas: society, politics, people's psyches, and so on.

The problems we face in interpreting popular culture texts involve determining, first, which disciplines, methodologies, or approaches are most appropriate and second, applying these methodologies in interesting ways. If we look at popular culture texts from a literary perspective, many of them are not very good. (Of course, we can say the same thing about most novels, even serious ones.) But if we look at popular culture texts in terms of how they generate meaning, at the way the media affect them, and at their impact on society and politics, the situation changes considerably.

As I suggested earlier, when literary scholars, philosophers, psychologists, and others recognized that culture, of all kinds, has consequences, and when postmodern philosophers explained to everyone that America, a pop culture society if there ever was one, was postmodern, the situation changed. Cultural Studies developed and people from many different academic disciplines started analyzing and "taking seriously" everything from detective stories to Madonna, from shopping malls to jokes. It is to this latter topic, a subject I have always considered significant, that we now turn.

5

What's in a Joke? A Microanalysis

Why do people laugh? What does our laughter tell us about ourselves and others? These questions have interested some of our greatest minds, and thinkers as diverse as Aristotle, Plato, Kant, Hobbes, Darwin, Schopenhauer, Bergson, Freud, Bateson—and one might go on end-lessly—have offered a variety of different answers to them. In this examination of humor I will deal with two basic topics: first, comic devices or techniques of comedy found in humorous texts such as jokes (that is, what makes us laugh) and second, what these texts reveal about the cultural, social, and political arrangements in the societies in which they are found (see Douglas 1975: 90–114). I will begin by dealing with a number of the basic theories of humor, under which the ideas of a number of different thinkers can be subsumed.

Basic Theories of Humor: Why We Laugh

The superiority thinkers, as represented by Aristotle and Hobbes, suggest that humor involves lowly types, people made ridiculous or, as Hobbes put it in his classic statement, humor involves a "sudden glory arising from some sudden conception of some eminency in ourselves; by comparison with the infirmity of others, or with our own formerly" (Piddington 1963, 160).

Probably the most widely held theory of humor involves the notion of incongruity, namely, that there is a difference between what we expect and what we get in jokes, cartoons, plays, and other humorous works. Thus, Schopenhauer suggested that we laugh at the "sudden perception of the incongruity between a concept and the real objects which have been thought through it in some relation, and laughter itself is just the expression of this incongruity" (Piddington 1963, 171–72).

A third theory deals with the psyche and, as explained by Freud in his book *Jokes and Their Relation to the Unconscious* (1963) involves the unconscious, masked aggression and various intrapsychic economies that humor provides (see Grotjahn 1966). Lastly, there are what might be called—by people like Bateson—cognitive and semiotic theories, which deal with paradox and the way the mind processes information and finds meaning in texts (Bateson 1972 and Fry 1968).

What Makes Us Laugh:
Forty-Five Techniques Found in Humor

All of these theories tell us why people laugh, in general, but they cannot explain what it is that makes people laugh at a joke or a line in a play or at any humorous text other than in very general terms. In order to gain an element of specificity in locating what people laugh at, I made a content analysis of a representative sampling of joke books, comic books, dramatic comedies, cartoons—that is, humorous texts of all kinds—to search for the mechanisms or devices in them that generate laughter.

I discovered some forty-five techniques of humor that fall into four categories: language, logic, identity, and visual phenomena or action. I would argue that these forty-five techniques, in combination with one another (and in certain cases when reversed) can help us find, with more precision than was possible before, what it is that generates humor in texts (Berger 1976: 113–15; Berger 1987: 6–15; and Berger 1993).

This notion that techniques are important in generating humor is not original with me, but I do not know of anyone who has elaborated the notion of techniques to the extent I have. Freud discussed the structural qualities of jokes and wrote about some of the techniques found in them. Jorge Luis Borges, in the preface to *A Universal History of Infamy*, talks about how he achieves his effects in his stories. He writes, "they overly exploit certain tricks: random enumerations, sudden shifts in continuity, and pairing down of a man's whole life to two or three scenes" (Borges 1972, 13). These forty-five techniques of humor are listed below:

The Forty-Five Basic Techniques of Humor

Logic	Language	Identity	Visual
Absurdity	Allusion	Before & After	Chase
Accident	Bombast	Burlesque	Speed
Analogy	Definition	Caricature	Slapstick
Catalogue	Exaggeration	Eccentricity	
Coincidence	Facetiousness	Embarrassment	
Comparison	Insults	Exposure	
Disappointment	Infantilism	Grotesque	
Ignorance	Irony	Imitation	
Mistakes	Misunderstanding	Impersonation	
Repetition	Overliteralness	Mimicry	
Reversal	Puns/Wordplay	Parody	
Rigidity	Repartee	Scale	
Theme & Variation	Ridicule	Stereotypes	
	Sarcasm	Unmasking	
	Satire		

A number of these techniques can be reversed. For example, insult turned against oneself becomes victim humor, and exaggeration when reversed becomes understatement.

This list of forty-five techniques of humor is, in certain respects, similar to Vladimir Propp's list of functions in *Morphology of the Folktale* (1968), though I had not read Propp when I worked out my list of techniques. They are dealt with in considerable detail in my *An Anatomy of Humor* (Transaction, 1993), which devotes a long, fifty-page chapter, "A Glossary of the Techniques of Humor: Morphology of the Joke-Tale," to describing and explaining each technique and offering relevant examples. I use a number of jokes in my glossary chapter, but only because they are short texts and relatively easy to deal with. I argue, also, that if one wants to be humorous, it is much better to use the different techniques to create one's own humor instead of retelling someone else's material, which is what we do when we tell a joke.

Jokes: Definitions and Explanations

A joke is conventionally defined as a short narrative text, meant to amuse, with a punch line. This punch line is a "surprise" and is what generates the humor. This surprise takes the first part of the joke and "opposes" it, we might say, by adding an unexpected element. The structure of a typical joke is shown below.

The Narrative Structure of a Joke

$$A \to B \to C \to D \to E \to F \to G*$$
$$\downarrow$$
$$H$$

A to G* represents the narrative, with each letter being a "jokeme," or basic unit of the joke and with G* being the jokeme that serves as the punch line. This punch lines generates some kind of meaning, H, which elicits laughter (when the joke is a good one). We move from a linear narrative or syntagmatic structure with G* and H to a paradigmatic structure in which there is meaning that is unexpected and a set of simple binary oppositions that can be elicited from the text.

To show how these techniques can be used to deconstruct jokes, let me analyze a joke. If pushed too far, analyzing a joke (or any other text) with these techniques might end up as overly mechanistic, but some of the techniques, such as allusions (to gaffes that celebrities or politicians have made and that kind of thing) involve social and political or, in more general terms, contextual matters. So, we do not merely anatomize texts when we examine the techniques found in them (Berger 1974). We cannot help but consider where jokes are told, what they are told about, and how the jokes relate to the societies and cultures in which they are told. The techniques are, then, a supplementary tool to understanding jokes and other humorous texts but an important one, since they help us understand how the humor is created.

Radio Erevan Jokes

With these caveats in mind, let us analyze a joke from the famous Radio Erevan cycle. Radio Erevan, or Yerevan, is an actual station in Soviet Armenia and is pictured, in the Radio Erevan jokes, as offering stupid, silly, or naive answers to questions that are asked of it by its listeners. These answers often reveal the inadequacies of Communism, Marxism, and socialism, and satirize Russian society and its institutions. One of the classic Radio Erevan jokes is mentioned in Alan Dundes's *Cracking Jokes*

(Dundes 1987, 163). The joke goes as follows, though I have slightly modified it from the version in the Dundes book.

> A listener asks "Dear Radio Erevan, would it be possible to introduce socialism into the Sahara?" Radio Erevan answers "Yes, it would be possible to introduce socialism into the Sahara, but after the first five-year plan, the Sahara will have to import sand."

This reply by Radio Erevan is a devastating and maliciously funny indictment of socialism.

Let me offer another example of a Radio Erevan joke.

> A listener asks "Dear Radio Erevan, could we have the Mafia in Russia? Radio Erevan answers, "Dear listener, we already have the Mafia except in Russia we call it the government."

Now that I've discussed the Radio Erevan joke cycle and offered some typical examples, let me turn to the specific joke I wish to analyze.

Techniques in the Radio Erevan Lottery Joke

> *Caller*: "Dear Radio Erevan, is it true that Comrade Gasparov won 10,000 rubles in the state lottery?"

> *Radio Erevan*: "Yes, it is true! But it was not Comrade Gasparov but Academician Smirnov. And it was not 10,000 rubles but 5,000 rubles. And he didn't win it in the state lottery but lost it gambling."

Let me use my techniques to see how the humor is generated in this text and then analyze it's social and political significance in some detail. There is often a good deal of variation in specific joke-texts, in terms of names used and that kind of thing, but the example below contains the fundamentals of the joke as I remember it. My informant was a Russian physician visiting the United States who I met at a dinner party.

The essential technique found in this joke is stereotyping. The Radio Erevan jokes are about Russia and its satellites and about the impact of socialism and communism on the lives of people living in Communist societies. Stereotypes are metonymic in nature and, more precisely, based on synecdoche, in which a part is used to stand for the whole or, in ethnic jokes, a small number of people, whether Scots, Poles, Irish, Jews, or Russians are taken as representative of all Scots, Poles, Irish, Jews, or Russians. The second most important technique used in this text is reversal and contradiction. Radio Erevan says "yes, it is true" to the caller, but then points out that the caller was mistaken about who was involved in the story and what happened. It is this "yes, it is true!" that is pivotal. It is the beginning of an extended punch line in which every part of the caller's story is reversed. If Radio Erevan had said "No," and then repeated the remainder of the joke, there would be no humor. But the "yes" of Radio Erevan is tied to the way people see it, the Communist party, and Russian/Eastern-European society. In this text the material leading up to the punch line is relatively short and the punch line element is extended.

It might be suggested that this text also is a parody of the kind of double-talk one gets from the Communist party, in which truth, according to some Marxist theorists, is whatever the Party says is true and the Party often speaks out of both sides of its mouth at the same time. Thus, if the party contradicts itself, both the original assertion and the subsequent contradiction are correct. Radio Erevan is telling its caller what he wants to hear, namely that he is correct, and then undermines every aspect of the caller's story.

The caller is revealing his ignorance, another commonly used technique: he's wrong, it turns out, about everything. In addition, there is the technique of revelation in which Radio Erevan inadvertently reveals the inadequacies of Communists societies, where a bureaucracy tells people what they want to hear, "Yes it is true," but undermines them and reveals that they know very little about what is really going on, even though they may think they do.

A polarity is set up in the joke between the caller and Radio Erevan, between truth and falsehood. Radio Erevan says "yes, it is true," to the caller, which is a falsehood since, in reality, the caller is wrong about everything. The caller asks "is it true" and recites a list of things that reveal his ignorance and turn out to be false. This polarity is shown the following chart:

CALLER	RADIO EREVAN
asks question	gives answer
seeks validation	confirms that questioner is right
is it true?	yes! (but not really)
Comrade Gasparov	Academician Smirnov
won	lost
10,000 rubles	5,000 rubles
state lottery	gambling

This joke, I would suggest, reflects the cynicism that many Russians felt about Russian society and the Communist party and the way it lied to them about so many things and is a humorous but biting indictment of Russian politics and society in the Communist era.

A Microanalysis of the Radio Erevan Lottery Joke

Now I would like to turn to a microanalysis of the joke and discuss what the jokemes reveal. There are a number of jokemes or elementary units of meaning in this text that deserve discussion. We may think of each jokeme as a kind of signifier and consider what it is that they signify. These basic units will be enumerated and a number of them will be discussed in terms of what they reveal about social, technological, cultural, and political matters.

I also understand that the callers in these jokes typically have a mock Jewish accent and the answers are made in an Armenian accent, which would have significance for Russians and Eastern Europeans hearing the jokes told in the languages of these countries, but not for Americans (Powell and Paton 1988, 53). When we think about these jokes, we should consider a given Radio Erevan joke in the context of the Radio Erevan joke cycle and the way Radio Erevan typically answers questions and consider these matters in terms of Russian society and culture.

1. A caller. 2. Dear Radio Erevan. 3. Is it true. 4. Comrade 5. Gasparov. 6. won. 7. 10,000 8. rubles 9. State lottery. 10. Radio Erevan. 11. Yes, it is true. 12. But. 13. Not Comrade Gasparov 14. but Academician Smirnov 15. not 10,000 rubles 16. but 5,000 rubles. 17. didn't win lottery 18. but lost the money gambling.

Making Sense of the Jokemes in the Radio Erevan Lottery Joke

A caller. If there are callers, there must be telephones. From other jokes in the series we know that there is at the very least the opportunity for people, presumably members of Radio Erevan's audience, to make phone calls to the station.

Dear Radio Erevan. There is a radio station in a province of Russia that, as a branch or representative (might we say symbol) of the Russian government, offers "official" answers to questions put to it by its listeners. The "dear" suggests that listeners do not hold the station in awe but have, instead, a familiar and affectionate feeling for it.

Is it true? A listener is asking whether a story that he has heard is correct. This question suggests that the caller believes that Radio Erevan offers truthful answers to the various questions put to it and, in addition, by implication, knows a great deal about what is going on in society. The answers Radio Erevan gives are often truthful but naive and revelatory and, as such, a great embarrassment to the Russian power structure.

Comrade. This term is a signifier that suggests Marxist communist societies, and most particularly Russian society, where status inequalities are supposedly played down and the official credo is an egalitarian one—"from each according to his ability to each according to his need." To the American, this term calls to mind various stereotypes of Russian society: heroes of labor, babushkas, socialist realism, caviar, endless lines, vodka, the KGB, and that kind of thing.

Gasparov. To an average American or westerner, this is a Russians sounding name and thus a signifier of Russian-ness. Those in Russia and its satellites might make more of the name: it might have ethnic or religious or some regional significance.

Won. This term tells us that some kind of a contest took place in which a person can win something and winning something means, of course, that it is also possible to lose something. We may also infer that gambling in some form exists.

10,000. This is a rather large number, which suggests that something of consequence might have transpired. But the situation is rather vague since 10,000 dollars is a good deal of money, while 10,000 Italian lira or Mexican pesos (and perhaps Russian rubles) are not worth very much at all.

Rubles. This is another signifier of Russian-ness, which, along with the term *Comrade* and the name Gasparov reinforces, in the listener's mind, that the story deals with "things Russian"—Marxism, communism, Russia, and possibly its satellites.

State lottery. We know now that Russia has a state lottery and that the caller thinks comrade Gasparov has bought a lottery ticket and won 10,000 rubles. The "state lottery" here suggests several things: that the Russian state uses gambling to gain revenues and that people gamble, perhaps because their situation is so desperate that they see no way out of their circumstances except through luck and chance.

Radio Erevan. See "Dear Radio Erevan" above.

"Yes, it is true." This confirmation, as I pointed out earlier, is the pivotal statement in the text and the joke's punch line. Radio Erevan, seen in the joke as the official spokesman for the Russian government, not only answers "yes," but redundantly adds "it is true," thus reinforcing its answer. This answer sets the stage for the "qualifications" (actually reversals) that follow in which every aspect of the caller's question is shown to be incorrect.

But. This term suggests either a contradiction or some qualification or other aspect of the answer previously given is coming. In essence, the joke tells the caller he is correct but then undermines him by showing that he was wrong about every aspect of the story he asks the station about.

Not Comrade Gasparov. Here's the first contradiction in the caller's story.

but Academician Smirnov. Here we find that the caller was mistaken about who was involved in the story. It was not Comrade Gasparov but Academician Smirnov. Smirnov also has a Russian sound to it (it's a brand of vodka that is very popular) and reinforces out notion that we are dealing with Russian society and culture.

Not 10,000 rubles. This is the second point about which the caller was wrong, even though he was told he was right about the whole story.

but 5,000 rubles. Here we find that the caller did not know how many rubles were involved and, in fact, it was half as many rubles as he thought. The actual number here is not important: the joke works with 20,000 or any other number except for 10,000, though it should be considerably different from 10,000 to be effective.

And he didn't win it at the lottery. Now we discover that the money was not won at the lottery, as was presumed to be the case.

but lost it gambling. This is the conclusion of the joke and the final contradiction. The caller, it turns out, was wrong about everything.

Political Implications of the Radio Erevan Lottery Joke

We can move a few rungs up the ladder of abstraction and look at this joke symbolically. We may look upon the caller to Radio Erevan as a representative or symbol of the Russian public in general, and the question about Comrade Gasparov winning the lottery as an example of how it thinks it knows what is going on in society. The people asks the Russian government for information—for verification of its information and the government tells the people, cynically, that it is correct and really does know what is going on. Actually, of course, the joke reveals that the people know nothing and are wrong about everything.

But the fact that this is a joke that pokes fun at the Russian government and shows that the people see through the cynicism of the government. It is the government that is actually in the dark, so to speak, since it does not realize that the people recognize it for what it is and are laughing at it. Thus, there is a final reversal. The government is toying with the people and laughing at their gullibility and ignorance and the way they can be manipulated (by being told what they want to hear, "yes, that is correct," or what the government wants them to hear, since it controls Radio Erevan and by extension the mass media). In fact, however, the people are mocking and ridiculing the government and its blindness in assuming it has duped the people.

Humor's Uses: Control and Resistance

Humor is a double-valenced agent: it can be used, in some circumstances, as a means of control and regulation, but it also is a force for resistance (Powell and Paton 1988). In societies where there is sexual repression, such as the United States, a goodly percentage of the jokes have a sexual dimension to them, while in societies where there is political repression, the jokes frequently focus on political, social, and economic matters.

The Russian people and those in Eastern European countries that were dominated by Marxist governments used humor as a means of dealing with the repression they felt and many of their jokes tend to be political ones—though they did not neglect sexual jokes, and there are even some Radio Erevan jokes that deal with sex rather than with politics. Or, to be more precise, they deal more directly with sex than politics, for there is always the satirizing of bureaucracy and the Russian/East European governments that hovers in the shadows of the Radio Erevan sexual jokes. Let me offer an example of a Radio Erevan sexual joke.

A listener asks "Dear Radio Erevan, can one use a glass of water to prevent pregnancy?" "Yes," replies Radio Erevan. "Before or after sex?" asks the caller. "Instead of," replies Radio Erevan.

Conclusions

In this essay I have asked "What's in a joke?" and have suggested with my microanalysis that there's generally a great deal more in a given joke than we might imagine. In jokes, which are relatively simple texts, we often find a number of humorous techniques operating in concert to generate, in good ones, laughter. Jokes reveal a good deal about social, economic, political, and technological matters in the societies in which they are told as well as what it is that all humans have in common. As such, jokes and humor in general deserve—dare I say it—serious attention.

6

Eight Scholars in Search of an Interpretation

Jokes are, as I suggested in the previous chapter, commonly defined as humorous stories with punch lines that are meant to generate laughter. They are one of the most common ways that people communicate their sense of humor to others—and amuse, or attempt to amuse, others. We must remember that jokes are seldom, if ever, made up by the person telling the jokes; they are almost always being "retold" and sometimes the teller isn't particularly good at telling jokes. Sometimes the jokes aren't very good (that is, very funny), either. There is also the matter of being told a joke one has heard before and having to "fake" a laugh. Once you've heard a joke, it isn't funny any more.

Eight Ways of Analyzing a Joke

There are, folk wisdom tells us, many ways to skin a cat (though I can't imagine why anyone would want to do so). Likewise, there are many ways to analyze a joke. Each of these "ways" is tied to the perspective or perspectives of the person making the analysis. To show this, I will offer a joke and then present eight different interpretations of the joke, each one based on a particular discipline or perspective.

I should point out, in passing, that jokes and other forms of humor often make fun of, insult, degrade groups of every sort—gays, straights, Jews, Muslims, Christians, Asians, African-Americans, Anglos—you name it. Often, the most interesting (from a scholarly point of view) are the most hostile or negative, so my use of jokes is not meant as an endorsement of the opinions and attitudes reflected in the jokes. If I restricted myself to jokes that didn't offend anyone, to the kind of "cute" jokes found, for example, in *The Reader's Digest,* I wouldn't have much to talk about.

Let's assume that eight scholars, from different departments in a university, are having lunch and one of them tells the following joke.

THE GAY MEN AT THE BAR

A man walks into a bar. "I'm Jim," he says to the bartender. "I'm gay. Will you serve me?" "Sure," says the bartender. "What will you have?" "A beer," says Jim. The next day Jim walks into the bar, with another man. "This is my brother Bob," he says to the bartender. "He's gay. Will you serve us?" "Of course," says the bartender. "What'll you guys have?" "Two beers," says Jim. The next day Jim and Bob walk into the bar accompanied by another man. "This is my brother Sam," says Jim. "He's gay. Will you serve us?" "Yes," says the bartender. "What do you guys want?" "Three beers," says Jim. After the bartender serves the men the beers he asks "Does anyone in your family like women?" "Of course," says Jim. "Our sister Sally does! But she doesn't drink."

Let's see, now, how each of our scholars might analyze this joke. These analyses will be brief and are meant to suggest the kinds of things people with different disciplinary perspectives or ways of making sense of the world concern themselves with when dealing with a joke or any text (the term conventionally used in literary studies for any work, such as a story, novel, poem, television program, and so on).

The Rhetorician

For our purposes, the rhetorician will focus on the techniques used to generate the humor in this text. Rhetoric is traditionally understood to be the science of persuasion. I have modified things and focussed on techniques that "persuade" us to laugh. The most important technique, I would suggest, is one I call "Disappointment and Defeated Expectations." The punch line in this joke, "Of course," suggests that at least one member of the family is heterosexual, but it turns out not to be the case, for the member of the family that likes women is a woman, and thus the family remains firmly homosexual.

In this respect, it is most unusual and thus we find the technique of eccentricity, comic types, and that kind of thing, at work, also. In addition, there is the repetition, in which we are introduced to the first, second, and third brother, thus heightening the significance of the question by the bartender ("Does anyone like women?") and of the punch line ("Of course...our sister Sally does...").

Semiotic Analysis

One of the important techniques semioticians use when they deal
with texts is to consider their paradigmatic structure—the set of oppositions found hidden in them (some would say read into them) that give
them meaning. Remember that concepts have meaning, according to
Saussure, due to their relationships with other concepts; nothing has
meaning in itself. The most basic relationship, for all practical purposes,
is polar opposition. Thus, a paradigmatic analysis of this joke would
yield the following set of oppositions:

NORMAL	DEVIANT
Heterosexuality	Homosexuality
Bartender	Brothers and Sister
Males like Women	Females like Women

The joke is based on this set of linked notions that are found under
each main concept. Listeners to the joke don't necessarily bring this set
of oppositions to mind, but they must recognize it if the joke is to make
any sense and the punch line is to be effective. When the bartender asks
whether anyone in the family likes women, the question assumes the
polarity between normal and deviant (we cannot use negations, such as
abnormal, in making our oppositions because they don't tell us enough).
The term *deviant* is actually problematic, and it might be better to use a
term such as *different,* which is not negative. But in humor, of course,
insults and stereotyping go on all the time, and using the term *different*
would dilute the opposition in people's minds.

The bartender assumed, obviously, that he was asking about males in
the family who liked women, about people who were, so-to-speak, "normal." The punch line only makes sense in that context, and its humor
comes from the way it defeats our expectation of normalcy.

Communication Theory

Communication theory is a very broad field that is continually evolving and generally in a state of "ferment." One of the most famous models of communications was elaborated by Roman Jakobson. It involves
an addresser, an addressee, coding and decoding of a message, and re-

lated matters. According to most communication theorists, a message has information to the extent that it has some kind of a surprise in it. If you tell people what they already know, there is no surprise and there is no information.

Thus, all jokes, since they have (by definition) punch lines, contain information. In this joke, the information conveyed by the punch line is that the sister of the gay brothers is a lesbian and thus, everyone in the family is gay.

We must also consider the matter of aberrant decoding, a situation in which a person does not interpret a message the way the sender wants, expects, or intends the message to be interpreted. For a joke to work, the addressee or receiver must understand the message and have the same assumptions the addresser or sender has. Thus, when the bartender asks, "Does anyone in your family like women?" the addressee must interpret that question correctly and assume, correctly, that the bartender is talking about heterosexual relationships. That is what sets up the punch line, "Of course. Our sister Sally does...but she doesn't drink." That explains why she hasn't come to the bar with the brothers.

Psychoanalytic and Psychological

From the psychological and psychoanalytic perspective, it is the sexuality of the members of the family that is of paramount importance. The heroes of this little story are, it turns out, gay men, all of whom are members of the same family. The psychoanalytic perspective on homosexuality, as explained in Hinsie and Campbell's *Psychiatric Dictionary* (fourth edition) is as follows:

> Freud pointed out that fear of castration, intense Oedipal attachment to the mother, narcissism and narcissistic object choice, and identification with sibling rivals with secondary overcompensatory love for them are important etiological factors in male homosexuality. (1970, 350)

The authors point out that some believe this behavior is genetically determined, though most researchers do not.

In any case, this joke would suggest that at the heart of the family is an imaginary strong mother who has been, the theory outlined above suggests to those familiar with Freudian psychoanalytic theory, the major factor in shaping the behavior of the sons. What this joke does, however, is place homosexuality in a different light, as something relatively normal. It plays with the listener, who is tricked by the punch line. The bartender has really asked, in a roundabout way, isn't anyone in your family normal (that is, heterosexual)? But what's normal in one family is not normal in another. Seen this way, the joke is liberating and frees us from being bound by conventional ideas and beliefs.

This notion that humor can be "liberating" is a very important one, for it suggests that humor has intrinsic therapeutic value, which may explain why so many people feel the need to experience humor on a daily basis. According to statistics I've seen, the average person laughs fifteen times a day.

Sociological Analysis

Here, I will use an important sociological concept, functionalism, to deal with the joke. Functionalism looks at the way phenomena contribute to the maintenance of some entity. Phenomena can be seen as functional, dysfunctional, and nonfunctional. They also have manifest functions, that are recognized and latent functions, that are not recognized. In addition, some phenomena can be seen as being functional alternatives. They provide alternative or different ways of doing something, of taking care of some function. (Many sociologists rejected functionalism because it suggested that phenomena had to be functional for entire societies; in later versions, it is attached to smaller entities, such as groups, and not generalized to entire societies.)

What are the functions of this joke for the teller and the listener, we may ask? First, telling the joke helps build a sense of togetherness, helps integrate the teller and the listener into a group (those listening to the joke). At the same time, it may be somewhat dysfunctional in that it pokes laughter at gay people, though in a way that I suggest is not harmful.

The manifest function of telling the joke is to amuse others, to be looked upon favorably as someone who has a sense of humor, who is amusing and entertaining. We can say this about joke telling in general. But the latent function of the joke is to establish more strongly, to firm up the teller's (and listener's) heterosexual identity, to demonstrate that one is "normal" by laughing at those who are supposedly not normal, who are deviant. But the joke is not really a hostile one; it is amusing and tricks the listener, whose assumptions are shown to be false. So the joke demonstrates that one is not a hater of gay people but, instead, one who might be seen as somewhat sympathetic to them.

Finally, telling this joke can be seen as a functional alternative to hostile and perhaps even violent behavior. Humor is a means of dealing with aggressive tendencies a person might have verbally rather than physically and telling jokes is a way of dealing with hostility in an acceptable, relatively speaking, manner.

Philosophy

Philosophers, when it comes to dealing with humor, have generally concerned themselves with the nature of humor in general, its ontological status, and that kind of thing. Aristotle argued that we laugh at people we see as ridiculous, as inferior to ourselves. He is one of the fathers of the "superiority" theory of humor. From this perspective, the humor in the joke comes from our being able to feel superior to the gay brothers and their lesbian sister.

Bergson argued that humor involves "the mechanical encrusted on the living," and suggested that this manifests itself in many ways, one of which was comic types. By this he meant people who are fixated, rigid, and inflexible, such as misers, misanthropes, and the like. Wherever you have a type, he wrote, you have humor. The gay brothers in this joke represent comic types; there's something mechanical and rigid here (all members of the family are gay) where there should be flexibility and variety. The question the bartender asks, as a matter of fact, is based on this notion of flexibility and variety. But the punch line shows that the family is all gay, thus defeating our expectations of normalcy, flexibility, and so on.

Political Science

It is useful here to consider political cultures and the work of Aaron Wildavsky. He has suggested, in a number of essays and books, that there are four political cultures found in democratic societies (he actually has revised things and added a fifth one, but it is small and not significant for our purposes). These cultures are formed due to the nature of the prescriptions groups place on their members and the boundaries that exist among groups. We end up with four political cultures: egalitarians, (hierarchical) elitists, (competitive) individualists, and fatalists. According to this theory, people sometimes change political cultures (if, for example, they aren't getting the "payoffs" they expect) and are not locked into a given group for life, though fatalists generally find it difficult to escape from that position. (Wildavsky's ideas will be discussed in more detail in a later chapter .)

I would argue, pushing things to extremes perhaps, that a given joke, based on the values it supports or attacks, should appeal primarily to one of these political cultures (or people moving toward a given political culture), since it reinforces their beliefs. Conversely, it should not appeal to the other groups since it attacks their values.

In this context, the joke would be seen as essentially an egalitarian one, since it presents homosexuality in a relatively benign manner. The joke, we might say, ultimately "normalizes" homosexuality and, by doing so, appeals to egalitarian values, which stress the things that unite people rather than those that divide them, and the equality of needs we all have. An elitist joke would have made gays objects of ridicule and suggested that gays are inferior to heterosexuals. A fatalist joke would have suggested that being gay was a matter of bad luck or something like that, and that there was nothing for gays to do except resign themselves to their fate, to persecution and that kind of thing. A competitive individualist joke might involve something like seeing who could bash gays more.

We might also remember that humor can be used to control people (especially in small groups) or to resist control. The joke might be seen as a means of resisting control. The gays, who are the heroes of the joke, do show a bit of anxiety about their marginal status ("We're gay. Will you serve us?") but also feel at ease, since each member of the family is gay. Gay bashing jokes are attempts to stigmatize homosexuals and isolate them and, in doing so, we must recognize, control them. Jokes that treat gays as relatively ordinary members of society, as no more eccentric or weird than others, have the opposite effect and are a form of resistance.

A Feminist Perspective

Finally, let me offer what I think would be a feminist perspective. The joke assumes a masculinist and phallocentric world—one in which normalcy involves men liking women and, presumably, having sex with them. Remember that the punch line is based on a question the bartender asks the brothers, "Does anyone in your family like women?"

This question, as I've indicated earlier, assumes a heterosexual orientation in contrast to the three brothers, each of whom is gay.

When the bartender asked this question, he thought he was asking whether there were any males in the family who were heterosexual. Asking this question, it could be argued, privileges the phallus and, in addition, focuses attention on male sexuality. It indicates the existence of a patriarchal society in which women are of secondary importance in the scheme of things. This is the case even though all the children in the family (that we are told about) are homosexuals.

We might note, also, that Sally, the sister, is only mentioned; she is not actually brought into the bar, like each of the three brothers. Thus, she ends up playing the traditional feminine role: she is a bystander, a person on the sidelines, who is talked about but who does not actually participate in the action in the joke. This is so even though her lesbianism is the basis for the punch line.

Conclusions

This brings us to the end of our survey. I have tried to suggest how each perspective, discipline, methodology (or whatever) might make sense of the joke about the three brothers in the bar. Each perspective examines a different facet of the joke, looks at different aspects of the joke, and while a joke may not be completely illuminated by a given perspective, each one does offer important insights that, when put together with other perspectives, does a good job of explaining and interpreting the joke in a more complete and interesting manner.

Note: In addition to analyzing the joke about the gay men in the bar, this chapter also calls our attention to (and serves as a brief introduction to) some of the more important concepts and methods one can use to analyzing popular culture, media and everyday life. In dealing with these subjects, from a qualitative perspective, we must use concepts and methods found in a variety of disciplines, sciences, what you will, to analyze various phenomena (fads, fashions, curious kinds of behavior) and to find meaning in texts (it has to be elicited by the "reader") and to relate what is found to social, political, and cultural considerations. As you progress in this book, you will find analyses that explain some of these methodologies in more depth and apply them to everything from television commercials to the comics.

IV
Comics: Introduction

In this section, I offer an analysis of the cultural significance of some of the more important American comic strip and comic book heroes and heroines, from Krazy Kat to Dick Tracy, from Superman and Batman to Mr. Natural. The title and subtitle of chapter 7 makes my point—comics are not just kid's stuff, which means if we learn how to read them, we can use them to make a critique of our culture and society.

I suggest that when we read comics, we must be mindful of the graphic style of the artists who draw the strips, the nature of the narrative structures in the strips (that is, their story lines), and the dialogue and other uses of language in the strips. Comic strips are generally defined as narratives, told in pictures, with continuing characters and dialogue generally in balloons. Reading them, as cultural critiques, involves taking all of these matters into consideration. I also point out that, unlike television shows or films, comic strips are a print medium, are relatively easy to find, and are a wonderful source for the cultural historian.

As an example of how a comic strip or comic book can be interpreted, I offer an in-depth analysis of Superman, our first and most famous comic book superhero. He made his first appearance in 1938, so he's been around for almost sixty years. Superman, I point out, is a rather complicated figure. With most comic book heroes, the hero figure is the disguise. Superman disguises himself as Clark Kent and, thus, has to make his celebrated dashes into telephone booths to strip off his clothes and become (that is, reveal his true identity as) Superman.

I also deal with the interesting and coincidental parallelism between the Superman origin tale and the American experience. There are, it turns out, a number of similarities between Superman's origin, coming to America from a planet that is breaking up, and the Puritans coming to America from a "corrupt" society.

Chapter 8 deals with a comparison between Ignatz Mouse, the hero of *Krazy Kat,* and Mickey Mouse. I use this as a means of dealing with

Disney's contribution to American popular culture, in general. I point out that there are traits of anal eroticism in Disney, a notion found in Richard Schickel's excellent biography of Disney, *The Disney Version*. This anality is also manifested in Disneyland and Disney World. The fact that Disney is so popular raises an interesting question: is Disney connecting, somehow, to widespread but unrecognized anal elements in American culture and society? Or is something else happening?

In chapter 9 I deal with the healthful benefits derived from humorous comic strips. The theory behind this chapter stems from my work on humor, and from the list of forty-five techniques discussed in the semiotic analysis of the Radio Erevan joke. The point I make is that it is the humorous techniques at work in the comics that lead to psychological benefits, not the topics dealt with.

I point out that humorous comic strips (and, by implication, humorous texts of all kinds) have biological, intrapersonal, and interpersonal benefits. The funnies, then, can have and often do have therapeutic value and it is possible that we unconsciously seek out comic strips that help us cope with the problems we face.

7

Not Just Kid's Stuff: How To
Read the Comics as Cultural Critiques

Ignatz Mouse, the brick-throwing hero of *Krazy Kat,* is in jail, having creased Krazy's noggin with his brick; and Offissa Pupp has put him there. Pupp spent more than thirty years trying to prevent Ignatz from throwing a brick at Krazy in one of the great existential epics of early twentieth-century American popular culture. From 1913 until 1944, when he died, George Herriman drew *Krazy Kat.* Herriman's language was so remarkable, his art style so distinctive, and his sense of humor so original that the strip, unlike a number of others, could not be continued after his death.

Krazy Kat is considered by many followers of the comics to be the greatest strip created in America, but it is only one of the countless number of comic strips that have appeared here, from the late 1890s to the present. American comic strip and comic book artists have created a vast mythology of characters who have amused and entertained us. Without being aware of it, these artists also provided a valuable resource for historians, sociologists, and others interested in the way popular culture both reflects and affects American society.

In the case of *Krazy Kat,* for instance, two themes tend to pervade the strip: first, a tendency to value illusion over reality and second, a sense of rebelliousness and unwillingness to accept the validity of authority. Krazy, for instance, takes her numerous beanings by Ignatz as signs of love. This is because in ancient days another cat named Krazy, the daughter of Kleopatra Kat, was beaned with a brick (carrying a declaration of love on it) thrown by a mouse who loved her. This experience of bricks as signifiers of love lingers in Krazy Kat's feline memory. Ignatz doesn't know this; he is a willful, mischievous mouse who hurls bricks because he wants to hurt Krazy, but ironically, each "creasing" only reinforces Krazy's romantic illusions.

Ignatz spends a great deal of time in jail, but he never learns his lesson, never stops throwing bricks. He is a rebellious soul who refuses to submit to authority. (I will have more to say about Ignatz when I compare him with Mickey Mouse in chapter 8.) This antiauthoritarianism, this feeling that authority, somehow, is not valid, is a common trait of many of our classic comics—from *Maude the Mule* to *Beetle Bailey*.

In all battles between "inferiors" and "superiors," it is the inferiors who win, whether it be mules making fools of humans or privates making fools of gluttonous sergeants and wacky generals. The antiauthoritarianism reflected in American strips is not universal. It is quite different, for example, from the attitudes reflected in classic Italian comics of the Thirties to the Fifties, which tend to value authority and see those in positions of superiority as deserving respect and rightfully dominating those below them.

A Note on Attitudes about the Comics

You can see from this discussion that if we look at comics in terms of the way they reflect cultural attitudes and values, there's more to them than meets the eye. For many years comics were seen as "kid's stuff." They were thought to be "mere" entertainments, as relatively trivial matters that had no social significance and didn't deserve serious consideration or analysis by scholars (or anyone else, for that matter). In the past few decades, however, we have come to realize that the comics have more to them than we originally imagined. This material was always there; we just never bothered to look at the comics critically, because we were blinded by elitist notions that comics are and must be "junk."

The term *comics* is a misnomer; many strips are not funny. They also do a wonderful job of reflecting social values and attitudes as filtered through the consciousness of the artists and writers who create them. Most comic strip artists are simply trying to make a living by creating strips that people will like. They usually aren't aware that their work has any sociological or political relevance.

Walt Kelly, who drew *Pogo* and satirized McCarthy and many other powerful political figures, argued that his work was pure fantasy and had no social or political meaning to it. I doubt that he actually believed that, but that was the pose that he took. Many comic strip creators take the same position. "We're only trying to entertain people."

Artists and writers never are conscious of the full significance of what they are doing; this applies even to those who think they are, such as Garry Trudeau, who draws *Doonesbury*, or the many underground comic book artists who have satirized American culture and society. That is why critics exist—to explain what artists and writers have done. Samuel Beckett was asked what the meaning of *Waiting for Godot* was. "If I knew," he replied, "I'd have told you." As a critic once put it, "trust the art, not the artist." See what you can find in the strip and don't be put off by artists or writers who say (though they may believe what they are saying) that they are only trying to entertain or amuse their readers.

Unlike films, radio programs, and television programs, comic strips and comic books are relatively easy to find and to analyze. They are a printed record covering more than ninety years of American history and are as close as the nearest library with microfilms or microfiches of local and regional newspapers, or your local comics store. Now there are many books about comics and collections of important comics, such as *Little Orphan Annie, Dick Tracy, Li'l Abner,* and *Superman*. They are beginning to appear in CD-ROMs, as well.

Analyzing the Comics

When we analyze comics, we consider their art or graphic style, their narrative structure, and their use of language. What values and beliefs are stressed? What attitudes do we find? Are certain groups stereotyped, and if so, what are these stereotypes like? Are allusions made to social and political matters? Are some groups underrepresented and others overrepresented? How, for example, are women, children, Latinos, Blacks, Jews, Asians, and old people portrayed?

A look at some of our earliest comic strips shows that they were full of vicious stereotypes of members of minority groups. The artists who drew these strips were just reflecting commonly held attitudes and, no doubt, gave little thought to what they were doing. But stereotypes, sociologists suggest, have very powerful effects on people—both on those who are stereotyped and those who participate in the stereotyping (by accepting the stereotypes).

So the comics, though we may still think of them as "kid's stuff," are much more than that, and have played an important role in recording and perpetuating many deeply and commonly held beliefs and attitudes. It is only in recent years that minority and ethnic groups have had any success in attacking stereotyping, which still exists, especially when it comes to the way women are portrayed in the comics.

The First Generation of Comic Strips: The Innocents

Comic strips and comic books are quite different. I will deal with comics strips first, and then discuss comic books. American comic strips have passed through a number of different stages. Our earliest classic strips, such as *The Yellow Kid, The Katzenjammer Kids, Little Nemo,* and *Mutt and Jeff,* which appeared until the Twenties, can be described as innocent. They tended to be humorous, lighthearted, and simple and probably are responsible for our notion that comic strips are simple and childish. If we look beneath the humor, however, to what the strips revealed about American society, we find some interesting things.

The Yellow Kid and *The Katzenjammer Kids*

The Yellow Kid, for example, reflected an important theme in American culture—abandoned children, left to their own devices. This theme is connected to another one that plays an important role in the American psyche. Americans, it can be argued, are "spiritual orphans" who have abandoned their motherlands and fatherlands, to strike out on their own. They are free to create their futures, but the price they pay for this freedom is alienation and isolation. Sadly, the matter of abandoned and abused children still remains a problem in American society. What *The Yellow Kid* shows is that it is nothing new.

In *The Katzenjammer Kids* we find Hans and Fritz, the kids in the strip, always stealing pies and playing tricks on people. They are the typical "naughty boys," and have to play this role to achieve male identities, since goodness and morality in American society tend to be associated with femininity. The kids are in constant conflict with their parents and with adults in general—and are the focus of the strip. The strip provides an early reflection of generational conflict and child centeredness, two important American traits. Because the kids do not accept authority as valid, they don't internalize our adult values and don't grow up; they also never find a way to deal with their aggressive feelings, except in childish ways.

The Second Generation of Comics Strips:
The Modern Age Comics

The second generation of comics, what might be called the modern age strips, covers many of the classic American strips—*Krazy Kat, Little Orphan Annie, Dick Tracy, Buck Rogers, Blondie, Flash Gordon, Pogo,* and *Peanuts.* These strips are much more complicated. Some are humorous but many are not. They deal with everything from a crime-obsessed detective battling a bestiary of grotesques to a little boy named Charlie Brown and his dog Snoopy.

Little Orphan Annie: *a Political Morality Tale*

Although most of its readers probably didn't recognize it, *Little Orphan Annie* was a strip with a strong ideological message. And why not? The comic strip, after all, is a kind of print medium that can carry many different genres—action adventure strips, science fiction strips, domestic comedy strips and, in the case of *Little Orphan Annie,* a child-centered adventure story that camouflaged a political morality fable. It reflected the ethos of the Coolidge era and championed the values of small-town America and big business.

In this strip, Daddy Warbucks (who grew to look more and more like Eisenhower) was a billionaire who befriended Annie. Warbucks was always involved with secret missions upon which the fate of the free world always depended. Annie frequently complained that if businessmen like Daddy Warbucks would only be left alone and not hindered by governmental bureaucrats and red tape, things would be much better. Hers was a voice crying in the wilderness for her values were out of synch with a modern, bureaucratized, urbanized America.

Dick Tracy

Dick Tracy was a much different kind of strip. Tracy was a detective who battled, to the death—or, more precisely, to their deaths—dozens of criminal grotesques that came flooding out of Chester Gould's fertile imagination. The physical ugliness of these characters mirrored their moral ugliness, and provided an easy means of distinguishing the "good guys" from the "bad guys."

Gould's style of cartooning also contributed to the morbidity and diffuse sense of terror in the strip; he used very strong blacks and whites most of the time. The strip had a visual intensity that fit in with the demonic nature of the characters and events in the stories. Tracy is a super-ego figure, par excellence. He reflects a sense of guilt and an anxiety about evil that pervaded (and still pervades) American society and its popular culture. America, so this view suggests, is full of criminals and evil and every manifestation of this evil must be rooted out so our society can be made perfect. Tracy is one of a long line of avengers who pursue evil with relentless energy and determination and who remind us that we must be eternally vigilant.

Blondie: *The Classic Strip of Domestic Relations*

If *Dick Tracy* was the archetypal procedural detective strip, *Blondie* was (and still is) the classic strip of domestic relations in America. Dagwood is a representative figure in our popular culture, an "irrelevant" male. At one time, before he married Blondie, Dagwood was a playboy. But after his marriage, he became, quickly, a rather childish figure, trying to eke out a bit of comfort lying on the living room couch or raiding the refrigerator.

One of the conventions of American popular culture is that marriage is destructive of male authority, which explains why so many fathers in the comics and situation comedies are buffoons, who nobody takes seriously. Dagwood Bumstead has no sex life (that we are aware of) and spends his life being abused by his boss and dominated by his wife and kids. Yet, despite his endless defeats and humiliations, he is cheerful and good humored. He refuses to acknowledge his situation, and is unable to be truthful about his real feelings. It has been estimated that Dagwood "wins" his various battles about 15 percent of the time, but you'd never know that from the way he acts.

Blondie is one of the most popular strips in American comicdom; it has been amusing us since 1930, though a new writer-artist team is doing the strip. Quite likely one of the reasons we like the strip is because it mirrors, in interesting ways, our lives—the relationships we have with our bosses, our wives and husbands, and our children.

Many sociologists suggest that comics and other kinds of popular culture should be understood in terms of the uses they serve and the gratifications they provide people. From this perspective, *Blondie* is popular because, curiously enough, it helps us see ourselves more clearly. At the same time, in Dagwood it may be providing a role model for men that teaches them to avoid acknowledging their feelings by adopting a stance of cheerfulness. That is how Dagwood copes, but it may not be the best way to deal with problems.

Peanuts

Peanuts is a different matter, but it also has a serious aspect to it. Created by Charles Schulz in 1950 (yes, it's been around for more than forty years), it deals with the experiences of a group of young children and a dog, Snoopy. These characters, such as Charlie Brown, Linus, Lucy, Shroeder, and Snoopy function as "naive commentators." Their passions mirror those of adults (who are never seen) and enable us to see our follies and crazy beliefs in a bit of perspective.

Schulz is a genial commentator on the human condition and uses Snoopy and all the other characters in *Peanuts* to poke fun at our behavior. There are several inversions in the strip: children act like adults and a dog acts like a human and is full of personality and spirit. The strip, like all comics, has changed over the years; Schulz's line is much more fluid and his characters look quite different and, especially in the case of Snoopy, have developed and refined their personalities.

The characters in *Peanuts* have moved from being mere comic strip figures and now have become part of our folk culture. Some scholars have also found a religious significance to *Peanuts* and a number of books and articles have been written on this aspect of the strip. Is there, in the background, these scholars ask, a diffuse sense of guilt and a notion that humans are "sinners"? Foolish sinners, but sinners nevertheless.

American children now grow up reading *Peanuts,* having Snoopy soft dolls, sleeping on *Peanuts* sheets, and surrounded by his characters. At the center of all this is Charles Schulz, a genial genius who read about an art school on a matchbook cover and sent away for information. The rest is history.

Doonesbury: *The Voice of the Liberals is Heard in the Land*

The last comic strip I would like to discuss is Garry Trudeau's *Doonesbury*. There is some debate about whether *Doonesbury* should be classified as a comic strip or as a political cartoon. Whatever it may be, *Doonesbury* is a strip that deals very directly and consciously with social and political matters. Trudeau, a Yale-educated cartoonist, is merciless in the way he satirizes businessmen, celebrities, social types, and politicians—especially conservative politicians such as Ronald Reagan and George Bush. (He also attacks liberal politicians when he feel they deserve it.) His strips are both funny and savage, in the best tradition of a long line of comic strip artists, cartoonists, comedians, and other kinds of humorists who have taken American politics and society as their subject.

Trudeau does not draw particularly well, but he has a brilliantly inventive mind. Like most humorists, he is a force that cannot be restrained, whether by propriety or good sense. There is, in the great humorists (we saw it in *Krazy Kat* as well), a wildness and irreverence that shows no concern for traditional pieties. From time to time certain editors refuse to run his strips. But Trudeau carries on and refuses to make compromises. This, it would seem, is the price we pay for having humorists. If they were able to restrain themselves, they probably wouldn't be humorists.

Humor as a Means of Control and Resistance

Humor, as I suggested earlier, can be a force for control and a force for resistance. In some cases, especially in small groupings, humor can coerce people into behaving in certain ways; in other cases, humor crystallizes popular opinion and strengthens the feelings people have that they should resist those with power. *Doonesbury*, I would say, is a force for resistance in American society. Trudeau satirizes and ridicules presidents, politicians, well-known personalities, and social practices and in many respects can be described as a spokesman for the liberal conscience in America.

There are countless other important strips that could have been discussed; we have created many strips since 1895, when *The Yellow Kid* appeared, and generations of Americans have grown up reading the comics in the newspapers. A look at strips from the Thirties and Forties shows that they had larger balloons and used many more words. In recent decades, we have moved away from narrative strips to daily gag strips, since the comics can't compete very well with television when it comes to telling stories.

But the newspaper comic strip remains popular. Many Americans, adults as well as children, start off the day reading the comics. (President Reagan is alleged to have done so.) Then, with the "serious" reading of the day taken care of, they move onto the front page or the business section or the sports section. We might only spend a few minutes each day on the comics, but when you add this up over the course of many decades, you can see that the comics play an important part in our lives. (Our attachment to the comics is so strong that during a newspaper strike in New York a number of years ago, the mayor read the comics, over the radio, so adults and kids wouldn't lose track of what was happening in their favorite comics.)

Caped Crusaders: Costumes in the Comics

Probably the most famous costume in the comics is that of *Superman*, the so-called "man of steel." His costume more or less set the tone for other comic-strip and comic-book heroes and heroines who followed, though they were all anxious to avoid copying him too closely (and getting sued). As Jim Steranko says in his *History of the Comics* (vol. 1, p. 39):

> Superman was a bold, bright figure displaying the three primary colors—red, yellow and blue, with poetic legitimacy. Not only would every costumed hero to follow be patterned after the Man of Steel's powers, but his costume would, of necessity, be some blend or synthesis of Superman's own.

The superhero's costume serves to differentiate the hero from the ordinary person, in general, and the character's heroic persona from his nonheroic persona, in particular.

In the case of Superman, who was the first significant costumed superhero in American comic books, the situation is quite complicated because unlike other superheroes, the superhero persona (I am using persona in its theatrical sense, in which it means "mask") is the real one and the Clark Kent persona is the disguise. With most comic-book superheroes, it is the everyday identity that is real and the superhero identity that is created when they put on their costumes. That is, most super-heroes put on their costumes and become transformed from ordinary persons into figures with super powers. (Some, of course, are always in costume.) With Superman, however, it is just the opposite and he must strip off his everyday clothes to reveal his true identity—often by ducking into phone booths—before he can go into action.

Superman made his first appearance in June, 1938, so he has been around a long time—and so have the host of other comic book superheroes who followed after him. These heroes provide their readers with images that speak directly to their unconscious, with characters who possess marvelous powers quite similar to those found in fairy tales. Though comics have mythic dimensions, it strikes me that more often than not, comic-strip heroes are more like those found in fairy tales than in myths per se.

As association is made between heroic costumes and super powers. In most cases putting on a costume signifies possessing powers and thus a physical transformation accompanies a sartorial one. It is a complicated matter because often the heroes, as a result of all kinds of scientific mumbo-jumbo, are powerful at all times. But they cannot use their powers, generally, until they are in costume. Often this is because they cannot give away their disguises. So the costume signifies both possession of superpowers and the ability to use them, in many cases.

What is at work here is what might be described as magical thinking—the belief that extraordinary and supernatural phenomena are at work in the universe. According to Bruno Bettelheim, children need to believe in magic at certain periods in their lives in order to help cope with a frightening and terrifying world in which they find themselves small and relatively powerless figures. This explains, in part, why comic books are so popular with children. These comics help youngsters "cope" with the world in a manner analogous to the way fairy tales function. In *The Uses of Enchantment: The Meaning and Importance of Fairy Tales,* Bettelheim discusses the kinds of satisfactions fairy tales provide. If you substitute "comic-book heroes" wherever Bettelheim says "fairy-tale heroes," you can see how important these heroes are for children. He writes, in his chapter "Vicarious Satisfaction versus Conscious Recognition" (1976, 57):

> The fairy-tale hero has a body which can perform miraculous deeds. By identifying with him, any child can compensate in fantasy and through identification for all the

inadequacies real or imagined, of his own body. He can fantasize that he too, like the hero, can climb into the sky, defeat giants, change his appearance, become the most powerful or most beautiful person—in short, have his body be and do all the child could possibly wish for. After his most grandiose desires have thus been satisfied in fantasy, the child can be more at peace with his body as it is in reality. The fairy tale even projects this acceptance of reality for the child, because while extraordinary transfigurations in the hero's body occur as the story unfolds, he becomes a mere mortal again once the struggle is over.

Costumes, then, allow children to return to reality and accept their bodies and situation. The comic-strip superhero's costume is very functional and psychologically gratifying in that in enables youngsters to have power fantasies and to return to normalcy with relative ease.

Notice the importance Bettelheim gives to being able to change one's appearance and to the body. Costumes enable children to escape the limitations they feel so acutely—they are relatively small and weak in a world dominated by "giants" (read adults here). The passage by Bettelheim quoted above might well describe a typical Superman adventure in which, after all kinds of heroic exploits, he once more assumes his disguise as Clark Kent, the "mild-mannered" and relatively obscure reporter. At the conclusion of one episode, in which, as Superman, he rescued Lois Lane from a disaster and was rewarded with a "super kiss" from her and expressions of her undying love, we find the following dialogue.

Clark Kent: "Lois...That wasn't a nice stunt you pulled on me. But I like you just the same.

Lois Lane: "Who cares.? (—The spineless worm! I can hardly bear looking at him, after having been in the arms of a *real* he-man.")

The very last panel in this episode features an advertisement telling children that in order to win prizes in a Superman contest, they have to be a member of the Supermen of America.

Children can gain valuable benefits from reading about Superman. Clark Kent *seems* weak—but underneath the appearance of weakness is the reality of superpowers. Someday, like Clark Kent, the young child will strip off his veneer of weakness and powerlessness and show what he can do.

Probably the second most recognizable comic book super hero is Batman, an iconic (that is, he resembles a bat) figure who battles against a variety of grotesque villains, also iconic, such as the Joker and the

Penguin. At the conclusion of the origin tale of Batman, Bruce Wayne speculates about the kind of disguise he should adopt:

> Criminals are a superstitious, cowardly lot, so my disguise must be able to strike terror into their hearts! I must be a creature of the night, black, terrible... A...A...A Bat! That's it! It's an omen. (A huge bat has just flown in his window.) I shall become a *BAT*!

The last panel of the origin story shows Wayne in his Batman disguise, silhouetted against a bright, full moon, and three bats flying about.

Like many other super heroes, Batman provides youngsters with a young sidekick hero to identify with—Robin, though it is Batman who captured the imagination of children the most. (The relationship that existed between Batman and Robin has been the subject of considerable speculation by psychoanalytically inclined critics, I should point out.) During the Batman rage of a number of years ago, many children in my neighborhood used to tie a towel around their neck and play Batman. It was always the youngest and weakest children who were forced into the Robin role.

In the forty years since Superman was first created there have been legions of important comic book heroes, each with distinctive powers and costuming. Thus, the Flash had the power of incredible speed and was drawn as a winged Mercury figure. The Green Lantern had a rather elaborate and long cape with a Green Lantern emblem, Hawkman had wings (and thus the power of flight) and a hawk facemask, and Captain America had a costume that approximated the American flag, with white stars and red, white, and blue colors.

Most of the early superheroes had rather simple identities—they were good guys (or women, we must not forget Wonder Woman) who fought crime and, when appropriate, foreign villains such as the Nazis, the Japanese, or Russians and other Communists, and their sympathizers and cohorts.

In recent years, however, comic book figures have lost their simplicity and their innocence—they've lost their virginity, it seems, as well as (in many cases) their capes. Thus a character such as Spider-Man is much more complex than earlier figures, though his costume is rather typical—using spiderwebbing motifs to signify the powers of the hero. But regardless of the changes made in comic books, a glance through almost any of them reveals characters with fantastic costumes and remarkable powers, battling opponents equally splendiferous and incredible. A glance at Marvel Comics's retinue of characters reveals that costumes are as elaborate and incredible as ever and that caped and uncaped crusaders are still battling villains of the most awesome and terrifying nature so that mankind (and womankind) will survive.

The subliminal message that children learn from reading and looking at comic books is that clothes are important signs of personality and character, and that there is a strong connection between fashion and fantasy and identity.

Superman and the American Experience: A Case Study

A look at the two-page origin tale of *Superman* shows that there is a remarkable similarity between Superman's origin tale and what might be described as America's origin tale. Superman was born on a doomed planet, Krypton. He was sent on a long, perilous voyage, in a small space ship, and landed in America. A kindly old couple, the Kents, found him and adopted him. "The poor thing!—It's been abandoned," says Mrs. Kent. He demonstrated superhuman powers and was taught by his foster parents to hide his strength (lest he scare people) and use it to assist humanity. When the Kents died, Clark Kent (Superman's disguise) decided to dedicate his life to "helping those in need."

This story, curiously, parallels the experiences of our Puritan forefathers, who abandoned what they saw as a corrupt society, traveled in small vessels across a vast ocean to a new world where they had great power, and had a strong sense of mission. They feared corruption by the old world and their values—individualism, achievement, equality, the importance of willpower—have played an important role in American culture for more than 300 years. They also were conscience ridden and this, too, was instrumental in the shaping of the American psyche.

It is probably only a curious coincidence that two schoolkids thought up a hero named Superman whose story parallels that of the Puritans, but Superman's values are probably reflections of the dominant values found in American society in the Thirties, when he was created. Note, also, that Superman can only be weakened by exposure to Kryptonite— that is, his old world. Americans felt, for a long time, that European culture and values weakened and corrupted American ones (a most interesting similarity).

Superman has changed over the years. The first drawings were quite crude; later on, he become a very muscular and slickly drawn figure. His powers increased, also. He flew (instead of "leaping tall buildings at a single bound"), he had X-ray vision (and so could root out criminals, no matter where they hid), and so on. One of the most significant aspects of Superman, as I pointed out earlier, is that Clark Kent is the disguise. The mild-mannered, bumbling reporter is only a mask for the superhero hidden beneath. This is a pose that many Americans adopt for themselves; underneath our facade of ordinariness, our disguise, is an heroic being, just waiting for his or her big chance. There is, unfortunately, all too often a split between our dreams and our actual achievements. When we reach our thirties and forties, this often leads to a sense of bitterness and depression over having "failed," somehow, to show our true colors and achieve our goals.

Spider-Man and the Tormented Psyche

Stan Lee, the creator of Spider-Man and The Fantastic Four (and scores of other superheroes and superheroines) is probably the most influential writer of mainline comic books in recent years. It was he who created Spider-Man. This comic book (and strip) features Peter Parker, "Midtown High's only professional wallflower," who is bitten by a radioactive spider and becomes a superhero with remarkable spiderlike powers.

What is remarkable about Spider-Man is that unlike previous comic-book heroes, he is three-dimensional; he suffers from anxiety and guilt, he often feels lonely and alienated. In an early episode he refuses to stop a thief who runs right by him. "From now on," he tells a policeman, "I just look out for number one—that means—ME!" As a result of his behavior, his uncle is killed by the thief. Spiderman learns, from this, that "with great power comes great responsibility," and that failure to act often has negative consequences. He is, then, a much more human kind of figure. Many of Lee's other heroes were also rounded and humanized. It was this innovation that made it possible for us to see comic-book figures in a new way, and led, quite likely, to graphic novels such as *The Dark Knight*.

Ultimately, this humanization of the heroes and heroines made it possible to make serious, full-length films about these characters. The success of the Superman films led to several Batman films, which were an enormous commercial success and to films about Popeye (which was an important utopian strip), Dick Tracy, and other heroes. What has happened is that we now are able to see these heroes (and there are, regrettably, relatively few heroines) as legitimate heroes, and not as one-dimensional cartoon figures. These heroes, like all heroes, are popular because they speak to our needs, because they give us models to imitate and identify with, because they reflect and reinforce fundamental American beliefs and values.

Underground Comics and the New Wave Comic Artists

Heroes such as Superman and Batman are popular with many Americans. But there are a number of heroes and heroines who are found in strips and in books who represent the opinions of critics of society and of various subcultures. The earliest of these counterculture comics were known as "underground" comics, and featured characters such as Mr. Natural, The Fabulous Furry Freak Brothers, and Trashman, to name just a few.

Mr. Natural and many of the other underground heroes satirized American middle-class culture as well as the fakery found in the counter culture. Their heroes reveled in "free" sexuality and a permissive attitude toward drugs, antimilitarism and a comic revulsion towards politics and most aspects of American society." But underneath it all could be seen a kind of joyless and compulsive sexuality as well as a degrading attitude toward women (and a comedic nihilism). Crumb, the creator of Mr. Natural, has been attacked for his sexism, but claimed (in a celebrated strip) artistic "freedom."

A newer generation of comic artists, a number of them women, has continued to satirize American politics and society, but in a manner that is more polished and not created to offend and outrage people. I am talking about artists such as Linda Barry, Victoria Roberts, Gary Panter, Bill Griffith, and Matt Groening.

Griffith created "Zippy the Pinhead," Groening invented weird characters who "hellishly" satirize contemporary American society, Victoria Roberts has a strip *Little Women* and appears regularly in *MS* magazine, and Gary Panter has a character, "Jimbo," who inhabits a world that has been devastated by nuclear bombs. These artists and many others use the comic strip form for telling commentaries on our values and beliefs, our fads, and fantasies.

Traditionally we distinguish between cartoons, which are in single frames and have dialogue underneath, and comics, which have continuing characters, many frames, and dialogue (generally) in balloons. These artists would all be classified as comic-strip artists, but they do not always follow the conventions of the comic strip or comic book. But neither did Herriman, for that matter. Their work often appears in books as well as magazines and other periodicals.

Final Considerations on the Comics

It is hard to come to any conclusions about a body of work that covers more than ninety years and thousands of artists and writers without resorting to "glittering generalities." Still, if I were to choose one characteristic that seems central to American comic strips and comic books (and American culture), it would be our widespread antiauthoritarianism. We do not respect our so-called "superiors" and feel that authority is, generally speaking, not valid.

This is a heritage of our egalitarian value system; we may not have achieved an egalitarian society yet, but we are committed to doing so. In America we hold it to be self-evident that all men and women are created equal. The artists who create our comics often attack us for not doing a better job of realizing this goal. They do this by being satirical, by trying (and often succeeding) to outrage us through the use of pornography, and by championing (not always consciously, I might add) a general antiauthoritarian view of things.

All cultures can be thought of as carrying on a "dialogue" with themselves and there are American comic strip and comic book artists who attack the rebelliousness and antiauthoritarian motifs found in so many of our comics. There are (or, more precisely were) strips such as *Dick Tracy* and *Little Orphan Annie*, which tend to support authority, though "conservative" strips are fewer in number. Most of the time, none of these social and political themes are evident to the readers, who are merely looking for entertainment. But the themes reflected in comics probably do, in subtle ways, reinforce the values of their readers.

Heroes play an important role in our lives. We identify with them, we internalize their values, we try to imitate them. It has been suggested by psychoanalytic theorists that the child is the father to the man. It is conceivable, then, that our first heroes, the heroes of our childhood and adolescence, in subtle ways help shape our sense of ourselves and our ideas about politics and society. Youngsters and increasingly young adults read comics, collect them, and think a good deal about their heroes and heroines and the adventures they have. So these paper heroes are much more important than we might imagine. When you know a person's heroes and heroines, you know a great deal about them.

Americans are not alone, of course, in having comic strips and comic books. There are brilliant comics in many countries; some comics, such as *Tintin* and *Asterix,* which are from Europe, are international favorites. The comic book industry is an enormous one all over the world; most of the European countries publish a large number of magazines and books of comics. Disney's comics (about which I will have a good deal to say in the next chapter) are widely read in Europe and South America, and have been attacked by Marxists, as a matter of fact, for spreading capitalist beliefs to unsuspecting readers. That is the thesis of a book called *How To Read Donald Duck: Imperialist Ideology in Disney Comics.*

UNESCO was involved with the publication of a book, *Comics and Visual Culture,* which dealt with comics in countries such as Japan, Kenya, Italy, America, Mexico, India, Russia, France, and Britain. The study examined the way comics "socialize" young people—how they teach them values, beliefs, and roles. It found that comics tend to reflect the societies in which they are created and have an impact on people of all ages and social rankings.

In Japan, for example, hundreds of comic magazines, known as *Manga,* are published each month which appeal to various groups, from young girls to adult males. More than ninety *Gekiga*—erotic comic magazines— are published and they are widely read. There are also *Songoku,* high-quality religious comics, and everything else in between. Japan is but one of many countries that has a flourishing comics industry.

In recent decades, sociologists and communications scholars have become increasingly interested in the comics. In Europe, Umberto Eco, the famous semiotician and novelist, has written extensively on the comics, and so have many other scholars. there is a great deal of work going on in America, too. There are now many books about the comics as well as collections of important comics.

Who knows how many other remarkable new characters are being born in the imaginations of the writers and artists who create our comic strips and comic books? Their characters are about to join that pantheon of American comic strip and comic book heroes and heroines with whom we have grown up and who have merged into our lives and affected us in ways that we are only beginning to understand.

8

Of Mice and Men:
An Introduction to Mouse-ology
(and a Study of Anal-Eroticism in Disney)

This chapter deals with the two most important mice in American comics—Herriman's Ignatz Mouse from *Krazy Kat* and Walt Disney's Mickey Mouse. In addition, it deals with important themes in Disney as reflected in his animated films and theme parks. Disney's characters, for the general public, seem to be embodiments of innocence and Disneyland is nothing but a clean amusement park. Psychoanalysts and cultural critics, on the other hand, have found other elements in Disney's work that raise interesting questions about what animated Disney, what effects his cartoons, films, and parks may be having on people, and what the great popularity of Disney might mean. Here, I investigate what might be described as the "dark" side of Disney, and compare Mickey Mouse with Ignatz Mouse, to my mind a much more humane and admirable comic-strip mouse.

A Mouse to Meet Technology's Needs

Mickey Mouse is one of the most popular comic-strip characters in the history of American popular culture and one of the most significant creations in animated films. What significance does this squeaky-voiced rodent have? What does he tell us about ourselves, our culture, our society, our ethos, and our mythos? Why is this mouse such a monumental figure for pop culturists, mythologists, culture critics, and Disneyologists?

This report should be looked upon as a contribution to the study of pop culture mice, a field to which I will give the neologism "mouse-ology." It also deals with Disney and, since his films and parks are so popular, by implication, the American psyche. (The troubles that the Disney park in France are having suggest that people in other cultures don't always relate to Disney's work the way Americans do, though his comic-strip characters are popular in many different countries.) Let's allow Walt Disney himself to describe Mickey Mouse's origin tale:

> His head was a circle with an oblong circle for a snout. The ears were also circles so they could be drawn the same no matter how he turned his head.
>
> His body was like a pear and he had a long tail. His legs were pipestems and we stuck them in big shoes [also circular in appearance] to give him the look of a kid wearing his father's shoes.
>
> We didn't want him to have mouse hands, because he was supposed to be more human. So we gave him gloves. Five fingers looked like too much on such a little figure, so we took one away. That was just one less finger to animate.
>
> To provide a little detail, we gave him the two-button pants. There was no mouse hair or any other frills that would slow down animation. (Schickel 1968, 95).

All of this was necessary because Disney, so Richard Schickel reports in *The Disney Version,* had to produce some 700 feet of film every two weeks; thus he needed a character who was easy to draw.

We already see here the germ of Disney's passion—his fascination with technology and his willingness to let the requirements of machines dictate what he would do with his creations. Technology's inner necessities shaped Mickey Mouse, Disney's first significant creation, just as they were to shape his other efforts, including Disneyland. Mechanization had already taken command, decades before the idea of audioanimatronics had entered his head.

Were I a doctrinaire Freudian (as I have been accused of being), I'd feel compelled to speculate, at the very least, about the significance of Mickey Mouse trying to wear his "father's shoes." Is there some kind of a hidden Oedipal aspect to this? What about the symbolic castration—lopping off one of Mickey's fingers (on each hand) because five fingers looked like "too much" on a small character? Could these "birth traumas" be, in some way, connected to the sadism and cruelty one often finds in Mickey's actions (masked, of course, by a veneer of genial humor and nonsense)? That squeaky voice of his? Is he one of the castrati?

The mouse is a familiar character in folklore and popular culture. A mouse gnawed through the ropes holding a lion, who had saved the mouse at an earlier time, and three blind mice, obviously not then castrated (even symbolically), ran after a farmer's wife—with disastrous results. (I will not go into the messy details about this matter.) We've also had a Mighty Mouse figure and, of course, that remarkable and magnificent mouse, Ignatz (hero of Herriman's brilliant comic strip *Krazy Kat*), about whom I'll have more to say later.

Mice are small, timid, dirty rodents with a passion, so we are told, for peanut butter and cheese. They have been anthropomorphized for centuries, but they have not always ended up like Mickey Mouse, though to be fair, I would imagine that media mice (as well as other creatures), like him, have mirrored many of their cultures' dominant values and preoccupations obediently and unobtrusively.

It is remarkable that Mickey Mouse's great triumph in *Steamboat Willie* was in 1928, more than sixty years ago. Since that time Mickey Mouse has been a character of some consequence and he, as well as his celebrated creator, "Uncle" Walt Disney, are worthy of considerable attention.

Considering the importance and impact of Disney's comic strips, film, and theme parks, there has been relatively little written about him and his impact on culture and society. Richard Schickel wrote *The Disney Version: The Life, Times, Art and Commerce of Walt Disney* in 1968, and there is an issue of *The South Atlantic Quarterly* "The World According to Disney" (Winter, 1993) that deals with his impact, and there have been occasional articles and books, but for all intents and purposes, he has been neglected.

The All-American Rodent: Like Father, Like Mouse

The myth of America is that we can all be successful if we are willing to work hard enough. We can all emerge from the poverty and obscurity in which we are born and with a bit of luck, pluck, and virtue, reach a stage in which we can, like Benjamin Franklin (who is an important role model for us, here), dine with kings. Or at least with movie stars and other showbiz celebrities. This is the American dream, which argues that social class is irrelevant and that individual will power is the crucial factor in determining success.

There is, in the American psyche, a voracity, a hunger for experience, a lust (and I use the word with its sexual connotations in mind) for success, and the symbols of success so that others will know that one is successful, which generates tremendous energy and dynamism. But also some other, less wholesome, consequences.

Disney was a small-town boy from the midwest with all-American values, whose life is a testimonial to the fact that some people who are born in ordinary circumstances can "make it." There seems little doubt, when you examine Disney's life and his work, that he was afflicted with a great and overwhelming desire to be a success, which might account for his well-documented compulsiveness. Much the same applies to Mickey Mouse, whose quest for experience seems Promethean or, at least, Kerouakian. Mickey's biography reads like something you might find on the dust jacket of a successful beat poet's book, describing his life and numerous occupations, travels, and adventures before he became a member of the literary bourgeoisie.

Here's Schickel's description of Mickey Mouse's career:

> The temporary solution to the problem of keeping Mickey fresh and amusing was to move him out of the sticks and into cosmopolitan environments and roles. The locales of his adventures throughout the 1930's ranged from the South Seas to the Alps to the deserts of Africa. He was, at various times, a gaucho, teamster, explorer, swimmer, cowboy, fireman, convict, pioneer, taxi driver, castaway, fisherman, cyclist, Arab, football player, inventor, jockey, storekeeper, camper, sailor, Gulliver, boxer, exterminator, skater, polo player, circus performer, plumber, chemist, magician, hunter, detective, clock cleaner, Hawaiian, carpenter, driver, trapper, whaler, tailor and Sorcerer's Apprentice. In short he was Everyman and the Renaissance Man combined, a mouse who not only behaved like a man but dreamed dreams of mastery like all men. (1968, 117)

In short, he was a kind of homemade Leonardo Da Vinci—and like Leonardo, Mickey's sexual proclivities, and those of his creator as well, are of some interest.

It is pretty obvious that Disney can be described as having many personality traits of the anal erotic. In his famous essay of 1908 entitled "Character and Anal Eroticism" (in a collection of Freud's essays, *Freud: Character and Culture,* edited by Philip Rieff), Sigmund Freud described anal erotics as follows:

> The persons who I am about to describe are remarkable for a regular combination of the three following peculiarities: they are exceptionally *orderly, parsimonious,* and *obstinate.* Each of these words really covers a small group of series and traits which are related to one another. "Orderly" comprises both bodily cleanliness and reliability and conscientiousness in the performance of petty duties...."Parsimony" may be exaggerated to the point of avarice; and obstinacy may amount to defiance, with which irascibility and vindictiveness may easily be associated. (27, 28)

These three characteristics are often connected with an eroticization of (and intense interest in) the anal zone.

In his essay "The Wonderful World of Disney—Its Psychological Appeal," psychiatrist Michael Brody discusses anality in Disney's work. (Ironically, this paper was delivered to a convention of psychiatrists at a meeting held at Disneyland.) Brody writes:

> The story of the two frivolous brother pigs and the contrasting hard-working pig [in "The Three Little Pigs"] chased by the hungry, big bad wolf, provides not only possibly a parable of the hard times of the early 1930's, but the virtues of obsessiveness. Plan, prepare, isolate and be orderly. Only the pig who builds a traditional house of brick saves the other two "silly pigs" from being eaten by the Big Bad Wolf.

> Anal themes are used defensively to lessen the anxiety of oral aggression, represented by the wolf's desire to eat the succulent pigs.... There is also the compulsive repetition in the story, going from house to house with the wolf and pigs saying the same phrase. This anality reaches its zenith when the wolf is punished by the huge mechanical spanking-machine. (1975, 2, 3)

Brody points out that we find anal themes and messages in many other places in Disney, with the "often-kicked-in-the-butt Jiminey Cricket and the exaggeratedly buttocked Tinker Bell" (1975, 3), to cite a couple of other cases. Schickel says much the same thing. He writes, "Disney's interest in the posterior was a constant. Rarely were we spared views of sweet little animal backsides twitching provocatively as their owners bent to some task" (1968, 146). Disney's anality really manifested itself in his great creations, Disneyland and Disneyworld. There, as Schickel puts it, Disney's "lifelong rage to order, control and keep clean any environment he inhabited" (1968, 15) could really take hold. He had "sanitized" the classics in his films—sometimes injecting anal resolutions to stories (as in the case of "The Three Little Pigs" cited above). This was one of the ways he "cleaned up" various stories (and "cleaned up" at the box office as well, of course).

Beneath that folksy "Uncle" Walt exterior, beneath his pseudo-geniality and amiability, dark forces were at work. Disney's need to control and manipulate would eventuate in Disneyland and Disneyworld (the latter the same size as San Francisco). In these parks, the ultimate in "clean" family entertainment, people could be (generally, without being aware of it) controlled, directed, regulated—whatever you will. As Brody put it, "Disney strove for control over his work and destiny. What could be more natural than a huge, controlled playground where all could be Disney-regulated" (1975, 6). Employees in these parks attend training school for "smile and behavior regulation," and it is "con-

trol, not amusement, [that] seems the central theme in both the California and Florida parks" (1975, 6).

This marked a new development in Disney's desire for mastery and
control. The very art for he chose to work in, animation, is one in which
the creator has great control. You can make animated figures do whatever you want them to do. As Schickel writes:

> Of course, for a man as intense as Disney in his desire to control his environment,
> animation was the perfect medium, psychologically. You can redraw a character, or
> even a line in his face, until it is perfect; you need never settle as the director of the
> ordinary film must, for the best an actor—imperfect human that he is—can give
> you...animation, to borrow from the unfortunate jargon of psychology, is a
> compulsive's delight. (1968, 161)

Thus, Disney progressed from animation to amusement parks, in his
attempt to gain control over himself and others.

The ultimate move, for him, was the creation of those grotesque
audioanimatronic figures. With them he does away with the vagaries of
human personality and pushes the logic of control to its final and perhaps most absurd realization.

Disney also prided himself on the fact that Disneyland and Disneyworld
were so clean. He is reputed to have come to Disneyland evenings to pick up
litter that his sanitation workers had missed. What he created, "his" anti-sep-
tic wonderlands, were gum free, dirt free, and only slightly totalitarian. It may
be, of course, that without recognizing it, Disney tuned into something buried
in the psyches of his patrons—a desire to be controlled as a means, unconsciously of course, of dealing with their conflicts—pre-genital and otherwise.
We must ask ourselves whether the various aspects of anal eroticism found in
Disney struck some kind a chord buried deep in the American psyche or, at
least, in the psyches of a large number of Americans?

Children might find anal themes pleasant and take delight in barn-
yard humor. But what about adults who "love" Disneyland, the "happi-
est place on earth" and go there often? How do you explain the fact that
many high schools celebrate proms at Disneyland? Does it provide a
momentary regression, in the service of our egos, or is there something
other than regression involved (namely, recognition)?

The Mouse I Love

The mouse I love is Ignatz Mouse, Herriman's malevolent, antiauthoritarian, incorrigible hero who heaved a brick at a lovesick Krazy

Kat (in the comic strip of the same name) for thirty years. The situation in Krazy Kat is complicated in the extreme. Ignatz loves throwing bricks at Krazy, who takes the bricks as signs of love. This is because thousands of years ago Cleopatra cat was creased by a brick thrown by her lover and the memory has lingered on. There is a third major character, Offissa Pupp, who loves Krazy and hates Ignatz. Pupp spends his life trying to protect Krazy from Ignatz, and arresting and throwing him in jail when he does "crease" Krazy with a brick.

We have, then, a mad and wonderful triangle of protagonists and antagonists and bricks. Ignatz is a brick-throwing menace who refuses to acknowledge the validity of authority and pays for his anarchistic, antisocial acts by spending a great deal of time in jail (separated from his wife and children, I might add).

There are, I would argue, two important themes in this strip: the triumph of illusion over reality (as shown by Krazy's belief that the bricks are signifiers of love) and antiauthoritarianism (as shown by Ignatz's brick throwing). Ignatz is, in many respects, the opposite of Mickey Mouse and has infinitely more personality and spirit—and good humor. Mickey (like his creator) is so enterprising and so conventional, despite his frenetic behavior, that he becomes rather boring. That is why Disney felt trapped by Mickey and had to push him into a voracious quest for experience—and to find other characters, such as Donald Duck.

Ignatz, on the other hand, is an "autonomouse" character, who seldom fails to interest us and has cosmic as well as comic significance. I think Ignatz is an infinitely greater mouse, a more interesting mouse, and despite his anarchism, a much less threatening and destructive mouse. Mickey represents pseudo-individualism and the illusion of freedom. Created to accommodate the necessities of mass production, designed to titillate the lowest-common denominator, he now rules a "magic kingdom" in which human beings are manipulated and controlled, without their being aware of it.

That Mickey Mouse is one of the most widely known "heroes" in the world of pop culture and entertainment is something I find troubling. For the Disneyean worldview, as reflected by Mickey Mouse and Disney's other creations, including his amusement parks—compulsive, conservative (if not reactionary), entrepreneurial, mechanistic, and perhaps even sadistic (at times, at least) is not the only way of showing what this country stands for. Ignatz Mouse would be, to my mind, a much more representative and appealing representative "hero." There is, of course, an element of compulsiveness in his behavior. He did, let us remember, spend thirty years throwing bricks at a poor, lovesick Kat and doing whatever he could to evade the rules and regulations of his society.

He was not a "Disneyfied" or even "dignified" character. But that, precisely, is his strength. There was an element of playfulness and humor about his behavior that showed he was not a victim of compulsions. If Mickey was the instrument of a "rage for order," then Ignatz was the instrument of a "love of disorder and chaos...of a messy world of wonderful, mixed-up characters." In the chart that follows I show the differences between these two mice:

MICKEY MOUSE	IGNATZ MOUSE
sadistic	playful
obedient	anarchistic
constrained	free
pseudo-individualistic	autonomouse
asexual	sexual
anal (reflects)	phallic

This chart suggests the differences between the two characters. I may have exaggerated things a bit, but I think it does a pretty good job of showing the dominant personality traits of each mouse—and what each mouse reflects about his creator and his psychological makeup.

If Ignatz Mouse had a theme park, it would be considerably different and, I would imagine, a lot more fun. There certainly would be more of an opportunity to *do* things (as opposed to spectate, go on rides, etc.) and test one's skills. At brick throwing, at the very least.

Conclusions

We are left with a problem. Does Disney's widespread popularity (in America and in many other lands, where Disney's characters are extremely well known) reflect some kind of a camouflaged and diffused anality buried deep in our psyches? It has been argued by certain Marxist media critics that Disney's work champions bourgeois capitalist values and is, ultimately, an instrument of cultural imperialism. It is possible that there is some kind of a connection between bourgeois values, capitalism, and anality? Is the anal personality type, then, one of the (if not the) basic personality types in modern capitalist societies, which would suggest, in turn, that Mickey Mouse is a symbolic figure who is truly representative?

Let me conclude by pointing out a second consideration that Freud discusses, relative to anal personality types. This has to do with the fact that, as Freud puts it,

> the connections which exist between the two complexes of interest in money and of defecation, which seem so dissimilar, appear to be the most far-reaching....
>
> In reality, wherever archaic modes of thought predominate or have persisted—in ancient civilizations, in myth, fairy-tale and superstition, in unconscious thoughts and dreams, and in the neuroses—money comes into the closest relation with excrement. (30, 31)

There is, then, reason to believe that the character traits connected to anality by Freud—orderliness, parsimoniousness, and obstinacy—have a certain functionality in the modern world as far as making money is concerned. The cost, in terms of other aspects of life, is another matter.

Freud concludes his essay by suggesting how people cope with anality in their lives—either by "unchanged perpetuations of the original impulses, sublimations of them, or reaction-formations against them" (33). That is, some people (such as Disney) never abandon their anal personalities; some redirect the energy from their anality into other areas; and some turn against anality, and like a drunk on horseback, swerve over to opposite extremes.

I would like to think that most of us learn to outgrow our anality, though residues of it may linger in our psyches and are sometimes activated. Disney, his creations like Mickey Mouse and Disneyland, do not help us resolve or deal positively with anal traits but, instead, help solidify this element in our psyches. Mickey Mouse is not like that mouse that gnarled the ropes that constrained the lion in the famous folktale, freeing him. Instead, Mickey Mouse helps forge the chains that we use, without recognizing what we are doing, to bind ourselves (in more ways than one).

9

The Funnies Are Good for You!: The Healthful Benefits of Humorous Comic Strips

The comics have been a part of American life for almost a hundred years. It has even been suggested that comics are an "American idiom" in that they became very popular in America and we created some of the most memorable and remarkable examples of this art form. People of all ages read the comics and for many young children, comic strip characters, in the form of Snoopy dolls and other stuffed animals and toys, have a reality all their own.

From *The Yellow Kid* to *Calvin & Hobbes*

From *The Yellow Kid*, generally held to be the first American comic strip, to *Calvin & Hobbes*, probably our most interesting new strip, we have produced an incredible number of comic strips—both humorous and serious. Most of the newer comics now are gag strips, with a new gag or something humorous each day, but other comic strips have continuing stories that last weeks or months.

In recent years scholars in America and elsewhere have been examining these comics for what they reveal about society, our values and beliefs. I've written several books on the comics—*Li'l Abner: A Study in American Satire* and *The Comic-Stripped American*—and numerous articles on them. There are quite a few scholarly books that have come out about the comics recently. There are even courses in universities devoted to the comics. Just twenty or thirty years ago the idea that literature professors, sociologists, or psychologists (or any scholars) would find comics interesting and worth studying was considered laughable. Comics, we were told, were what you wrapped garbage in (before, of course, we had garbage disposals and trash compactors).

American comic-strip artists have created a number of remarkable humorous strips. Among the greatest are *Krazy Kat, Blondie, Li'l Abner, Little Nemo, Doonesbury, Beetle Bailey,* and *Peanuts.* We also have a number of interesting new artists and strips (some of which are not nationally syndicated in the papers) such as Bill Griffith's *Zippy,* Matt Groening's *Hell* comics, and Victoria Robert's *Little Women.* Not only have we produced extraordinary funnies over the past seventy or eighty years, we are still producing great funnies.

What We Get From the Comics

I used to have a bit of fun with my friends who were curious about what a professor was doing studying the comics. "When you read the funnies," I said, jokingly, "you're just trying to amuse yourself, have a laugh, and indulge in innocent escapism. But when I read the funnies, I'm doing research." (For some scholars, as I've suggested in this book, the idea that what I do is research on the comics is an oxymoron.)

Although I was kidding, and playing on people's incredulity, I was actually telling the truth. My research, of course, involved considering why people read the comics and what they "got" from reading them. What they got from the funnies, most immediately, of course, was a laugh (or a chuckle). But, at the same time, they also got messages about values, beliefs, attitudes they should or should not have—as reflected in the things the characters in the funnies did and what they said. These values and beliefs, their relation to historical events, and similar topics are the subject of most of the books on the comics. (If you are interested in this aspect of the comics, you might find a recent book by M. Thomas Inge, *Comics as Culture,* worth looking at.)

Let me focus our attention here on the laughs we get from the funnies. I believe these "laughs"—when a strip is good enough to make us laugh—are of great significance and not just a trivial matter. That is because, as we have recently discovered, and as the work of a number of researchers into various aspects of humor demonstrates, humor plays much more important role in our lives than we have previously recognized.

The Uses of Funnies

I would like to propose a radical hypothesis. What I would like to suggest is that without being aware of what we are doing, we use funnies to deal with various problems we have, to cope with pressures we face, and to fight stress and anxiety. We often find particular episodes of strips that help us deal with specific problems. The funnies, then, are a therapeutic tool that millions of people use. They do not use the comics consciously to help them deal with their problems and life's aggravations, but more or less intuitively, they recognize that the comics do play a positive role in their lives.

We find, for instance, that we "like" a particular episode of some strip and often cut it out of the paper to show our friends or tack up somewhere. That episode somehow "speaks" to us—the same way a particular fairy tale speaks to a child at a certain point in his or her development. In a sense, then, the funnies we like and, in particular, the episodes of these funnies we find memorable, are clues to our psychological states.

Instrumental Humor

Humor has, I would suggest, instrumental qualities, then, and is a good way for us to deal with various problems we face. We love to laugh and this desire to be amused, to experience humor and the laughter that is generally associated with humor seems to be universal and also, it seems, insatiable. No matter how much we've laughed at a cartoon or comic strip or joke, we want to laugh some more, and are ready for the next cartoon or comic strip or joke that will amuse us.

Without being aware of what laughter does, we seek it out, to deal with needs we don't even know we have. I suggest that humor helps us on four levels and will use examples from the funnies illustrate how things work:

1. I will consider humor at the biological level—what it does for our bodies.

2. I will deal with its intrapsychic or intrapersonal effects and offer an explanation of how humor heals, of how it helps us, as individuals, cope with everyday problems.

3. I will deal with humor's role in our interpersonal relationships, and discuss how it helps us deal with other people.

4. Finally, I will deal with the way humor helps people cope with anxieties and difficulties at the social and cultural level.

The notion that humor has healthful benefits is not new. The well-known work of Norman Cousins, who used humorous films to recover from a serious illness, has been documented in his book *Anatomy of an Illness as Perceived by the Patient*. Since the publication of this book, the notion that humor has an important role to play in our physical and mental health is now fairly well accepted. We have been told, many times, that "laughter is the best medicine," but most of seldom think about how humor works, how it helps us heal ourselves.

The Importance of Humorous Techniques

There are a few things to keep in mind when we think about how humor heals. What is important in creating humor is not the subject (though it plays a role) but the various techniques that humorists use to create humor. I've seen, for example, the same joke told about a military officer in one joke book, a dean in another joke book, and a businessman in a third joke book. What generated the humor in the joke was the various techniques found in the joke: things like insult, exaggeration, ridicule, wordplay, misunderstanding, and mistakes. You often find a number of different techniques at work in a given joke— or any other example of humor—which is why it is so difficult to make sense of humor.

Consider, for example, *Krazy Kat*, which was discussed in the previous chapter. The strip was about a mischievous mouse, Ignatz Mouse, who loved to throw a brick at Krazy Kat (who took being "creased" on the head by a brick as a sign of love), and a policeman, Offissa Pupp, who loved Krazy and tried to prevent Ignatz from throwing the brick. This went on for more than thirty years. Herriman made wonderful use of language. In one of his strips, the story is told in just four words— transgression, apprehension, retribution, and procrastination.

There are many different techniques that humorists use (generally not consciously) to create humor. In addition to the techniques mentioned above, some of the more commonly used techniques are: eccentricity (zany characters), facetiousness, absurdity, repartee, sarcasm, stereotypes, unmasking, exposure, imitation, impersonation, and parody.

I suggest that it is these comedic techniques, as found in humorous comics (and other humorous works), that do the work of generating the mirth and laughter that helps us cope with our problems. It is the techniques (listed in chapter 5) that are therapeutic, not the topics dealt with.

The Biological Benefits from the Funnies

Any humorous strip that leads to a laugh or a chuckle is good for us. That is because laughter has proven physiological benefits. Consider a typical episode from *Calvin & Hobbes*. The episode may not lead to explosive laughter, but it probably generates a mild chuckle in most people. This touch of laughter has, it turns out, physiological consequences of some value.

As William Fry, a psychiatrist who has spent many years studying the physiological effects of humor, explained in a lecture:

> Mirthful laughter has a scientifically demonstrable exercise impact on several body systems. Muscles are activated; heart rate is increased; respiration is amplified, with increase in oxygen exchange—all similar to the desirable effects of athletic exercise. ("Using Humor to Save Lives," 1979)

He adds that stress and anxiety are also lowered by laughter. We've always had a notion that laughter was, somehow, good for us—but until the last decade or so, when scientists conducted experiments, we never realized how good laughter was for us or how this laughter affected us.

The daily newspapers are now full of humorous comic strips; every strip in the *San Francisco Chronicle,* for example, is now a gag strip. Though these strips may not always be funny, the general impact of these strips (and cartoons such as *The Far Side*) is quite beneficial from a biological or health-enhancing perspective. (Cartoons, as I pointed out earlier, generally have only one frame, have captions below the frame [not dialogue in balloons], and do not have continuing characters.)

Laughing at Ourselves

When we move on to the intrapersonal level, to that dialogue that we carry on in our heads with ourselves, comics also play an important role. Because funnies are, by definition, "not serious," they can deal with important problems we all face and yet not raise alarms in us and trigger defense mechanisms. It is analogous to the role fools play in Shakespeare's works. Because they are fools, they are allowed to speak the truth—but nobody pays attention because they are, by definition, fools and not to be taken seriously.

Consider Matt Groening's episode on "Parents Out of Control" in his strip *Life in Hell.* In this episode a character reflects, in a monologue, on all the terrible things some parents do to their children. "They can really screw up your mind," his character says, "because they're the only parents you know. So you think this is the way the world is, but it isn't. And you end up growing up all weird and damaged and unhappy and stupid."

What Groening is offering, in actuality, is a disquisition on the problems many people face as the result of growing up in families that psychologists now describe as "dysfunctional." (Since it would seem that just about every family in America can be described as dysfunctional, there's some question about whether the term has any meaning.) Had Groening written this material in an essay, it would not be taken quite the same way by his readers. The humor, the funny characters, the nonidealized view of life, quite likely are of benefit to large numbers of people who recognize themselves in his strip and can laugh at characters like the poor soul who is enduring this "childhood in hell" and at themselves.

In the same light, the series of comics *My Day,* by Victoria Roberts, deals with (and spoofs) the lives of famous individuals. Her strip on Jorge Luis Borges, the avant-garde, modernist writer, is most instructive. Borges awakens to find himself in a labyrinth, and then spends a literary day, ending up with a toothache at night. He makes comments about his age, his not getting the Nobel Prize, about the food habits of Americans and the English, about his feelings, and so on. There is an existential quality to his musings and activities; for example, he gives a prize to novelists, but it is based on the quality of the paper in the books, not the novels themselves.

This strip suggests the absurdity of life—if we look at it too seriously. The moral of the strip, from a psychological point of view, is that we must not be too uptight about things, we must accept an element of the ridiculous in our lives, and enjoy the simple things—the bliss of a good cup of Columbian coffee or of the taste of peppermints. This capsule biography pokes fun at Borges and through him at people in general. As we laugh at Borges and think about his comments about life, we gain some valuable insights about how to live and learn something quite valuable—how to laugh at ourselves.

The Groening and Roberts strips are just examples of the kind of thing we experience daily as we read the comics. We learn that being overliteral (a favorite technique of humorists) is silly, that being rigid is destructive, that there's an element of absurdity in life that we have to keep in mind. The cartoonists bestow on us benefits that are similar to those that certain Hindu doctors give when they compose fairy tales to deal with problems their patients have.

As Bruno Bettelheim explains the matter in *The Uses of Enchantment: The Meaning and Importance of Fairy Tales*:

> In a fairy tale, internal processes are externalized and become comprehensible as represented by the figures of the story and its events. That is the reason why in traditional Hindu medicine a fairy tale giving form to his particular problem was offered to a psychologically disoriented person, for his meditation. It was expected that "through contemplating the story" the disturbed person would be led to visualize both the nature of the impasse in living from which he suffered, and the possibility of its resolutions. (1976, 25)

I would argue that our humorous comic-strip artists function in ways analogous to the Hindu doctors mentioned above, except that the comic-strip artists create their tales for the general public, not specific individuals, and are probably not conscious of the impact of their creations on people.

Laugh and the World Laughs with You

We now move to interpersonal relations, those that involve other people. As the comics we have examined to this point show, the world is full of absurdity and nonsense. Adopting a philosophy of "what fools these mortals be" (including ourselves in both categories) helps downgrade the seriousness of some of the things we and others do and say that otherwise might be looked upon as hostile or insulting.

Many of the comics focus on interpersonal relationships. In some cases, as in the *Doonesbury* strip, we have sexual relationships as the subject of the strip. The hero of one episode asks, innocently, for a goodnight kiss. He is immediately attacked as being a "male chauvinist pig" by his date, who raises her left hand (in solidarity with women, we must assume) and glares at him.

Doonesbury is a very controversial strip, and some editors see it as being so political that they place it on the editorial page. Most newspapers place it on the comics page. For, even though it often deals with politics, it also spoofs education, family life, and relations between people and the media, among other topics.

Interpersonal relationships are the subject of many comic strips. Consider *Beetle Bailey*, for example. Here we have a lazy private, Beetle, a gluttonous sergeant, an insecure lieutenant, and a daffy general, all interacting with one another and each pursuing his private passions. One of the basic humorous techniques involves creating characters who are eccentric, who have manias that shape their behavior and affect all their relationships.

Snoopy, for example, tends to have one dominant concern—his food. He may take on all kinds of roles and identities, but the one constant in his career has been making sure his food dish is full and, whenever possible, getting treats to eat. Linus, of course, has his blanket and Charlie Brown has his insecurity. In *Peanuts* all these characters, with their problems and passions, are thrown together and have to find some way of making do. Schulz's genius is that he has found ways of capitalizing on his characters and creating a strip that has universal appeal, since it speaks to the passions that all of us have.

What is particularly interesting about the comics is that many of them have lasted for forty or fifty years or more, and we start reading them when we are young and continue reading them into old age. *Krazy Kat* went from 1913 to 1944, *Blondie* started in 1930 (and still is being published, though the artist has changed, of course), and *Li'l Abner* started in 1934 (and ended in 1977). Both *Peanuts,* which started in 1950, and *Doonesbury,* which started in 1970, are still going strong.

The Social Dimension of the Funnies

It could be argued that if the funnies help people on the biological level, help people deal with personal anxieties and worries, and help people with their relationships with others, they are already having a considerable social impact. Funnies that deal with relationships between men and women, with family life, and with politics have, implicitly, a social dimension. But the comics often focus directly and explicitly on social concerns.

In 1985, for example, a group of comic-strip artists got together and dealt with the theme of world hunger. Their strips were auctioned off and the money was donated to relief efforts. The strips were also collected into a book, *Comic Relief.* This effort was the idea of Garry Trudeau, who got a number of comic-strip artists to deal with the theme of world hunger.

Robert Crumb contributed a parody of a typical magazine advertisement on the back of *The Best of Rip Off Press* (Volume One) that is amusing but also worth thinking about. We see Crumb pointing a finger at us. "Don't you think it's time to Stop Watching T.V.?" he asks? He suggests that if people want a media injection, they should read Motor City Comics. He writes:

> These comics BREAK THROUGH the TV-INDUCED STUPOR, for this is ANTI-MEDIA! It's got the MEDICINE for the BLUES, and has been known to turn MENTALLY ILL persons into HEALTHY, GOOD-HUMORED FREE-THINKERS.

Crumb was making fun of television (described by Newton Minnow as a "vast wasteland") and being satirical about the benefits that reading Motor City Comics conferred on people.

But, ironically, he was correct, many would suggest, about the negative impact of television on individuals and American society and he was also right about the value of reading—though most of us would include reading more "elevated" forms of literature here, in addition to the comics. (Comics are a form of literature and often help people learn how to read. Better to read comics than nothing at all, I would argue.) The SAT scores of American students in reading and mathematics declined in 1991 and some have suggested that one reason this happened was because American students spent too much time watching television (high school students average close to twenty-one hours of television watching per week) and too little time reading and doing homework (high school students on average only spend about five hours a week doing homework).

Crumb's parody, then, had a great deal of truth to it. His drawing of a person watching television and getting "bad vibes," "lies," and "paranoia" is not as far-fetched as it might seem. The "goodness," "humor," and "honesty" that he showed emanating from Motor City Comics are, as I have demonstrated, found in many of the funnies we read. They help us become healthy and good-humored and, like all humor, free us from any number of hangups and anxieties.

As Harvey Mindess, a psychologist interested in humor, has pointed out in *Laughter and Liberation,* "a flourishing sense of humor is fundamental to mental health. It represents a source of vitality and a means of transcendence second to none" (1971, 15). It frees us, he tells us, from conformity, from a sense of inferiority, from being overly rational about things and from being too serious about our lives—among many other things.

We don't, as a rule, hear jokes every day. We don't always see situation comedies when we watch television. We don't always choose comedies when we go to the movies. But most of us read the comics in the newspaper every day, and have a chuckle or two as we follow the exploits of Beetle Bailey, Snoopy, Calvin, Cathy, or any of the other characters in the strips we read. These brief moments of mirth are extremely valuable to us on a number of different levels.

That is why we consider people like Charles Schulz or Mort Walker or Garry Trudeau or Bill Watterson "national treasures." The funnies are not only for children and are just not simple-minded diversions. Our brief escapes into the make-believe worlds of *Peanuts* and *Doonesbury* and *Calvin and Hobbes* and *Cathy* and *Mr. Natural* make it possible for us to function better in the real world. The funnies are gifts to us from humorists of great skill, and in some cases, genius, that play a much more profound role in our lives than we have previously imagined.

V

Television: Introduction

Media events can be defined as occurrences that, because of their importance or the amount of interest people have in them, are given considerable coverage by television as they unfold. A media event, then, involves television coverage of something that is happening; the coverage is simultaneous. In addition, the media event deals with core values in society, with fundamental beliefs and the events either reinforce our belief in these values or lead to some alteration in them.

I have chosen three media events to deal with: the first is the Gulf War, the second is the Democratic National Convention in 1990, and the third is the coverage of the arraignment and preliminary parts of the O. J. Simpson trial. In dealing with these media events, I try to suggest how complex they are, and how they lend themselves to different interpretations.

Thus, in my interpretation of the Gulf War, I take the same approach I did in analyzing the "Gays in the Bar" joke (which used eight different methodologies) but I expand my analysis to eleven ways of looking at this "television war," as it has sometimes been called. These perspectives—indeed, all the different ways of looking at things found in this chapter—come from the way the events were covered in the media or from interesting parallels that can be made between the events and other phenomena, whether it be different media events, programs, films, comic-strip characters, and so on.

My analyses show how polysemic these texts are, how they lend themselves to many different kinds of interpretation, a phenomenon that can be described as the *Rashomon* phenomenon. In this film, all the characters offered different and contradictory interpretations of what happened in a grove between a woman, her husband, and a bandit. This is the point the reader-response or reception theorists make; I discussed their theory in some detail in the first chapter of this book. Their central idea, that different readers see different things in a text, makes good sense. Whether the different things these readers see are very different or essentially the same is an unresolved question in literary and cultural theory.

In chapter 11 I deal with the question of the relationship that exists between the medium of television and terror. I repeat a number of the points I made in my article in *Television as an Instrument of Terror*, that television, as a medium, leads to disorientation, the liberation of impulse and hyperkinesis, and a kind of psychic mobilization.

I point out that television generates cynicism and skepticism in its viewers, and can lead to what I call a "vicious cycle" in which the viewing of certain television programs by young children (with adult conflicts that are too difficult for the children to handle) leads to psychological problems and dependencies in their later years that they then use television to try to overcome.

In addition, I suggest that much of the programming on television generates what Henri Lefebvre called "unacknowledged compulsions" in people and these compulsions are a subtle form of terror—not recognized by those who create the programs or watch them.

I conclude with a discussion of postmodernism and what Lyotard has described as basic to postmodernism, "incredulity toward metanarratives." If we reject the basic theories and systems of belief that we held in earlier days, what do we have to fall back on? How do we order social and political life? I also point out that the postmodern lifestyle described by Lyotard relies, ultimately, on purchasing power, and it is the lack of purchasing power that is one of the sources of the terror, I would argue, that many Americans feel.

But not only the poor are terrorized; everyone feels uneasy in this world of "choice," for no matter what we have, there is more to be had. There are newer versions of everything and there are new products—new styles of clothing, new lifestyles—to be consumed (and new politicians, to be elected, and dumped when we get bored with them, as well). It is for these reasons I argue that television is an instrument of terror.

10

Three Media Events

According to General "Stormin' Norman" Schwartzkopf, war is the "most complex thing in the world." The Gulf war was, if you think about, quite a remarkable achievement. The United States military establishment transported, in short time, the equivalent of a mid-sized city and our government formed alliances with governments in the Middle East who hadn't been terribly friendly with one another and, of course, our strategists planned a successful military campaign.

But complex things, we must recognize, often cause problems for many people. We have a need, often, to make sense of things by comparing them to things we know (see X in terms of Y, as I put it in an earlier chapter) or by simplifying them and using schemas to help understand them. As a result of the way the media covered the war, using various military and political commentators and experts to help us understand what was going on and what the implications of the conflict might be, I would suggest that there are at least eleven ways of making sense of the Gulf War (if not more).

Event One: Eleven Ways of Looking at the Gulf War

When we have different experts with different points of view explaining something, we have what I've called "The *Rashomon* Effect." In the Gulf War coverage we had professors, retired generals (in abundance), think-tankers, journalists, diplomats, and many others discussing the war and, as often as not, disagreeing with one another. Let me offer a number of different ways that people interpreted and explained the Gulf War to the American public.

The Gulf War as a Video Game

Some of the visual images shown and reshown on television encouraged us to think of the Gulf War as a giant "for real" video game. We saw numerous scenes in which "smart bombs" hit doorways or the ventilating shafts of bunkers (though, as we found out later, many of the so-called "smart bombs" missed their targets, but, of course, we weren't shown the misses). Because we hardly saw Iraqi casualties, the war took on the appearance of a somewhat surrealistic video game and led to a spurt in the sales of video games that simulated war in the Middle East.

Our fascination with televised wars and violent video games has now become domesticated. We have now, unfortunately, taken to turning many parts of America into battlegrounds and in October, 1994, someone actually took an assault weapon and fired a number of rounds at the White House.

The Gulf War as Arabian Nights

We can see the Gulf War as a modernized form of fairy tale. It is possible to apply the ideas of Vladimir Propp, who wrote a book on the basic components of fairy tales, to the war. Propp suggested that most fairy tales (he actually studied only certain Russian ones, but his theory covers other kinds as well) involve a hero, who is generally sent on some mission. This hero has many helpers, obtains the use of magic weapons given to him by a donor figure, fights with a villain and defeats him, and so on. Propp actually listed thirty-one different functions—actions done by heroes, villains, and secondary characters. Many of these functions can be applied to the Gulf War. (I will also apply Propp to *Star Wars* later in this book.)

At the end of the fairy tale, Propp has a function in which the hero weds the princess and ascends the throne. At the end of the Gulf War, stopped after 100 hours (a nice round number by George Bush, but, it turns out, a day or two too soon), he seemed likely to be re-elected (the moral equivalent of ascending the throne) and had, for a short while, enormous popularity. He seemed, at that time, unbeatable. Eventually the economy soured and so did Bush's popularity, which shows that fairy tales don't always end happily.

Bush didn't know that; Clinton did.

Kigmyism

Kigmies were fantastic creatures created by Al Capp that were found in some episodes of *Li'l Abner*. Kigmies, it turned out, loved to be kicked and thus satisfied a need found in most people who delighted in having someone to kick.

We can see the tactics of the Iraqi army as being Kigmylike. They seemed to love to be kicked—or, in this case, bombed, machine-gunned and attacked by rockets and other such devices. Unfortunately, this attitude (or whatever we wish to call it) led to the deaths of thousands—perhaps hundreds of thousands—of Iraqi soldiers in a slaughter that we didn't see or learn about until after the war was over.

The Iraqis also had something of a reverse-Kigmy attitude, since they were brutal and "kicked" those weaker than them just as they were Kigmyized and were "kicked" by those more powerful.

In America we often talk of "kicking ass," which suggests that we need Kigmies, or functional alternatives, to assuage our desire to be violent and dominating.

The Gulf War as a Chess Game

In this metaphor, George Bush and the coalition and Saddam and his allies moved armies (the equivalent of pawns) around and countered one another in something resembling a chess match. Saddam didn't use his Queen (poison gas) and was defeated by players who hadn't lost important pieces and who had a better command of the game.

Some have suggested that Saddam and the Iraqi army, though one of the biggest in the world, wasn't in the same league as the coalition's military forces, and never could have won. The only question, these critics suggest, was how many pawns Saddam might have taken in a game in which he had no chance to win.

Psycho-Saddam-Analysis

Various psychologists, psychiatrists, and other experts spent a good deal of time analyzing Saddam's personality—and such matters as the rate at which he blinked his eyelids during certain television interviews he had. Some experts in psychology labeled him a sociopath; others suggested he was closer to being a serial killer. His rhetoric, including such famous phrases as "the mother of all battles," led some to see him as a megalomaniac (perhaps with unresolved Oedipal problems?).

Semioticians analyzed his facial expressions to offer some clue as to what he was thinking. What did his smiles mean? Was he cracking up under the strain or were his smiles examples of something as banal as being in good humor? Elements of pyromania were later detected, after he set fire to the oil wells in Kuwait.

Franken(stein)Saddam

This is a variation of Psycho-Saddam-Analysis in which we see Saddam as a monster figure, with touches of Adolph Hitler and Frankenstein, killing masses of people and hiding in a bomb-proof shelter. If Saddam was the monster, who was the Dr. Frankenstein figure who created him, out of bits and pieces of dead bodies?

The Gulf War as a Media Event

The war wasn't, it would seem, planned as a television media event, but it rapidly became one. When the attack by the coalition started, people were glued to their television sets, as legions of retired generals and other military experts gave opinions on this and that. There were, after a while, numerous televised press conferences, at which military spokespersons showed video clips of "smart bombs" doing their stuff and other footage.

At first there were few visual images to be seen, so much of the programming turned out to be discussion and analysis, with various experts playing military *Rashomonism*. The Gulf War turned out to be the kind of thing television does best—a media event—with television covering some matter of national or international significance, as it took place.

The War as a Medical Procedure

The term *surgical strikes* was often used by the military as they described various bombing raids. Saddam and his cohorts were presented as "cancers" to be cut out so the patient, the Middle East, could be cured. Saddam and the Iraqis were also made to be what might described as "pathological tubers," to be rooted out by the American "Wart Hog" airplanes.

What we discovered was that we didn't get all the cancer and Saddam, the "disease," has reappeared, and by moving his troops near Kuwait in the Summer of 1994, created major problems for everyone involved in the Middle East. The disease has gone out of remission. (Could Saddam's play have really been a plan to make Bill Clinton look good and George Bush look bad? That's too devious, one would imagine, for even someone as sly as Saddam.)

Armageddon

Fundamentalists saw Saddam as an anti-Christ figure and the war in the Gulf as Armageddon, signaling the second coming of Christ. Orthodox rabbis, on the other hand, argued that God "hardened" Saddam's heart (the way God hardened the Pharoah's heart several thousand years earlier) so he wouldn't withdraw his army, which made it possible for the coalition to devastate it.

The fact that the war ended on Purim also had significance for the rabbis, calling to mind the miraculous salvation of the Jews from an earlier Saddamite figure, Haman.

The Malevolent Jack-in-the-Box

Here we see Saddam characterized as a kind of evil Jack-in-the-Box, who had somehow escaped from his confinement (the box being Iraq) and had to be put back in it. This notion also has implications dealing with learning to accept limits. Certain conspiracy theorists argued that Saddam was actually encouraged to spring out of his box by the American ambassador to Iraq, who seemed to have suggested that America would not construe an Iraqi invasion of Kuwait as a "big deal."

Others suggested that we were looking for an opportunity to put Saddam back in his box and when he invaded Kuwait, he gave us the opportunity to do so. Thus, he played into our hands.

The Comedic Perspective

It might be argued that my description of the previous ten ways of looking at the Gulf War has a comedic dimension to it, showing how many different ways the war was presented to the public. This might be seen as a way of dealing with anxiety and coping with horrors beyond our imagination. Many tragedies, such as the Discovery explosion and the O. J. Simpson trial, give way to series of jokes, which help people cope with their feelings.

The actual invasion of Kuwait turned out to be a nonesuch, and instead of having fierce battles, the war was much closer to shooting fish in a barrel. Thus, the huge buildup, all the talk about Saddam's army (fourth largest in the world) and his special forces, ended in an anticlimax. The anxieties people felt turned out to be mistaken. In a bizarre way, the invasion was almost comic.

A Note on Methodology

The eleven ways of dealing with the Gulf War all were suggested by words people used in interviews and briefings and images shown on television and in newspapers and magazines. The American public wanted to make sense of what was going on in the Middle East, an event that was evolving before them, that bewildered them, raised a great deal of anxiety and had, at first sight, all the elements of a tragic drama.

It will take a good deal of time before we make sense of this war and are able to see it as more than the media event it became.

Event Two: The Passion Play in Madison Square Garden

The 1990 Democratic National Convention in New York ended on a rare note of party unity and with a heightened significance—caused by Ross Perot's surprise withdrawal from the race. He had watched the convention and, some suggest, became disheartened by the Democratic party's "revitalization," as he put it. The convention didn't get gavel-to-gavel coverage and some pundits have even speculated that 1990 will be the last one in which the conventions get substantial television coverage. I seriously doubt that this will happen because, though the outcome of the convention was known, there's more to conventions than simply nominating a candidate. The convention, I would argue, was wonderful television, as well.

A Passion Play, Not Just a Media Event

It's true that the Democratic National Convention was a media event, one that was carefully scripted and which functioned, in some ways, as one long commercial for the Democratic party. Some journalists complained that there was no "news" coming from the convention, no conflict, no suspense. They miss the point. The convention itself was the news. The medium may not be the message but in this case, the process was the story.

Whatever else it might have been, the convention was a powerful and frequently moving passion play. This was suggested by all those shots of delegates with moist eyes or, at times, sobbing, as they listened to the speakers, and the cheering and the sense of exultation that frequently surged through the delegates.

In the Middle Ages, Huizinga tells us (in *The Waning of the Middle Ages)* people experienced extreme emotions—they wept as preachers spoke of the Last Judgment or the Devil, and were exultant as they were told about salvation. One merely has to substitute George Bush and the Republican party for the devil and you have the same kind of experience at the Democratic Convention.

The convention was a ritual, a gigantic, spectacular rite of bonding and of reinforcement of beliefs. It was also a pep rally, in which the party faithful celebrated their new leaders and their new identity—as a centrist, moderate party. After years of ideological purity and electoral defeat the Democratic party had, so it seems, decided that it was time to "end ideology" and redefine itself, if it were to regain the presidency. (Some, of course, question whether the Democratic party has really moved to the center and cast off it's "liberal" ideology.) Would the enthusiasm and passion of the delegates move the American public? Would those voters who had abandoned the party "catch the fever" and rejoin with the party? Would they vote for Clinton and Gore?

On the Power of Oratory

In an age of television, when most of what we see on television is dramatic, we tend to underestimate the power of oratory. But words can move people today, just as they did in the Middle Ages. Not all of the speakers were able to excite the delegates, but there were some memorable speeches. Zell Miller, the governor from Georgia, gave a rip roaring and, at times, humorous speech. He talked about his youth in a small town in Appalachia, and of the difficulties he faced in getting an education. He also had a wonderful way with words and had some nice digs for George Bush.

Jesse Jackson gave a passionate speech that had the delegates shouting and stomping and many of them crying, as he talked about the pain many people are experiencing in America. Mario Cuomo gave a brilliant speech, enthusiastically supporting Clinton and savagely attacking Bush as the captain of a ship, heading toward the reefs, who is unaware of the seriousness of what is happening and who has a naive faith that an invisible hand will alter the currents in some mysterious way so the ship will be saved. There was something rather poignant, also, about both Jackson and Cuomo; both men, doctrinaire liberals, were now on the sidelines, almost irrelevant, left behind by the "new generation" of younger democrats, who had seized control of the party.

Albert Gore recounted the story of his son's terrible accident in very moving terms and Bill Clinton talked about his humble beginnings in Hope, Arkansas and his love for his family in a long (fifty-three minutes) and, at times, tedious speech. I assume he felt that since he had the attention of the American public and free television time, he'd make the most of it. The speech was substantive and had some good moments and good lines, but it did get a bit wearing.

Clinton had given a relatively long nominating speech at the 1988 convention that had bored people and that had become something of a joke. His acceptance speech was even longer. But this time, of course, he was not nominating someone else but trying to give the American public some kind of an idea of who he was and what he stood for.

All the speakers had learned from Ronald Reagan, the so-called "great communicator," that it is useful to get personal and to tell stories, which gives speeches emotional color and resonance, and above all, to avoid abstract, ideological "lectures." Generally speaking, the Democrats had learned their lesson and the emotions, the tears, the enthusiastic cheering of the delegates was a powerful message that the Democrats were unified and optimistic.

A Revolution or a Repositioning?

The question that remains, as I suggested earlier, is whether Clinton and Gore were really moderates or only liberals in "sheep's clothing," and whether the Democratic party had changed in major ways or was merely marketing itself differently. In this respect, the flap about Jerry Brown speaking was significant. He refused to endorse the candidates and was not going to be allowed to speak, even though he had a number of delegates committed to him. A way was found to allow him to speak, though not in prime time, and he gave a rousing talk, "speaking truth to power," attacking the entrenched interests and the role that money plays in financing campaigns.

He had a grim, almost possessed look on his face at he spoke. He didn't mention Clinton or Gore and stormed out of Madison Square Garden when he had finished. Brown had been a seminarian and there was something of the fight between the forces of God and the forces of Satan in his demeanor and his talk. Most of the commentators reviled Brown as a "sore loser" and someone who was not a "team player." Brown's speech, full of rather classic ideological populism and liberalism served Clinton well, ironically, since it helped define Clinton as a moderate and reinforced the view that Clinton and the Democratic party had, indeed, moved to the center.

Clinton and Gore also were on a crusade (a word that was used from time to time) to save the country. To do this they needed the elusive Reagan Democrats, the Joe Sixpacks who had been lured into the Republican party and now, as Clinton put it, were getting "the shaft." Would Clinton's *new covenant,* a term whose religious significance must not be underestimated, lure them into the party? Or would the dismal economy push them there? Or would they stay put, afraid that things would get worse rather than better with the "tax and spend" Democrats?

Chivalry is Not Dead: A Hero Goes on a Crusade

Bill Clinton, having undergone the ordeal of the primaries and having proven himself, like a mythological hero, had set out with a trusty companion, Al Gore, on a quest. It was to defeat the dragon George Bush and the dreaded Republican party, and rescue the damsels in distress—American women. Clinton was bringing a lot of them with him in his crusade. He received a rousing send-off in a carefully choreographed media spectacular that generated a large (and somewhat temporary) "bump" for him in the ratings.

A Wrestling Match Is About to Begin

As I watched Clinton and Gore in Madison Square Garden, I could not help but think of other media spectaculars, also carefully choreographed, that sometimes go on there—professional wrestling matches, which are also, in many respects, passion plays. Clinton and Gore reminded me of two "clean" (no breaking the rules) wrestlers who are a tag team and are usually matched against a team of bigger, dirty wrestlers.

The good wrestlers are attractive, muscular, but only weigh 230 pounds or so and they are matched against hulking brutes of 350 or 450 pounds. These evil wrestlers usually massacre the clean ones, often attacking their unsuspecting opponents even before the "match" begins. The villains here would be Bush and Quayle, with all the millions they have to use for negative television commercials and their penchant for dirty tricks.

Sometimes, however, just to make life interesting, the good guys are about the same size as the villains and are scripted to win. They have dynamism, speed, remarkable holds, good teamwork, and so on. In this wrestling match metaphor, Clinton and Gore had just entered the ring and were flexing their muscles and warming up. Bush and Gore were on their way to the ring from the dressing room, whispering to one another as they planned their attack.

They would have the Republican convention—a vicious, snarling convention full of religious zealots and reactionaries (such as Pat Buchanan) who blabbed about family values to an anxiety-ridden group of delegates who were afraid that many Republican politicians would be going down the tubes with Bush and Quayle in the elections.

Then the match was joined. Clinton and Gore were taking their bus trips and trying to lure the swing voters to their camp. Bush decided that family values weren't selling and was talking about trust and his plans for the economy. He brought in the "miracle worker" James Baker to run the campaign and coordinate foreign and domestic policy—a job that the president is supposed to do.

We know the results: after twelve years, the Republicans lost the presidency, proclaiming it was the best thing that ever happened to them, since the American public would find out what it was like having a Democrat in the White House. Clinton won, but only had something like 40 percent of the votes (since it was a three-man race). George Bush disappeared from the public view, for all practical purposes, and Dan Quayle, defined by the media as a kind of village idiot, started planning his campaign for the Republican presidential nomination in 1996—as did many other Republicans.

Event Three: Overdosing on O. J.

What is one to make of the television coverage of the famous O. J. Simpson "chase" and his hearings that followed afterward? How do you explain the fact that the television networks pre-empted their regular programming to cover his famous "run" and his hearings?

We generally don't see this kind of coverage except for matters of national or international importance, such as the Watergate Hearings or the Gulf War. So how does one explain the fact that the whole nation became transfixed, as it were, by proceedings involving a former football star, actor in commercials and minor films, who was accused of brutally murdering his wife and a young man who was with her? In this segment I will explore the meaning of the case and deal with a number of the questions about American culture that it raises.

Hero or Celebrity?

Many of the commentators described Simpson as a "fallen hero," and evoked comparisons with Shakespeare's *Othello* (a black man who strangled his white wife) or with mythological Greek heroes who suffered tragic fates. But was Simpson a hero? A *hero,* as we traditionally understand the term, is someone who does something of consequence for society, whose acts are not self-centered and not tied to self aggrandizement.

Heroes are courageous and selfless and take risks for the good of others. Simpson was a wonderful athlete, what we sometimes describe as a "star," but his athletic prowess does not make him a hero. Nor are all the other wonderful athletes heroes, per se.

It is true that the term *hero* is sometimes loosely used for people who are outstanding in some particular field, but there is a world of difference between "sports heroes" and real heroes. Many sports heroes, so we've discovered, lead less than exemplary lives off the field. We used the think that sports somehow ennobled people and taught them good values (like the importance of teamwork) and decency; now we realize that many athletes are not the kind of people whose behavior should be emulated and that sports often teaches athletes that they should be willing to do "anything" to win and get ahead.

Simpson can, as a result of his commercials and some minor acting roles he had, be described as a celebrity—someone who is known about by many people for one reason or another. The Latin term *celebritas* means famous. Celebrities are people who are looked at by the general public, which is fascinated by them and tries to emulate them in various ways. Bishop Berkeley wrote "to be is to be perceived." With this in mind, we can say—pushing things to extremes, of course—that celebrities, people who are perceived, who are looked at, are somebodies, and those who look at them, who are the perceivers, are philosophically speaking, nonexisting nobodies.

O. J. and Simpson: A Dr. Jekyll and Mr. Hyde Phenomenon

The American public thought it "knew" Simpson, but it turned out that the "O. J." it saw, the "nice guy," was a *persona*, a mask. There was, it has been suggested, always a tension in him between his blackness and his more or less "white" posture. (People who are black-skinned but have "white" souls used to be called "Oreo cookies—dark on the outside, white in the inside"—at one time, but I've not heard the term for a while.) He was, it turns out, a wife beater who also continually cheated on his wife and, quite possibly, brutally murdered her and a young friend.

Social scientists use the term *para-social relationships* to describe the feeling people have that they "know" the actors and actresses they see on the television screen or in films. This, of course, is quite ridiculous. Actors and actresses are performers who pretend to be certain kinds of characters. O. J. was, I would suggest, the performance, the disguise; Simpson was the real person—a deeply troubled and not particularly nice person, it turns out.

For many years O. J. had been able to keep Simpson under control or, at least, out of the spotlight, but finally, it seems, the O. J. persona cracked and Simpson gained control. We could get a sense of the real Simpson in the recording of the 911 phone call his wife made to the police and get some idea of what the real Simpson was like in the pictures of her bruised face.

This kind of split between personality and real character is not too different from what we find with most people. We adopt, so this theory suggests, a persona to mask our real self, a privatissima that is buried deep in the unconscious realms of our psyches. That is why the admonition "know thyself" is so difficult to do, even though it sounds very simple. Knowing someone else is every more difficult. As Richard Corliss wrote in "It's Already the TV Movie":

> On Friday he listened to the coroner's droning, explicit testimony of the wounds that caused Nicole Simpson's death. Raw emotion played on his features, but what emotion? We have spent thousands of hours watching cop shows and love stories, intuiting feelings from faces. A glance at O. J. proved that there are some secrets even TV cannot reveal. (*Time,* 18 July 1994)

Corliss's point is well made. We think we know what the actors and actresses we see on television are "really" like, but we are mistaken. We cannot read character from the faces of performers of from the faces of people we meet in our daily activities.

In Simpson's infamous suicide note, we find the following lines, which reflect this matter:

> Don't feel sorry for me, I've had a great life, great friends.
>
> Please think of the real O. J. and not this lost person.

The lost person, of course, was the real Simpson, not the O. J. persona. Why Simpson was unable to maintain his performance as O. J. is the puzzling question.

Dramatic Fascination

I'm not sure whether the O. J. Simpson story is a tragedy or something better described as pathetic. I say this because we generally understand a tragedy to involve the fall of a great man or woman, and Simpson, whatever else he was, was not a great man. We use the term *tragedy* loosely nowadays, and to the extent that anyone acts in a destructive or self-destructive way, it probably is reasonable to use the term *tragedy*. If the story is not a tragedy for Simpson, it certainly was one for the two victims.

The America public has spent, relatively speaking, enormous amounts of time watching the famous "run" (and, in some cases, cheering him) as the car with him in it, driven by his friend "AC," Al Cowlings, proceeded down the highway, followed by police cars, with a number of helicopters from news stations flying overhead.

We have been fascinated by the chase and the hearings because, among other things, the story is a really dramatic one. Why watch made-up stories when real-life stories are so much more fantastic? What mystery story writer would ever get away with things like having the suspect purchase a fake moustache and beard? In some respects, the situation is so preposterous, has so many bizarre twists to it (and strange people involved) that it seems almost comic.

The reason this story fascinates us is that it is, really, a terrific drama. There is conflict, between the defense lawyers and the prosecution, about everything and all kinds of questions about whether or not certain matters, like blood spots and DNA testing, should be accepted as legitimate evidence. There are also interesting actors and actresses—the prosecuting attorney Marcia Clark was at one time a professional dancer and the defense attornies are very famous.

There are also the witnesses who were at the hearing, ranging from the enigmatic "friend" Brian Kaelin, who sort of hung out at Simpson's estate, to the detectives, the various criminalists (a new word for many people) and other experts, who came with their charts and other paraphernalia.

Simpson, a celebrity, is being represented by a team of "celebrity" lawyers: Robert Shapiro, Alan Dershowitz, F. Lee Bailey, and so on. Simpson is reputed to be worth $10 million, but by the time the trial is over, so conventional wisdom tells us, the lawyers will have all the money. What good would Simpson's money do him if he is found guilty and sentenced to life imprisonment, without parole (since the District Attorney will not ask for the death penalty)? Simpson might just as well spend all his money on the best lawyers he can find. (Recent news reports suggest that Simpson has spent most of his money, so far, on the trial and that he is "broke.")

A Psychoanalytic Explanation of Our Interest in Mysteries

One reason people like mystery stories, so psychoanalytically inclined critics such as Martin Grotjahn tell us, is because we are, in the deepest recesses of our psyches, would-be murderers ourselves. This repressed feeling is tied to our infantile states, when we experienced the Oedipus complex and wanted to "get rid of" the parent of the same sex, so we could have our mothers (or, in the case of women, our fathers) all to ourselves. This repressed hostility leads to a split in our minds: one part of us identifies with the murderer and the other with the detective, or in some cases, Grotjahn points out, the victim.

This curiosity started when we were young and wondered what went on in the bedroom between our parents. According to Grotjahn, most children get to observe the "primal scene." As he writes in *Beyond Laughter: Humor and the Subconscious*:

> The child's first observations of sexual activities are perceived as a lustful fight, a fight in which the male wins and the female is conquered and hurt—perhaps murdered?

> The attempt to learn the facts of life is later symbolized in the search for the detailed facts of the crime, which lead to the discovery of the murderer. The interest in mystery is a reactivation of the long-repressed interest in the bloody details of life and death, intercourse, menstruation, defloration, pregnancy, birth, delivery, and all the rest of it. (1966, 166)

Our fascination with mysteries and with the feats of great detectives represents, Grotjahn suggests, a displacement in our adult lives of our childhood curiosity about sex (especially sex between our parents) and related matters to crime.

In the Simpson trial, blood is playing a central role, since it can be used, so the prosecution asserts, to identify individuals involved in crimes. There were no witnesses that we know of, so the prosecutors are using laboratory tests to "prove" that Simpson was the murderer. The fact that Simpson is a well-known personality makes the case even more interesting to people than it ordinarily would since we all "knew" O. J. from his feats on the football field and his television commercials. The crime was, in a strange sense, a local one as far as the American public is concerned; it involved a person we all "knew"—parasocially, that is. But, in a sense, we all know one another in the "global village" we live in.

Guns and Knives

There is also an enigmatic aspect to it: why would a person who had, it seemed, everything, kill anyone? One answer might be that he had used violence against his wife before, and murder is, one can say, a stepped-up form of violence. But this murder seems to have been planned carefully; it was not, it seems, a matter of losing one's head, and killing someone in the heat of excitement. It may have been, nevertheless, a crime of passion.

Another matter that should be considered is the amount of violence on American television and in American society. This includes both nonfictional programs (like news shows and sports programs) and fictional programs—crime shows, children's shows, and so on. It is possible to argue that the all-pervasiveness of violence on television and in our films has desensitized us and made many of us more willing to murder people.

A story from Chicago about an eleven-year-old "hit child," less than five feet tall, murdering someone and then being shot in the back of the head, presumably by someone in his gang, got a good deal of attention, but what do one or two killings mean when something like 38,000 people are murdered in America each year?

There are hundreds of millions of guns (from handguns to automatic weapons) owned by Americans and attempts to control these guns have not been successful, due, in great part, to the power of the National Rifle Association. So we live in a society in which people have, on the one hand, been desensitized as far as shooting people is concerned, and on the other hand, find it easy to get their hands on guns.

The weapon used in the Simpson case murder was a knife, presumably so the murderer could avoid alerting people to what was going on. Knives are even cheaper than guns, but knives suggest a different sensibility. They are messier and, as we have learned from following the trial, it is not unusual for a person using a knife to kill someone to get cut himself or herself. Guns, especially automatic rifles and pistols, are the weapon of choice in the crime shows we see; knives are old-fashioned and don't convey the authority and power of the gun.

Commercials and Events of Magnitude

When I watched the hearings I was struck by the fact that for a number of hours there were no commercials. (Then, after a while, they started being run.) Broadcasts without commercials are signifiers by television stations that an event of some magnitude is occurring. The local television stations didn't have commercials during the most recent earthquake in San Francisco; when the commercials came back on, everyone knew that the crisis was over with.

Time magazine commented on the American public's seemingly insatiable interest in the O. J. Simpson hearings. As Richard Corliss wrote in "It's Already the TV Movie":

> Are we weary of this year? Has a single citizen of the global village od'd on O. J.? Apparently not. Every day for two weeks everybody was talking, everybody was watching. Last Friday, when the pretrial hearing reached its grisly climax, was Day 26 of American Held Hostage by its own lust for sensation. On ABC, CBS, NBC, Fox, CNN, ESPN2, and especially Court TV (the all-O. J. channel) the talkathon played six or more hours a day. Afternoon ratings soared 24% above their usual levels; prime-time specials were available for the law-impaired and the jurisimprudent. If you still couldn't get enough, you must have contacted Simpsonitis, an inflammation of tabloid curiosity. (18 July 1994)

Perhaps the most significant question the television coverage of the Simpson trial raises involves explaining the behavior of the American public. The matter of the amount of time the American public has given, and seems to be willing to give to this story, is quite remarkable. Let me offer some hypotheses.

What The O. J. Simpson Phenomenon Means

First of all, the O. J. Simpson trial is the ultimate police procedural. There are three different formulas found in detective shows. There is the classical formula, with a brilliant detective like Sherlock Holmes or Hercule Poirot. There is the "tough guy" formula, with a private-eye who faces danger in the course of solving a mystery. One of the best examples would be Sam Spade, the hero of *The Maltese Falcon*. There is the police procedural, which is found in the recent British series *Prime Suspect*. In police procedurals, there is a detective, but the detective relies to a great extent on work done by his or her colleagues, laboratory reports by coroners and criminalists, and so on. O. J. Simpson is the "prime suspect" but this case is not fiction but "real life," as they say. If we give the event a dramaturgical perspective we can say the O. J. is playing his most important role.

Second, and at the same time, there is a soap opera aspect to the story, in that it is quite melodramatic with all kinds of tortured and tangled relationships. We have an interracial marriage, philandering, murder, and the possibility of a suicide, right in the middle of the Los Angeles freeway system. It seems, in a strange way, unreal—almost like a parody of a soap opera. That may explain why people cheered O. J. as the car with him in it, and him holding a gun to his head, drove through the freeways of Los Angeles. It was more like a stunt for a picture than something real. In Los Angeles, as many have commented, it is often difficult to separate reality from fantasy.

Perhaps the Simpson trial tells us something really interesting, namely, that life imitates art more than art imitates life. The trial, like all interesting ones, echoes back to Kurasawa's great film *Rashomon*. That story, as I mentioned in an earlier chapter, also involved a murder, with a knife, but everyone in the grove where the murder took place—a bandit, a woman who was raped by the bandit (though he claimed she submitted willingly), and her husband—told a different story. Each character claimed to be guilty of the killing, including the murdered husband who, speaking from the grave through the voice of a shamanic woman in a trance, said he had committed suicide due to a broken heart. To further complicate matters, a woodcutter who observed the events told a story that differed from all the others.

Did Simpson plan what he thought would be the "perfect" murder? Is it possible that he is innocent and that someone else did it? Barring a confession and evidence in the bloodwork, we will never know. Did Simpson think he was, somehow, "above the law" and could get away with killing someone? If Simpson did kill his wife, he won't have the honor of being the first celebrity or famous individual involved in a murder. Unfortunately, he won't be the last, either.

The events involving O. J. Simpson have become the subject of numerous jokes—and part of American folklore. Let me offer some of the jokes:

O. J. Simpson calls and orders a limousine. "We'll have one for you in forty-five minutes," the limousine service tells him.
"That's okay," he says, "I've got time to kill."

The good news: O. J. Simpson is convicted and sent to jail.
The bad news: Michael Jackson is to take care of O. J.'s kids.

As if often the case, when there is a tragedy or something of major important, the joke makers become involved and one starts hearing jokes that allude, in various ways, to the event. It probably represents a way of dealing with collective anxiety. This happened, for example, when the Challenger exploded and seven astronauts were killed.

The Simpson jokes represent a means of dealing with events that are troubling or puzzling. We really don't know what to make of it all, and so we make jokes to deal with our anxiety. In the first joke, we can emphasize either "time" or "kill" in the phrase "time to kill," alluding to the murder of Simpson's wife. In the second, an allusion is made to the alleged pederasty of Michael Jackson. Allusion is one of the most common form of creating humor—calling attention to something someone has done in a manner meant to evoke laughter or mirth.

Regardless of how the trial turns out, Simpson has now become part of our contemporary American folklore. How long he will occupy our attention, and what the jokes will be like over the next few months, as the trial takes place, and new revelations are made, remains to be seen.

Media Events and Society

The three media events I have been discussing tell us something about our society, but what they tell us is not clear. This is because media events, which are characterized by, among other things, simultaneous transmission, provide different messages for different groups. They rearticulate our values but in doing so, offer articulations that are often ambivalent. As Daniel Dayan and Elihu Katz wrote in their article "Television Ceremonial Events" (Berger, 1987, 43), a media event

> has a performative nature. It consists of a ceremonially conducted alteration or reinforcement of society's central values; it offers a rearticulation or reaffirmation of the consensus that holds it together. It offers a symbolic manipulation of what Edward Shils calls its "center."

So the media events, according to Dayan and Katz, reinforce traditional values and affirm the core values of a given society. But, as reader-response critics keep pointing out, individuals and interpretive communities read texts differently. If the reader-response critics are correct, we can see media events as the site for varying and conflicting readings or interpretations, based on the beliefs of individuals and groups watching the media events. In addition, some media events offer different interpretations of themselves, as I suggested in my discussion of the Gulf War as a media event.

Because we see media events as they occur, there is an element of spectacle, and in some cases, drama to them, which helps explain why they are so popular. As Dayan and Katz explain, media events "allow their spectators to follow the event from within, to explore it, to vicariously become part of it" (Berger, 1987, 49). We watch others in media events, but they function, it might be said, as performers who take part in televised rituals that help us better understand ourselves.

11

Television as an Instrument of Terror II: Old Views and New Considerations

When I wrote my original chapter titled "Television as an Instrument of Terror" I made a number of points about the relationship that exists between television and terror. I would like to review some of them briefly, and then say something about how I feel about the matter now.

The Medium is the Problem

Television, as a medium, tends to lead to disorientation and confusion. (This argument, which leans on the ideas of Marshall McLuhan, will be discussed shortly.) I distinguish between the medium and the programs carried by the medium. It is the medium itself that primarily causes problems as far as disorientation is concerned, though in some cases the programming exacerbates things. We can now add cable and satellite television and videos to broadcast television to cover all our bases nowadays, as the communication industry is undergoing remarkable transformations and telephone lines will soon be bringing us all kinds of programming.

The Difference between Film and Television

Viewing television, which involves our making images out of ever changing patterns of dots, is different from viewing a film, which is a succession of still images or frames that are run very quickly and create the illusion of motion. When watching television we have to work very hard, so to speak, to "make" pictures out of collections of dots that we see continually forming and reforming on the television screen. In this sense, watching television is "work," though our eyes are able to do this work with remarkable ease.

Disorientation Due to Television

Television, as an auditory "all-at-once" medium, "envelops" us and contrasts with the linear, sequential, and implicitly more logical, medium of print that we can examine at our leisure. "It can be argued," I wrote, "that television is, by its very nature, illogical and disorienting." This perspective draws on the work of Marshall McLuhan, who argued that "the medium is the message" and that is was the impact of television on our sense ratios that was of significance. As he wrote in *Understanding Media: The Extensions of Man*:

> The effects of technology do not occur at the level of opinions or concepts, but alter sense ratios or patterns of perception steadily and without any resistance. (1965, 18)

It is, then, the medium itself, rather than the programs the medium carries, that is of primary significance.

The Problem of Impulse and Hyperkinesis

The overpowering immediacy of the medium of television and, I would add, of many of the texts broadcast on it, generate impulsive responses and thus television acts, in a way, as a kind of hyperkinetic trigger for viewers. How much difference is there between Pavlov's ringing a bell when he served his dogs a meal (to set them salivating) and the commercials for fast foods and other foods broadcast on television, with extreme close-ups and the sound of sizzling meat (to set viewers salivating)? Or all the soft-core pornography in the commercials and dramas to sexually excite viewers?

Commercials aim, generally speaking, at liberating impulses and evading the strictures of the ego and rational, logical decision making. They also interrupt the continuity of programming, so we become used to seeing programs in bits and pieces, and this may carry over into our lives. Perhaps we also see ourselves as fragments and, thus, our identities become difficult to establish and maintain.

I read recently, in a video trade publication, that people have eight-second attention spans when watching television, and if they do not see a new image or something different after eight seconds, they become bored and restless.

The Matter of Psychic Mobilization

Despite the variety of programs on television, beneath all the diversity of genres and shows, there are certain cultural codings that tend to unify us—even though we have an increasingly a multiracial, multicultural population. The people who create television shows argue that "they are only giving people what they want" but, in reality, I argue, television functioning as a socializing agent, has created a situation in which people "have been mobilized, psychically, to want what they get."

I'm not as sure now, as I was earlier, that television can mobilize people to the extent that I thought it could. But recent articles about the infamous Huffington-Feinstein television campaign quote people who, when asked about political matters, mouth, word for word, the slogans and phrases they have learned from the political commercials of the two candidates. This leads me to think that although I don't see there being a mass culture in America, as the mass culture theorists projected things, people are nevertheless affected in profound ways by what they see and hear on television.

Media Effects

I suggested that there were certain media effects—using the term *media* literally—that could be hypothesized. Television leads to disorientation, to confusion (from a lack of a fixed point of view), to impulsive behavior, and to the loss of a fixed identity and to de-individuation—though viewers had the illusion of individuality, since they supposedly exercised their "choice" in deciding what to watch. Or, to be more precise, their ability to *select* which programs to watch from those being broadcast.

This was leading, I added, to a situation in which Emerson's lines from his essay *Nature,* "I become a transparent eyeball; I am nothing. I see all," was coming true. Have we become an "occulocentric" society in which, for large numbers of people, doing and touching are less important than seeing?

Mediated Realities are not Always Truthful

Mediated realities are not always truthful. This is shown in the work by Kurt and Gladys Lang on MacArthur's homecoming in 1951 in which the televised portrayal of the trip was highly selective and provided an unreal picture of what actually happened. Someone, after all, always selects which images television broadcasts, so the camera might reveal the truth, but it doesn't necessarily reveal the whole truth.

Television and the Problems of Cynicism and Skepticism

Television leads to cynicism and skepticism in young people. At an early age, around eight or nine, children learn that commercials exaggerate or even "lie" about the products they advertise. Toys don't work as well as they do in the commercials, for example. Children then transfer this disillusionment, skepticism, and cynicism, I believe, to the people they are involved with in everyday life and to the institutions in society. These attitudes persist, I would suggest, into later life.

Thus, it might be argued that the cynicism and skepticism found in the American public about politicians and government is exacerbated by our television viewing—especially since we tend to watch a great deal of television.

Vicious Cycles and Television Viewing: Feeding Upon Dependencies it Creates

Television, I suggest, often leads to a "vicious cycle" in which young children, exposed to adult conflicts (on the programs they watch) that are too difficult for them to handle emotionally, become afraid of having serious relationships when they grow older. A study by Bradley Greenberg reveals, for instance, that there are 6.6 "sexual incidents" in a typical afternoon soap opera (that is, per hour). These incidents involve everything from extramarital sex to rape.

This kind of programming leads, ultimately, my theory suggests, to an unwillingness of young men and women to have strong emotional ties, to practicing nonrelational sex, and to strong feelings of anxiety and loneliness, which the afflicted parties try to assuage by turning to television to occupy their time.

It can be argued, then, that people become caught up in a vicious circle; television creates the very dependencies that people use it to overcome and they end up as "prisoners" of their television sets. This may account for the enormous amount of time, relatively speaking, that people spend watching television—about four hours a day for ordinary people and much more of "addicts."

Privatism and Psychologism

The world of television, studies have shown, tends to be a middle-class one. There are relatively few shows about working-class people or poor people. This leads to a distorted picture of American society. Also, the enormous number of commercials found on television tends to focus people's attention on their private concerns—their desires for goods and self-realization.

They become what I call "prisoners of psychology" who see everything in terms of individual will and volition, reduce everything to psychology (so to speak) and do not see problems in social or political terms. Society becomes an abstraction; there are only individuals.

Television Violence

In my original chapter I included a brief discussion on television violence, a topic that is much debated by media scholars. How much violence people see on television depends, of course, on how one defines violence, and studies with very narrow definitions of violence naturally find much less violence than studies that define the term broadly. However you define the term, the average television viewer is exposed to an enormous number of incidents of violence in a typical day's or week's viewing—whether it is comic violence on children's shows, dramatized violence in action-adventure shows, or "real" violence in news programs.

There is reason to suspect that this exposure to violence does have an impact on society, and in the years since I wrote my original chapter, the number of killings in America has really skyrocketed. School children bring guns to school and eleven- and twelve-year-old children murder people. Violence, of an increasingly deadly nature (due to the widespread availability of pistols and machine guns) is growing and approximately 38,000 people were killed in America in 1993 by guns. America is perceived by people in other countries as a dangerous place, and it is. Television is not the cause of all this violence but it is, I would suggest, a major contributing factor.

Television and Terror: Unacknowledged Compulsions

All of the factors discussed to this point play a role in generating "terror." I distinguish between terror, which involves the use of force by the state or other entities in a society and "terrorism," which involves the use of violence by small groups of people to disorient people, to make them afraid and to weaken their sense that their society is stable and that their government can protect them.

Television does not enhance our sense of possibility but does just the reverse—it hinders it when it does not destroy it. Its mass-produced fantasies tend to get in the way of our personal ones. (Some therapists report that television has invaded their patients' dreams.) Some people even use television characters to create their identities.

There are, I suggested, unrecognized compulsions that are shaping our behavior. I quoted from Henri Lefebvre's book, *Everyday Life in the Modern World,* "compulsion and the illusion of freedom converge," and "unacknowledged compulsions shape our lives." I also quoted from the German writer Hans Magnus Enzenberger, who wrote in an essay "The Industrialization of the Mind," that there is a "consciousness industry" whose basic goal is to sell people the notion that the existing order is worth keeping. He writes:

> All of us, no matter how irresolute we are, like to think that we reign supreme in our own consciousness, that we are the masters of what our minds accept or reject.... No illusion is more stubbornly upheld than the sovereignty of the mind. It is a good example of the impact of philosophy on people who ignore it; for the idea that men can "make up their minds" individually and by themselves is essentially derived from the tenets of bourgeois philosophy. (1974, 3)

Enzenberger and Lefebvre raise important questions. Are we free to make up our own minds about things (who to vote for, what to buy, what occupation to follow) or are we victims of our illusions about the "sovereignty" of our minds, living in a state that can be described as one of "terror" (though we may not be able to articulate it as such)? This terror, without our recognizing what is going on, shapes our consciousness and its unacknowledged compulsions, so the argument suggests, shape our behavior.

The Problem of Reading Television

This the gist of the chapter I wrote in the original version of *Television as an Instrument of Terror*. I still find the argument compelling, though I would admit that I have some thoughts about the degree to which television is an instrument of terror. In terms of its content, there is no question that the violence that permeates television does have the effect of making people feel that life in America is dangerous and thus experience a sense of anxiety, if not terror. Personally, I find it sickening and distasteful, and believe it has visceral effects on people—even though we know we are watching "make-believe" stories.

People who watch large amounts of television tend to think that there is more crime than there is and that the world is "crueler" than it is. In recent years in America, statistics suggest that the amount of crime actually has gone down, but because local news programs tend to focus on violent and sensational crimes, like murders, we have the perception that crime is more rampant than it actually is. Of course, it is our perceptions of the world that shape our beliefs and opinions, not the "reality" of the crime statistics.

There is a problem, however, with assertions about what people "must be getting" from watching or "reading" television programs. I am referring to a problem mentioned, from time to time in this book, that deals with the way different viewers decode what they see. According to the reader-response theorists, each reader brings the text he or she is reading or viewing into being and interprets it according to his or her education, background, fund of knowledge, and so on. If that is the case, how can any text, or any medium that carries texts (such as television) terrorize—or do anything—to people?

There are several ways of answering this question. First, it may not be accurate to say that every interpretation is different in important ways. Yes, people are all different and see things differently, but the differences may not always be significant. They may have, for example, visceral reactions to violence on television (and other matters like sexuality) that are not filtered out or processed by their cognitive processes.

Second, it may also be the case that people interpret texts in terms of their identification with socioeconomic, racial, religious and other groups and, in particular, political cultures, to which they belong. Since there are a limited number of political cultures (according to Aaron Wildavsky, just four), there is much more agreement by members of each of these four "interpretative communities" than the reader-response theorists would imagine.

So there is some question in my mind as to whether there is interpretative anarchy when it comes to reading and interpreting texts. The other extreme, the notion that we all respond exactly the same way to texts, what I call "interpretative absolutism" is also not tenable. What we are left with is a sense that while all readings of texts are different, the differences may not be that great, and certain commonalities exist. Human beings are all different, as far as what they look like and what their experiences are, but they are all similar in certain ways, too.

The Postmodern World and Terror

Postmodernism, defined by Jean-Francois Lyotard as (and I'm simplifying his argument to the extreme) "incredulity toward meta-narratives" (1984, xxiv) raises interesting questions about terror. As the term implies (though Lyotard doesn't necessarily accept this notion), postmodernism refers to the period that comes after modernism and refers not only to the arts but to all of culture. *Meta-narratives,* as Lyotard uses the term, refers to broad theoretical constructs that people accept and that offer generally accepted values and beliefs to guide their behavior.

If these meta-narratives are rejected, we have a crisis of legitimacy, since we no longer have broad rules and general belief systems to guide us. This leads to a rather chaotic kind of society and culture. As he writes:

> Eclecticism is the degree zero of contemporary general culture: one listens to reggae, watches a western, eats McDonald's food for lunch and local cuisine for dinner, wears Paris perfume in Tokyo and "retro" clothes in Hong Kong; knowledge is a matter of TV games. It is easy to find a public for eclectic works. By becoming kitsch, art panders to the confusion which reigns in the "taste" of the patrons. Artists, gallery owners, critics, and public wallow together in the "anything goes," and the epoch is one of slackening. But this realism of the "anything goes" is in fact that of money; in the absence of aesthetic criteria, it remains profitable and useful to assess the value of works of art according top the profits they yield. Such realism accommodates all tendencies, just as capital accommodates all "needs" providing that the tendencies and needs have purchasing power. (1984, 76)

It is this need for purchasing power that helps generate terror in people, for when they watch television, they see an endless number of commercials advertising this product and that service—all of which are, it is suggested, necessary for the good life.

But what of those people who cannot afford these products, who do not have the requisite purchasing power? How much purchasing power does one need, for no matter what you have, it is never enough. (In San Francisco, a baseball player who earns seven million dollars a year, which works out to almost $50,000 a game, went before a judge to cut his alimony payments, pleading that he was broke because of the 1994 baseball strike.)

There are always new needs being created and more expensive desires to be satisfied. Everything is reduced to what one can afford in a consumer culture and for those who cannot afford very much, let alone everything, there develops, I would say, a feeling of anguish, of powerlessness, of deprivation, a sense that one is, somehow, a failure, a feeling that can be described as psychic terror. In addition, those at the top of the socioeconomic pyramid wish to maintain their position and do so, LeFebvre argues, by repressing those beneath them—politically as well as psychologically.

Feeling Uneasy in a World of Choice

When anything goes, in a postmodern world (though some would describe our contemporary society not as postmodern but as late modernistic) the only thing that is stable is the dollar (or its equivalent in other countries), and if you don't have enough dollars, you can't play the game of consuming in a consumer culture very well—if at all. The more one watches television, the more commercials one sees promising the good life, sexual pleasure, happiness, and all kinds of other things, but the less one can afford, and consequently the more "terrorized" one becomes. As Henri Lefebvre describes the role of advertising, in *Everyday Life in the Modern World*:

> The time is past when advertising tried to condition the consumer by the repetition of slogans; today the more subtle forms of publicity represent a whole attitude to life: if you know how to choose you will choose this brand and no other.... [Y]ou are being looked after, cared for, told how to live better, how to dress fashionably, how to decorate your house, in short how to exist; you are totally programmed, except that you still have to choose between so many good things, since the act of consuming remains a permanent structure...consuming is no joke; well-wishing and helpful, the whole of society is with you.... We had misjudged society; all of us; it is maternal and fraternal; our visible family is duplicated by this invisible one, better and especially more efficient, the society of consumption that showers

considerations and protective charms on everybody. Who can be ungrateful enough to be uneasy? (1984: 107, 108)

The ironic sentence that Lefebvre uses at the end suggests the degree to which what he calls "the bureaucratic society of controlled consumption" terrorizes people. He writes "uneasy," but this is a subtle way of indicating something much stronger, namely, what I've described as terror.

Those who cannot consume are terrorized by feelings of inadequacy and failure and those who can consume have, at the other end of the spectrum, the problem (in some cases even terror) of choice to face at every instant, and anxiety about whether their choices are the "right" ones? Then, finally, they experience boredom, for when you can have anything you want, what you do you next? In a postmodern world, where anything goes, and you can do anything, how do you avoid boredom?

Conclusions

It may be that the term *terror* is too strong and that what I have been talking about is better described as diffuse feelings of anxiety, malaise, insecurity, disappointment, and relative deprivation. I think the term *terror* is, more often than not, correct. That is, because I believe that television—both the medium and the programs it carries—does exert immense pressure on people and, though they may not recognize it as such or be able to articulate it, really does terrorize them.

I had been reading Lefebvre's book and found his argument about terror pervading our everyday lives compelling, even though it strikes one, at first thought, as extreme. Thanks to technological developments, like VCRs, we can time shift and exercise more choice as far as the programs we want to watch (and we can rent and see films at home). We can also zap programs and go channel surfing to create our own mosaic television programs (a very postmodern activity).

But the fact remains that television is the dominant medium of our time, and with the development of cable and the promised 500 channels that will come into our homes, it is unlikely that things will change very much, so television and other programming brought to us on cable and soon through our phone lines will remain, aided and abetted by larger and sharper screens, with more compelling images, even more of an instrument of terror, that is, for those who cannot turn the television set off!

VI
Film: Introduction

The films I deal with in my discussion here are two of the more important films of the last thirty years. *The Terminator* was a low-budget film that made a star of its lead actor, Arnold Schwarzenegger, and made its director, James Cameron, a powerful figure in Hollywood. I describe this film as a "fatalist" one, using Aaron Wildavsky's typology of political cultures. He explains his theory as follows (quoted in Arthur Asa Berger, *Agitpop,* 1990, 5):

> The dimensions of cultural theory are based on answers to two questions: "Who am I?" and "How Should I Behave?" The question of identity may be answered by saying that individuals belong to a strong group, a collective, that makes decisions binding on all members or that their ties to others are weak in that their choices being only themselves. The question of action is answered by responding that the individual is subject to many or few prescriptions, a free spirit or one that is tightly controlled.

We end up with four political cultures: *fatalists* (numerous rules, weak group boundaries), *competitive individualists* (few rules, weak group boundaries), *hierarchical elitists* (numerous rules, strong group boundaries), and *egalitarians* (few rules, strong boundaries). Fatalists, who tend to be at the bottom of the socioeconomic ladder, think that luck and chance is basic. So, basically they are pessimistic and reactive.

In addition to discussing *The Terminator* as a fatalist text, I also deal with it in terms of the bipolar oppositions that inform it. If Lévi-Strauss and Saussure are correct, we can elicit a set of paired oppositions in all texts. I show that there are, in fact, numerous oppositions in this text, based on the opposition termination versus continuation, that help give this text its resonance. I also deal with the Terminator figure as a distorted or perverted kind of superego and argue that it reflects a diffuse kind of paranoia found in the American public in general.

Then I discuss *Star Wars* as a fairy tale, showing how Vladimir Propp's *Morphology of the Folktale* can be used to analyze the film. Propp argued that folktales (he studied a number of Russian ones) could best be understood in terms of the actions of the characters in them. These actions he called functions. He offered a list of thirty-one functions found in all the folktales he studied, which are useful for other folktales and other kinds of texts as well.

I offer an abbreviated list of his functions, then I show that a considerable number of Propp's functions can be found in *Star Wars*. This suggests that it is, in reality, a modernized fairy tale, and that, I hypothesize, may account for much of its popularity. We also learn, I point out, from *Star Wars* and the other films in the cycle, that heroes need helpers, that they cannot function alone. This message is one of the subtexts of the film. Like fairy tales, there are all kinds of fabulous and weird characters, with remarkable powers, in the film.

Fairy tales are important, Bettelheim reminds us, because they give young children courage and help them gain psychological strength. I also draw upon the ideas of critics who argue that narratives of all kinds are metaphoric attempts we make to understand the nature of life and gain a sense of our place in the universe.

12

The Terminator: A Case Study in High-Tech Paranoia

The Terminator is a science fiction film made in 1984 starring Arnold Schwarzenegger as a malevolent cyborg sent from future times to present-day American society, to kill a young woman, Sarah Connor. The purpose of this exercise is to prevent her from having children and starting a family whose offspring would exist in the future. In essence, the Terminator's job is to change history.

This kind of plot is a common one in science fiction. There was an episode of *Star Trek* in which Spock, Kirk, and McCoy had to let a beautiful young woman be killed in an automobile accident otherwise history would have been changed with results that would have been disastrous for the world. In this case, the heroes of *Star Trek* were time travelers whose mission was a positive one.

The Story

In *The Terminator,* the situation is different. The Terminator is a time-travelling cyborg, a robot with a veneer of flesh, which seems human, that is programmed to accomplish its mission and use whatever means are necessary to do so. A soldier, Kyle Reese, also manages to travel into the past to fight the Terminator, and the film is, in essence, a series of battles between Reese and the Terminator in which Reese attempts to save Sarah Connor from termination.

We know from a flashback of Reese's that Terminators torment people in the future and see a scene in which a Terminator has managed to get into an encampment of freedom fighters and machine guns people with wild abandon. In that scene, Reese sees a Polaroid photo of Sarah Connor, the progenitor of a long line of people, which was taken in the distant past.

The Terminator violates one of Asimov's laws for robots—that they will not hurt human beings. It (he) is a nightmare figure, half-machine, half-human (or seemingly human), that stalks Sarah Connor relentlessly and single-mindedly, destroying anyone or anything that interferes with its mission. The Terminator is a monster that reminds one of Frankenstein—it is not human though it approximates human form—but unlike Frankenstein, the Terminator has no emotions or feelings.

In essence, the plot of *The Terminator* is a sustained chase story in which the Terminator, played with a grim deadness by Arnold Schwarzenegger, relentlessly searches for and attacks Sarah Connor. There are innumerable automobile chases and close escapes. In one scene, Sarah and Kyle are apprehended by the police. A police psychologist interrogates Reese, who tells him about the Terminator in considerable detail.

The psychologist concludes that Reese is insane. In one ironic scene, the psychologist is shown leaving the police station just as the Terminator enters, to inquire about Sarah Connor. A short while later, he rams the police station with a car and, machine gun blazing, devastates the station. In the confusion, Reese escapes with Sarah Connor and they race off to a motel far from the city. When Reese goes to a hardware store to purchase some supplies to make bombs, Sarah makes the mistake of calling her mother. She actually talks with the Terminator, who has imitated her mother's voice and who jumps on a motorcycle and sets off for the city and the motel where Sarah and Reese are staying.

That night Sarah and Reese make love and, as it turns out, she is impregnated. The next morning there is a final denouement in which the Terminator, on a motorcycle, dodges bombs made by Kyle Reese. The final scenes, which are terrifying, show the Terminator driving a huge oil rig, all set to run down Sarah. Kyle has put a bomb in the rig and it explodes, turning the truck into a fiery blaze. One would think that would be the end of the Terminator, but such is not the case. The Terminator, stripped of its flesh and revealing itself as a glistening robot, emerges from the blaze and continues to chase after Sarah and Kyle.

The Terminator chases them into a metal factory. Kyle manages to put a bomb on the Terminator, which explodes, killing Kyle and ripping the Terminator in half. The top half of the Terminator, using its arms to crawl, continues to chase Sarah. She runs into a huge press, the Terminator follows, and just before the Terminator can reach her, to strangle her, she turns on the press and crunches the Terminator.

At the end of the film, we see Sarah, pregnant, heading toward some mountain in Mexico. When she stops for gas a young Mexican child takes a Polaroid photo of her—the same Polaroid photo we saw in Kyle Reese's flashback.

Thus, the story ends with the Terminator having been foiled and with Sarah Connor pregnant and about to start a line of progeny that will extend far into the future—into the time when many Terminators exist, killing people and spreading mayhem.

The Terminator as a Fatalist Text

The Terminator reflects a diffuse sense of paranoia that many people feel—especially those whom we may describe as "fatalists" (using Aaron Wildavsky's typology), who see life as essentially a matter of luck and believe that powerful forces are operating against them. *The Terminator* is, of course, an extreme example of the power of those who control society (and the various Terminators at their command) but the ambience of the film, the gritty quality of the parking garages and police stations, is the world of the powerless and fatalistic.

It is only Reese, a warrior with courage and determination, who is able to fight against the Terminator. It wipes everyone else out and seems unstoppable. The relentlessness of the Terminator's behavior is a major source of the terror. It is, being a cyborg, mindless, but it has an intelligence. We see computer readouts on the screen whenever the Terminator comes across a device or situation that needs to be understood. For example, a computer readout shows it the gearing structure of the oil truck and "teaches" the Terminator how to drive it.

Thus, it could be argued that *The Terminator* is a personification of the sense of despair and oppression fatalists have, a sense that the powers that run society are everywhere and are just about all-powerful (but not completely all-powerful, because there has to be room for luck and chance to operate).

There is also the matter of the anxiety we all feel about machines and, in particular, about machines in the future, which may be "intelligent" and may be mobile (that is, robots or cyborgs). Many science fiction stories deal with powerful machines or machinelike creations that have no emotions or feelings and which kill and destroy until some manner of stopping them is found. One thing that science fiction stories do is raise feelings of anxiety and fear (and sometime even terror), which they then deal with by finding ways of destroying the monsters and machines. This leads to a sense of well-being and hope.

Let me summarize, then, some of the fatalistic elements reflected in *The Terminator*:

1. Powerful forces attack us that we cannot (at least at first) deal with.
2. There is no let up. The Terminator is relentless and even when it is blown up, it still presses forward, trying to accomplish its mission.
3. One survives due to luck and chance. It is only such things that enable us to manage, given the nature of the forces that we must contend with.
4. Authority is useless. The police, for example, were both powerless and wrong. Sarah Connor survived in spite of the police, not as the result of their assistance. In fact, they actually did more harm than good. The moral is you can't trust the police. When they aren't useless they are harmful.
5. The concept of "termination" has a bureaucratic ring to it. The CIA reputedly uses the phrase "termination with extreme prejudice" when it wants to have someone killed and "termination" suggests that some entity, which has the right and power to do so, has decided to put an end to one's employment (or life).

Science Fiction Elements of *The Terminator*

The Terminator is an alien, but not a bug-eyed monster that is easy to detect, even though it may be powerful and scary. What is anxiety provoking about this creature is that it has a human form and thus is not immediately recognizable for what it is. There is also, as has been mentioned earlier, the anxiety about "intelligent" machines and what they might do if, somehow, they become independent or are programmed by some malevolent force.

(There is another source of anxiety relative to machines, namely, that they will end up controlling human beings, who will become "servoproteins" that are needed to do certain operations for these intelligent machines. This reversal is the source of considerable concern and even before we develop intelligent machines, many people in the computer business can be regarded as, in a sense, servoproteins.)

One interesting aspect of *The Terminator* is its hyper-phallicism. The chosen weapon of the Terminator (and of all Terminators, it is suggested in Reese's flashback) is the submachine gun. The substitute phallus of the Terminator is used to kill, not create life. Schwarzenegger, a giant, muscular figure, devastates the police station with his submachine gun. He races from room to room shooting everyone he sees, as he searches for Sarah Connor. She has been snatched by Reese, however.

The story also projects a bleak future, for it shows a society in which people who wish to be free are continually being hunted down by submachine gun toting Terminators. The flashback of Reese showed this society. It is only dogs that can distinguish between human beings and Terminators and they are used to sound alarms when Terminators approach.

The Terminator as a Metaphor

In a curious way, these stories about alien figures replicate what happens in our bodies when alien forces (germs, viruses, etc.) invade and we are attacked. Stories like *The Terminator* are metaphors for infection and disease and replicate the battles that take place in our bodies as "intelligent" alien organisms invade them and attempt to destroy them. The AIDS virus is currently the great "terminator" in present-day society and, as of now, there is no way to deal with this malevolent force successfully.

Disease, we may say, is the model of the alien killer and *The Terminator* and many other science fiction stories, can be looked upon as projections and manifestations of this model. Like the Terminator, these viruses and alien forces seek to kill us, though in so doing, as the biologists point out, they ultimately destroy themselves.

Finally, there is the matter of emotionless "intelligence," which is very scary. One of the reasons humans like dogs and other warm-blooded animals is that they have emotions and are animated, responsive creatures. Snakes and other reptiles, on the other hand, are single-minded predators and generally repel us. We fear intelligence without feeling because we all believe that it is our feelings and emotions that humanize us, that temper our reason and prevent us from mindlessly and perhaps destructively following the dictates of our so-called intelligence.

It should be noted that in *Star Trek*, Mr. Spock is portrayed as essentially logical and relatively devoid of emotion. (We are told there are certain periods when this is not so and Spock feels passions.) But Spock is not, actually, emotionless. His face is often expressive and he is portrayed as essentially human, but with those pointy ears symbolizing his relative lack of emotion. He gives, one might say, a human face to being without emotion.

Oppositions in the Text

It has been suggested by Lévi-Strauss that the function of mythic heroes is to mediate between opposing forces and, in some way, reconcile them. Although *The Terminator* is not a myth, it has elements of the mythic in it and in Sarah Connor and the Terminator it has two figures who are very different.

Let me spell out these oppositions below. First, the Terminator is a killer and Sarah Connor is the woman he wants to kill. (All the other killings are incidental, as a matter of fact.) The Terminator is a cyborg, a nonhuman thing, a robot that has a veneer of human flesh around it. Sarah, on the other hand, is a human—and a warm and loving one, too—who gives birth to new life. The Terminator chases and attacks and Sarah and Kyle are chased and attacked. The Terminator is a tall, powerful male and Sarah is a (relatively speaking) weak female—though, as we see at the end, she is a courageous and resourceful one.

The Terminator represents the future, which has come into the past and Sarah, through her progeny, represents the past, which will extend into the future. She is pregnant with Kyle's child at the end of the film and we know that her line will play an important role in the future. The Terminator, as its name implies, represents death and is asexual while Sarah represents life and fertility. The Terminator is an alien cyborg (pseudo-human) and Sarah is a "real" human. The Terminator, as a machine, is emotionless. Schwarzenegger does a superb job of capturing this; he is very cold, matter of fact, and businesslike. Sarah, on the other hand, as a human, is loving and passionate. The Terminator is self-sufficient while Sarah needs help. Without Kyle she has no chance to survive. It is her survival that is crucial to the story, which, in the final analysis, deals with the central opposition of the story—termination versus continuance. Her survival is, in part, the result of Kyle's heroism and sacrifice, terms that would be meaningless to cyborgs. Though Kyle dies, he lives on through the child that he has fathered.

These oppositions, which it is suggested provide the central meaning of the text, can be seen in the chart below:

THE TERMINATOR	THE GIRL
Cyborg	Human
Killer	Victim
Chases	Is Chased
Male	Female
The future in the past	The past in the future
Death	Birth
Asexual	Sexual
Evil	Good
Emotionless	Emotional, loving
Self-sufficient	Needs help
Goal: Termination	Goal: Continuance
Is destroyed	Survives

It is these oppositions that are central to the text and which provide its meaning. It is the oppressiveness of the film, its portrayal of a powerful alien creature that has but one goal, which it pursues relentlessly, which leads me to suggest that it is a work best described as fatalistic.

The film, I've suggested, has a seamy quality; it is full of car chases, it takes place in parking garages, police stations, cheap motels and factories, all of which can be considered part of the underside of American culture, areas that may be quite familiar to people who tend to be fatalists. Worst of all, I would say, is the figure of the Terminator, a perverted super-ego figure that is relentless in its pursuit and seemingly all powerful.

A Psychoanalytic Interpretation of *The Terminator*

From a psychoanalytic point of view, the Terminator figure reflects a super-ego that has become distorted and destructive and is out of control. (I do not see it as an id figure because it is has no vitality and is not impulsive or anything like that. It is merely following instructions.) Sarah can be seen as an id figure in the most positive sense of the term, for as the Freudians tell us, we all need the id, which provides energy and, ultimately, life itself. Kyle Reese takes over the role of the ego, trying to mediate between the super-ego and the id, but because the super-ego is perverted and obsessive, Reese cannot use reason or logic but must fight it with its own weapons.

Many years ago, psychiatrists were called "alienists," for it was felt that disturbed or crazy people were, in a sense, aliens or even alienated. The plot of *The Terminator* can be seen as an externalization of the battles that go on, so the Freudians tell us, in our psyches between our superegos (guilt, conscience), our ids (desire, sexuality, impulse), and our egos (reason, survival).

When one element of the psyche is too powerful and our psyches are out of balance, so the theory goes, we find neuroses and other problems. One reason the film is so disturbing, I would argues, is because it reflects, in vague and disguised ways, a kind of unbalanced collective psyche, in which guilt and related matters have overwhelmed the id (our source of energy) and rendered it ineffective.

This may explain the reliance on luck and the sense of powerlessness that are associated with fatalist political cultures. The id elements are too weak and the ego is rendered ineffective by a distorted superego. *The Terminator* can be seen, from the psychoanalytic perspective, is a little morality drama in which a monstrous superego is destroyed by a valiant ego so that the id can survive.

None of this, I would add, is necessarily apparent to the typical viewer of the film. It is just another science-fiction film dealing with a killer alien that has a lot of excitement, action, and violence. What the psychoanalytic perspective does is offer us a sense of why the film has such a nightmare quality about it, why it is so disturbing. What I have suggested, also, is that our understanding of people who would be categorized by Wildavsky as fatalists may be enlarged by speculating about the psychoanalytic reasons for their present-mindedness and reliance on luck and chance.

The Terminator was described in one review as having a comic-book quality about it. This criticism may be due to the nature of the Terminator figure, but I would disagree. I thought the acting was quite good and the narrative certainly had a great deal of action in it. In recent years, as a matter of fact, the film has taken on something of a cult status and is now seen as an important film. It made the reputation of its director, James Cameron, and its lead actor, Arnold Schwarzenegger, who is one of the most important—and expensive—stars in Hollywood.

The Terminator may not be a classic and may not be placed on those lists of ten or twenty-five greatest films ever made, but *The Terminator* is a remarkably resonant and compelling film that reflects the diffuse paranoia and anxiety of many people and reveals, to those who examine the film carefully, a number of interesting things about American culture and society.

13

Star Wars as Fairy Tale

Films tell stories. Film is the medium through which the stories are told, and it is the remarkable things that can be done with this medium that have characterized many of the most popular films in recent years. But without a good script, without interesting and exciting stories, characters we can identify with, and dialogue that pleases us, all the technological know-how in the world leads to very little. If all we can say about a film is that the special effects were wonderful, we've not said that the film was worth seeing—or making.

The stories told on film tend to fall into certain genres: detective films, spy films, love stories, war stories, adventures, science-fiction and fantasy stories, and so on. Within some of the genres there are sub-genres. Thus, adventure stories can involve police films, kung-fu films, and various other kinds of adventure films. These genres all have a formulaic dimension to them; that is, they are based on conventions that specify certain kinds of plots, characters, heroes, and villains, among other things.

The Morphology of the Folktale and Other Kinds of Tales

It doesn't matter whether the genre is spy (as in the James Bond films) or detective or western, there are certain things a story has to have to hold an audience's attention. That is, there is what might be called a core or essence to stories, whatever their nature; although they may differ in certain aspects, in important ways they are all alike.

In 1927 a Russian folklore scholar, Vladimir Propp, wrote a book, *Morphology of the Folktale,* which analyzed a number of Russian folktales in terms of the basic components he found in the tales. He did this because discussions of kinds of plots or basic themes led nowhere; everyone had different classification schemes and none of them were very helpful. The term *morphology* means structure and what Propp did was come up with the structural elements of folktales.

He called these components "functions" and described them as representing some kind of an action of a character "defined from the point of view of its significance for the course of the action" (1968, 21). He added, "Functions of characters serve as stable, constant elements in a tale, independent of how and by whom they are fulfilled. They constitute the fundamental components of a tale" (1968, 21). He also believed that the number of functions was limited. In his book Propp listed and described his thirty-one functions, pointing out that there are often a number of variations of a function.

For example, his first function is: "One of the members of a family absents himself from home." He offers three subcategories of this function: first, the person absenting himself can be a member of an older generation; second, the death of parents represents an intensified form of absentation; and third, sometimes members of the younger generation absent themselves. His book describes his basic functions and the variations or subcategories of the functions in considerable detail. Functions also can be reversed or inverted in some cases, he adds, to make things more complicated. His second function is: "An Interdiction is Addressed to the Hero." Other functions involve such things as a hero getting helpers and the use of a magical agent.

Many fairy tales begin with these two functions. For example, the parents of a princess go on a trip (absentation) and tell her not to open the door or look in a trunk or something of that nature (interdiction). Of course, as soon as they have left the princess forgets about the interdiction or pays no attention to it and then the trouble begins. She is poisoned by a witch or abducted by a demon or whatever.

What is interesting is that Propp's functions are also found in contemporary stories for the simple reason that Propp's functions apply not only to fairytales but to stories of all kinds. We may, at times, have to update Propp's functions a bit, but they can be used to explicate a number of contemporary films and other texts. In the chart below I offer simplified versions of Propp's functions. He suggests all stories have an initial situation (which he does not consider a function). Then he lists and describes his thirty-one functions. An abbreviated list of his functions follows. (Note: The initial situation is not considered by Propp to be a function.)

Propp's Basic Functions

Initial Situation	α	Members of family or hero are introduced
Absentation	β	Member(s) of family absents self
Interdiction	Υ	An interdiction is given to hero or heroine
Violation	δ	Interdiction violated
Delivery	ζ	Villain gets information about victim
Trickery	η	Villain attempts to deceive victim
Complicity	θ	Victim is deceived, helps villain
Villainy	A	Villain causes harm to member of a family
Lack	a	Member of a family lacks something
Mediation	B	Misfortune is made known, hero is dispatched
Departure	↑	Hero leaves home
Receipt	F	Hero tested by donor, gets magical agent
Transference	G	Hero led to object of search
Struggle	H	Hero and villain join in combat
Branding	J	Hero is branded
Victory	I	Villain is defeated
Return	↓	The hero returns
Pursuit	Pr	The hero is pursued by villain
Difficult task	M	A difficult task is proposed to the hero
Solution	N	The task is accomplished
Recognition	R	The hero is recognized
Exposure	Ex	A false hero or villain is exposed
Transfiguration	T	The hero is given a new appearance
Punishment	V	The villain is punished
Wedding	W	The hero is married, ascends the throne

Propp explained that there are two kinds of heroes: "victim heroes," who suffer from the actions of a villain, and "seeker heroes," who agree to go out in the world and liquidate some "lack" or do some task demanded of them. The heroes always defeat the villains but the kinds of plots they are involved with differ. Thus, we see different functions for different kinds of heroes, though often their tasks merge and seeker heroes have to defeat villains (dragons, etc.) to accomplish their task. Heroes generally need helpers and find donor figures who give them magical agents.

One of the traditional acts of the hero is to help "damsels in distress" or rescue them from villains (or both). In modern stories, it is possible to have an assertive and strong heroine, but generally speaking, the heroes are strong and active and the heroines are weak and passive. A figure such as Princess Leia is a case in point, perhaps an exception to the rule. In *Star Wars* she grabs a machine gun, zaps storm troopers and shows herself to be a strong person. (This stereotyping of women as weak and needing heroes to help them is changing, as women become directors and make the kinds of films they want to make, but such films still tend to be the exception, not the rule.)

A Proppian Analysis of *Star Wars*

The righteous warrior, then, according to Propp, has courage, imagination, inventiveness and, in addition, he generally has helpers (who often possess great powers) and has the use of a magic agent, which is supplied by a donor figure. (Think here of Obi One Kenobi as a donor figure giving Luke his father's light saber, which connects him to "the force" and confirms Luke as a Jedi warrior.) With his magic agent and his other qualities, the hero generally is able to defeat the villain, who often has greater power and superior numbers. This is what happens, of course, in *Star Wars*.

One thing we learn from Propp is that a hero generally cannot function on his own; he needs others, and though he fights for freedom or to accomplish some task to win the hand of the woman he loves, he is part of something bigger than himself. This is certainly the case in the *Star Wars* epic. Heroes are tied to their communities; villains, on the other hand, tend to be alienated and unloved, even though they may have sexual partners. These villains direct their repressed sexuality into a "lust" for power and domination. Villains often have women who work for them, and may even be their sexual partners, but generally they fear the villain more than they love him, or are attracted by his wealth and power. Villains generally are not young but are middle aged or older.

Heroes, on the other hand, tend to be young (or youngish) and are often motivated by romantic love—for the heroine. Obviously, a conflict between a young hero and an older villain over a woman has an Oedipal dimension to it that cannot be ignored. When the young hero defeats the older villain, the hero can then "marry" the heroine (or, in modern day stories, have sex with her) and "live happily after" until the next villain appears on the scene.

Let us look at *Star Wars* as a fairy tale. I will show in a highly schematized way that many of the functions discussed by Propp are found in modern stories because, as I pointed our earlier, Propp dealt with the basic components of stories of all kinds, not just Russian fairy tales. *Star Wars* and others in the Lucas epic are full of fairy tale elements, and it is well-known that Lucas was very interested in myths and legends and related concerns when he was writing the script for the films and making them.

What follows is a list of Propp's functions applied to *Star Wars*. This list could be easily extended and amplified, but I just want to show how easy it is to apply Propp to *Star Wars*.

Proppian Functions in *Star Wars*

Family introduced	We meet Luke Skywalker
Absentation	Luke goes looking for his droid
Interdiction	Luke warned about staying out in wilds
Violation	Luke stays out long time, involved with sandpeople
Delivery	Hans Solo's space ship is bugged
Departure	Luke goes off to mission to save Leia
Villainy	Vader's agents kill Luke's uncle and aunt
Receipt	Luke tested by Obi, gets Light Saber
Transference	Luke flies all over looking for Leia
Struggle	Luke and friends fight storm troopers on Death Star
Pursuit	Luke and friends pursued by ships from Death Star
Difficult task	Luke must drop bomb in little opening on Death Star
Solution	Death Star explodes
Recognition	Leia gives Luke, Hans medals

These functions, and others that could have been added, show the amount of fairy tale material found in *Star Wars*. That is because, I would suggest, the fairy tale is the prototypical tale, the UR (original) tale, from which other kinds of stories draw sustenance. Propp also discussed "moves" which might best be characterized as sequences of activities that can be repeated in different forms. Each battle scene in *Star Wars* can be seen as a Proppian "move," which means that plots don't necessarily have a straight, linear form but can repeat certain actions or events, in varied ways, over and over again.

On the Popularity of *Star Wars*

One reason that *Star Wars* was so incredibly successful (it had something like $500 million dollars in box office receipts in America) is that it is a modernized fairy tale. Thus, it speaks to the psyches of young people and adolescents, who can identify with its young hero, the way fairy tales speak to the psyches of children who are read these tales.

Like the typical heroes of fairy tales, Luke Skywalker has helpers and Lucas has created a remarkable and brilliant collection of weird characters, similar to the fantastic creatures found in many fairy tales, to help Luke and to battle Darth Vader and his minions.

This young man must battle to rescue a princess from a villainous older man—Darth Vader. We learn, in a later film, that Darth Vader is Luke's father, so the Oedipal aspects of fairy tales (Jack the Giant Killer and so on) is an important subtext of this film. Young males can identify with Luke Skywalker and young women with Princess Leia, deriving great comfort from their struggles and ultimate triumph over the forces of adversity.

In an essay in *Psychoanalytic Review* (74, 3, Fall 1987), entitled "*Star Wars* as Myth: A Fourth Hope?" Lucia Villela-Minnerly and Richard Markin explain that their analysis of the film

> is based on the assumption that movies are modern myths and that myths, fairy tales, and narratives in general are metaphorical attempts to understand and explain the perceived realities of our own selves, our origins, our future, our world. We believe it is often through these creative metaphors that we reach for that which is as yet imperfectly understood and attempt to expand our knowledge of the conscious and unconscious wishes, fears, and conflicts that underlie human dreams and human actions.

This statement is very similar to those made by Bruno Bettelheim in his book *The Uses of Enchantment*. In this book, as I mentioned earlier, he analyzes a number of fairy tales and shows how they speak to the needs of children and help them gain psychological strength and courage, to face the future.

Star Wars was popular, then, because it did such a brilliant job of telling a story that had great meaning to the people who saw it, even though they might not have been able to articulate what, in particular, it was doing for them. People said they liked it because of the action, because of the wonderful effects, because of the remarkably inventive characters Lucas created, and because of the superb acting in the film.

But more than most films, *Star Wars,* like myths and fairy tales, spoke, in subtle and appealing ways, to those realms of our psyches that we do not generally recognize and cannot access directly, giving us comfort and courage, to deal with the problems we all must face. *Star Wars* was, whatever else it might have been, a form of collective therapy—and that explains, I would suggest, why so many young men and women saw it over and over again.

Star Wars was the fourth film in an epic that Lucas said will need nine films to complete. He is working on the first three films and in the not-too-distant future, the pre-quels to *Star Wars* and then, later, the sequels will be appearing. We can only hope that he can create films that have the same psychological and cultural resonance as *Star Wars.* To a considerable degree, strange as it may sound, his success in creating these futuristic works hinges on the extent to which he continues telling modernized fairy tales. He needs to maintain *his* connection to "the force," too.

VII
Everyday Life: Introduction

Everyday life is a subject that has been of increasing interest to social scientists. I use, for example, ideas from Henri Lefebvre's study of everyday life, *Everyday Life in the Modern World,* in my discussion of television and terror. Much of what I've written about in my analyses of other aspects of popular culture really involves everyday life. A good deal of our everyday life—our leisure—is devoted to the mass media and popular culture, or influenced by it, so I often find it difficult to separate or distinguish everyday life from popular culture.

If we define everyday life as the routines we go through, the rituals we practice, the performances we put on in the course of our daily activities, and separate these phenomena from our media-culture we can give everyday life a modicum of autonomy as a concept.

I start my discussion of everyday life the way most people start the day—with food and, in particular, breakfast. I point out that America is a multicultural society and that there are many different "ethnic" breakfasts people eat in America. Nevertheless, there is a "classic" American breakfast that we find on the menus of many coffee shops and restaurants. This breakfast consists of orange juice, cold cereal with milk, coffee, toast, bacon, eggs, hash brown potatoes, and perhaps preserves.

I offer a deconstruction of this breakfast in an attempt to see what this breakfast "means" psychologically and culturally. I also deal with an interesting phenomenon: although cook books are full of hundreds or even thousands of recipes, many families use only a very limited number of them, as people eat the same thing (with minor variations here and there) over and over again.

In chapter 15, I offer a micro-primer on semiotic theory and use semiotics to deal with the difference between public and private space. I also offer a number of questions to consider in analyzing spaces of all kinds: what is the quality of the light in the space, what is the shape of the space, how big is the space, and so on.

From space I move on to my last subject, our material culture and technological warfare among everyday products. I start by enumerating how many different electronic devices and gadgets the average person has in his house or apartment. I came up with thirty electric or electronic devices in my house in a matter of minutes. Then I deal with the "warfare" that I suggest is going on between old and new technologies.

I discuss the battles for markets taking place between manufacturers of objects such as rubber sandals (Teva) and leather sandals (Birkenstocks), print encyclopedias and CD ROM encyclopedias, and thin-wheeled bikes and Mountain Bikes. There are incredible changes taking place in everything from the kinds of pots and pans we cook with to the fabrics we wear and the devices we use to listen to and record music.

The world divides, I suggest, into two camps: traditionalists and futurists, those who like the "good old" products and those who opt for the "new technologies." Traditionalists tend to use fountain pens, zippers, gas or electric stoves, phones with cords and vinyl LP records. Futurists opt for ball point or roller ball pens, velcro, microwaves, cordless phones, and CDs. The pace of change is so fast that we become blind to it, and products that were revolutionary five years ago are now old hat. Ironically, research indicates that despite all of our technological advances, we have less leisure time now than we did in earlier periods. This raises an interesting question: what good are all our wonderful new products? Are they improving our lives or are they doing something else, injecting an element of sterility in our lives? That is the question with which I end my analysis of everyday life.

14

Everyday Eating in America: Decoding Breakfasts and Making Sense of Other Dietary Practices

In a sense it is impossible to talk about "everyday eating" in America because the country is so diverse in so many respects. As a result of patterns of immigration, there are many different ethnic groups in America, many of whom have their own distinctive cuisines. (I have a friend who lives in a section of Los Angeles that he has suggested is really part of the "third world," and in the apartment complex where he lives there must be, conservatively speaking, a dozen different ethnic groups and nationalities.)

Then there is the matter of region. Some geographers suggest that there is not one America but eight different Americas ranging from the midwestern "breadbasket area" (where we might find the quintessential American cuisine, I might add) to a "Tex-Mex" area, bordering Mexico in Texas and California and other southwestern states, where there is an obvious Mexican influence on food preferences. The area north of San Francisco, along the coast, is an "Arcadian" utopian part of the country, where health foods and natural foods are *au courant*. In the other Americas, other kinds of food are popular.

We might also consider the matter of socioeconomic class, which plays a major role in determining food preferences and eating practices. Until fairly recently, it would have been possible to suggest that working class people tended to eat more fatty proteins and drink more beer than middle class people but there is reason to believe that the health revolution is beginning to impact on the working classes and I understand that construction workers have been known to ask for avocado and sprout sandwiches instead of the old fat-rich corned beef sandwiches that they used to eat in the good (that is fatty) old days.

In a certain sense, middle-class and upper-middle-class taste is becoming dominant and occupying the great middle ground between the food consumed by the very rich and that consumed by the desperately poor. Sociologists have shown that there is a connection between social class and obesity, with middle and upper class people tending to be slimmer than working class people. Obviously this has something to do with the diet of people in their respective classes. As evidence for this assertion let me quote from an article, "If She's Rich, She's Thinner," from the 11 April 1984 *San Francisco Chronicle*, written by Dr. Lawrence Power:

> For every $1000 above average the husband's income, the thinner his wife. This information comes from a survey of 5000 couples. Income was tabulated from employment records and fat was measured by skin fold thickness. For every $1000 above average the income, there was one millimeter less than average fat on the arms of the wife.... The richer, the thinner; so what else is new?.... Poor people were being interviewed about hunger and hard times and they were consistently fat.

There are several other variables to keep in mind. Thus age plays an important role in determining the way people eat. Adolescents, for example, tend to be notoriously obsessed about their bodies and skin complexion, but also tend to be addicted (in varying degrees) to fast foods, which contain a considerable amount of fat and other undesirable ingredients. A typical meal at a fast food restaurant of a hamburger, shake and french fries, is not the most ideally balanced meal imaginable. As these adolescents become educated or stop their education and join the working class, their food preferences change to a certain degree.

The point of all of the above is to suggest that any generalizations about "typical" American food are risky—in part because we don't know a great deal about what typical Americans are like and how they think about food or very much else (except when we ask in opinion polls, from which we often get conflicting results.)

Statistics can give us a certain amount of information, but we never can be sure how this or that individual will behave, even if we have all kinds of demographic information about him or her. Nevertheless, it is possible to make some generalizations about "typical" American eating practices and throwing caution to the winds (which some people claim is my typical way of operating), I will proceed now to do so.

Everyday versus Gourmet

There is a distinction which we must keep in mind, here, and that involves the difference between "gourmet" dishes and "everyday" eating practices, which is the subject of this discourse. Gourmet dining can be thought of as that which is *not* everyday eating; gourmet food more or less is "defined" by being the opposite of everyday food. One "dines" on gourmet food; one "eats" everyday food.

Let me explore the differences in the chart which follows and which pushes things to extremes that I recognize don't always exist:

EVERYDAY	GOURMET
Easy to prepare	Hard to prepare
Inexpensive	Expensive
Part of routine	Special occasion
American	Foreign (often)
Soda pop	Wine
Early evening	Late evening
Mechanical	Artistic

Gourmet cooking only has meaning because it is the opposite, more or less, of ordinary, plain, everyday cooking. Gourmet cooking, typically, is based on a sense of occasion, uses expensive and unusual foods, often has rich, complex sauces, and is concerned with style and aesthetics.

It is conceivable that one might be a gourmet cook (or be married to one) who spends a great deal of time cooking, in which case eating everyday cooking would turn into an "occasion," but it is doubtful that many people are able to (or want to) eat gourmet food all the time—especially if they are to remain thin, which, we now see is generally felt to be an obligation for middle and upper class people.

Ethnic Food

Ethnic food is a problematical element here. Generally speaking, we do not classify most ethnic cooking as gourmet; that seems to be reserved for French and possibly Italian food (and perhaps a few other cuisines) but ethnic food does play a role in defining everyday American food.

I would suggest that ethnic food is usually seen as a different kind of everyday food and not, generally speaking, as gourmet food. Thus, for the price of one dish at an expensive French restaurant, one can have a whole meal in a typical Chinese restaurant. A number of years ago, an editor was kind enough to take me to dinner at a medium priced French restaurant where we had a prix-fixe dinner for $30 each. For $30, five or six people could eat at a good Chinese restaurant. (Japanese food may be a different matter, and may be seen as gourmet food, since it tends to be more expensive than Chinese food and has a distinctive aesthetic about it.)

The Classic American Breakfast

If one traverses America and looks at what is offered for breakfast one sees that there is what might be called a "classic American" breakfast. It would include the following: orange juice, cereal and milk, bacon, eggs, hash fried potatoes, coffee, toast and jam, marmalade, and ketchup (for the potatoes). There are other alternative breakfasts (pancakes, waffles, etc.) but the bacon- (or ham) and-eggs breakfast is the standard or classic breakfast in America.

As a result of our interest in nutrition nowadays, and our concern about fat in the bacon and cholesterol in the eggs, many people would not eat this particular breakfast, but in the good old days, before the nutritionists came on the scene and made us conscious of the relationship between our diet and our health, we would have enjoyed this meal. Many people still do.

This breakfast is an idealized conception in our minds of what a breakfast should be like and our breakfasts approximate it to varying degrees in everyday life. The classic breakfast is, quite obviously, a hearty and very calorific meal—meant, it would seem, for people who exerted a great deal of physical effort in their jobs.

The classic American breakfast is really not suitable for anyone, but it certainly isn't suitable for people in modern America who live in an information society, in which more than 50 percent of the population spends its time with conferences, paperwork, telephone calls, and so on. This kind of a society demands a different breakfast for the average person and has got it with yogurt and other so-called "health" foods.

But our examination of breakfasts reveals something interesting and useful: many of our classic meals seem to be anachronistic—connected, perhaps, to the eighteenth and nineteenth century, when people had different kinds of jobs and lifestyles. I will analyze this breakfast structurally and show that this classic breakfast also reveals something rather interesting. This analysis follows.

Breaking the Breakfast Code: Deciphering the Meaning of the Classical American Morning Meal

Breakfast is the most mundane meal in the American cuisine, and in most cuisines. It means, literally, to break one's "fast," which presumably started the day before, after dinner. Midnight snackers and grazers (who eat a number of small meals during the day) have not fasted very long by breakfast, but that is beside the point; for most people, the time from the evening meal of the night before to breakfast is quite long—often eleven or twelve hours.

Now some people have fancy breakfasts. Sundays people may have champagne breakfasts. Others, on weekdays, merge their breakfasts and lunches into brunches. Many people hardly have anything; donuts and coffee or, for those in a hurry, some kind of an instant breakfast drink of bar. But there is, I would suggest, a classical American breakfast, which is relatively ubiquitous in America, and which a typical person wanting a "big" breakfast would have. (One sees this breakfast on the menus of countless restaurants.)

In order to "decipher" a meal we must find the way the fundamental elements in the meal are related; that is, we do not concern ourselves with what is eaten but rather with hidden (but meaningful) relationships among the various items. In other words, what we are looking for is the structure of the meal, which, I suggest, reveals some surprises.

In this kind of investigation we do not look at the classic American breakfast as a meal but rather as a *system*—a collection of units or elements that are structured in some way that ties them together but which frequently is not evident. Another way of putting this is that there is what might be thought of as a breakfast code, and our "mission" is to crack this code. I am assuming, of course, that there is a code; you can decide for yourself whether this is so when you have finished this mini-course in structural analysis.

Once I had convinced myself that there was some kind of a hidden structure in the American breakfast, I started looking for the key that might unlock it. I worked on this problem by first drawing pictures of each of the items involved. Then I listed each item: orange juice, coffee, cream, sugar, Corn Flakes, milk, sugar, and the like. For my first attempt at finding a set of interesting relationships I took the matter of whether each item was eaten *hot* or *cold*. Of the thirteen items in the classical American breakfast, eight are eaten cold and five are eaten hot. I could find nothing useful with this mode of analysis, so I moved on to *color*. All the colors are earthy, warm colors: orange, brownish black, light brown, yellow, and white. Color was another dead end in this particular case.

Perhaps, I thought, *shape* might reveal something? Most of the items had no shape, but, instead, occupied the shape given by their containers: juice, coffee, cream, milk, sugar. So what? Nothing, I thought, and moved on to *taste*. But I found it hard describing different tastes meaningfully.

How does one describe a number of different tasting items according to some principle of organization? Sour and sweet? Bitter and mild? Bland and tasty? I found I could not come up with anything that even looked promising, so I abandoned taste (the way many of our manufacturers of foods have) and moved on to *substance*. What are we talking about, I asked myself? Fruits, cereals, dairy products, meats, sugar.

Sugar? What is sugar? I asked myself. The dictionary gave me my answer. Sugar is a sweet, crystalline substance obtained mostly from the juice of sugar cane or sugar beets. Sugar is liquid that becomes a solid. That made me consider a category I had not thought of earlier, namely, that of solids and liquids. When I ran the items on the menu through the solids or liquids category, nothing remarkable emerged. Juice, coffee, cream, and milk are liquids; and toast, cereal, cooked eggs, bacon, and potatoes are solids. I couldn't find anything promising there, but there was something about this category that intrigued me.

Then it came to me. The fundamental matter is not whether something is a solid or a liquid but whether something becomes *transformed* from solid to liquid or vice versa. It was only when I took the notion of transformations between solids and liquids that I found anything interesting.

Let's start down the list. Orange juice is a solid that becomes a liquid. Coffee is a drink made from a solid, coffee beans. (I will argue, admittedly stretching things, that milk and cream are solids that become liquids, since a cow has been defined as a "machine that turns grass into milk and cream.") Sugar is a solid that becomes a liquid and then a solid again. Corn flakes is a solid that becomes a liquid and then made into a solid again. Butter is a liquid that becomes a solid. Eggs are liquid and become solid. The other items—bread, bacon, and potatoes—are solids that remain solids, while milk and cream are solids that become liquids.

Thus we find ourselves with four possibilities: some items are solids and become liquids and then become solids; some are solids and become liquids; some items are liquids and become solids, and some items maintain their identities.

Transformations in the Classic American Breakfast

Solid to liquid to Solid	Solid to Liquid	Liquid to Solid	Maintain
sugar	orange juice	butter	bacon
preserves	coffee	eggs	potatoes
corn flakes	milk/cream		

It doesn't make much difference, actually, whether you consider milk and cream as solids that change to liquids or items that maintain their original identities. What we must recognize, then, is that a breakfast is a study in transformations, and has a kind of magical quality about it. Is it not logical to assume that the people who eat this "classic" American breakfast believe that they can "transform" themselves? That they can change their identities in a manner vaguely analogous to some of the things they eat?

I am assuming, in this analysis, that food is a kind of code. This idea is not original with me—many people have worked in this field. As the distinguished British anthropologist Mary Douglas put it, in "Deciphering a Meal," if food is treated as a code, *"the messages it encodes will be found in the pattern of social relations being expressed. The message is about different degrees of hierarchy, inclusion and exclusion, boundaries and transactions across the boundaries"* (1975, 249, my italics).

In a society that conceives of itself as "classless," it must be possible for people to escape their original class identities and merge into other class identities, in particular the middle class. The problem that this merging causes is that one loses one's original identity; and there is a psychic cost to be paid, just as foods one eats for breakfast in America have lost their original identities. *The message of the classic American breakfast is disguise and endless transformation.* Is it any wonder, then, that the process of alchemy has been carried further with the creation of instant breakfasts that one eats or chews, the moral equivalent of the alchemist's dream of turning lead into gold? Space bars and instant breakfasts are the perfect foods for men without qualities who can be anyone, who believe that like the foods we eat, we too can transform ourselves into anyone or anything we wish.

Routine and Rite in Everyday Eating

Although cookbooks are full of thousands of recipes (and are one of the most popular kinds of books to publish), I would imagine that the average American housewife, who does most of the cooking in America, has a relatively limited repertoire of dishes she makes and that she repeats the cycle over and over again. There are reasons for this.

First, a large number of married women work and they do not have the time to labor over new and fancy dishes. Second, young children often are very conservative about what they like (hot dogs, hamburgers, etc.) and it is often easier to accommodate their tastes than argue with them. Third, many of the everyday meals people cook are dishes they grew up with and there is an element of historicity involved. There is also the matter of cost. A pound of hamburger costs less than a pound of veal, is easier to cook.

All of these reasons would lead us to understand why there would probably be a relatively limited repertoire of dishes made in the average family. Quite likely some kind of routine is established—chicken one day, hamburger another—from which there is relatively little variance. (An Englishman I met once told me his wife had something like eight different dishes she cooked, and she just went through the cycle week after week, with little change. I would suspect that such is the case with many people. It is easier to establish a routine like that than worry, from day to day, what to cook.)

Thus, ironically, we live in a world in which there are thousands and thousands of different foods to eat and ways of cooking them, but from this universe of possibility, we choose a very limited number of items and make do with them. This is no different from the way we behave in many other areas of our lives; from a vast array of possibilities we choose a fairly limited number of what might be called "actualizations," and live by habit and routine. While we may seek adventure and excitement in food (and other areas of life) we also seem to crave security and certainty. As I mentioned, many of the dishes we eat are tied to our childhoods. As I understand it, from the writings of anthropologists, food preferences once established, remain powerful throughout our lives.

It may be that the dishes we eat facilitate a regression (in the service of our egos, naturally and nutritionally) that provide emotional nourishment as well as the physical kind. In this respect, then, as in many others, the child's stomach is the "father" of the man's. Countering this is the matter of food trends, based on the discoveries of scientists and faddishness. One is often caught, then, between the comforts of the old "regressive" meals and the satisfactions of new "healthy" or trendy ones. Quite likely most of us alternate between the two polarities as we try to figure out how to reconcile our love of some fatty dish we crave (from our childhood) with our sense that we really should eat more bean curd and broccoli.

History haunts us in other ways. Octavio Paz has argued, in an essay called "Gastrosophy," that the Puritans have had a major impact in our cuisine, which is based upon purity and exclusions. We do not, as a rule, have sauces in everyday American cuisine; we add them (ketchup, etc.). Our collective passion for milk (which can be connected to a pre-genital innocent stage) also suggests that there are powerful psychological forces at work in our cuisine—forces that most of us do not recognize.

Obviously cultural history impacts upon personal history in shaping the American everyday cuisine. With the rise of ethnic pride, the typical or everyday American cuisine seems to be losing status as various ethnic groups now find it "in" to enjoy dishes that were once looked down upon as being non (or is it "un") American. WASP (White Anglo-Saxon Protestant) food now is "revealed" as bland and tasteless and ungratifying. When former president Richard Nixon mentioned that one of his favorite dishes was cottage cheese with ketchup, that was a revelation, I would say, more interesting than most of what came out of Watergate.

Holiday and Festival Fare

In America when we celebrate our holidays, religious and patriotic, we often have "traditional" meals that we eat. Let us take Thanksgiving as a case in point. It is a political holiday, which turns out to be the day before the largest shopping days in America, when people rush out and start their Christmas shopping.

The meal we eat is traditional—supposedly the meal that the Pilgrims ate many hundreds of years ago—turkey with various trimmings. A typical Thanksgiving dinner would include: a large, roast turkey (or perhaps a ham), stuffing, sweet potatoes, salad, cranberry sauce, corn bread, and pumpkin pie. (In different regions of the country this varies somewhat, but the turkey is generally the centerpiece of the traditional Thanksgiving dinner.)

In eating this meal we establish our identity with the Pilgrims; the dinner is an existential act that leads to a sense of solidarity and well-being. We return to the days of our founding fathers (actually this pre-dates them) by eating the same meal they allegedly ate.

What is interesting about our holiday meals is that they are not gourmet meals (except in certain ritzy groups, which eat at very expensive restaurants) but are, instead, elaborated ordinary meals. The main course is a large bird that conveys a sense of well-being to all, who can eat from it to the heart's content. But it is cooked the same way the conventional chicken is cooked. The meal is more complete, with more side courses and perhaps more desserts. But it is not different in nature from an ordinary dinner.

We would expect that a meal that is meant to reaffirm our political and national identity would be common and not gourmet (which is not associated with American cooking). The meal is meant to be hearty—socially, politically, and digestively. Once stuffed and satisfied with reaffirming one's identity as an American, it is easy to go out the next day on a shopping spree. That too, we now discover, is American.

American holiday cooking, then, is not much different from ordinary cooking, except in terms of the completeness or elaboration of the meal. Because of the size of the turkey, however, and the political, historical, or religious connections and connotations, the meal assumes a difference from ordinary ones.

Conclusions

We are, conventional wisdom tells us, what we eat. But what we eat is determined, generally speaking, by what we are. Change is introduced into this tight little system by various matters—who one marries, one's education, fads and trends in eating, new discoveries, rising up the social ladder, and so on. The average supermarket now carries some 20,000 products, though many of them are now non-food items, which are much more profitable.

Supermarkets are currently engaged in a battle with fast-food stores to determine who will get the higher percentage of available income that is to be devoted to food. Time is the crucial dimension, now, since such a large percentage of women work, and those who work more likely than not also find themselves burdened with cooking. Thus there is a big push into frozen dishes that can be cooked, almost instantly, in microwave ovens. Fast food has triumphed; the question now seems to be whether it will be us or someone else, who cooks our fast food.

Ironically, the development of frozen foods and microwaveable foods may lead to an expansion of the range of our eating. If you don't have to bother with preparing some interesting dish, and money is not an important consideration (which often seems to be the case now), it is just as easy to try something a bit exotic as it is to try Salisbury steak. Whether we will do so, or whether we are prisoners of our early food preferences, is something that remains to be seen.

15

Space as a Sign System: A Semiotic Approach to Private and Public Space

Although few of us think very much about public and private space, we all recognize that the two realms exist. Our homes (apartments or houses) are, we would say, our "castles" and are private. On the other hand, certain areas in our cities and towns we would generally describe as public.

The notion that there is public and private space calls to mind one of the most fundamental principles of semiotics, as enunciated by Ferdinand de Saussure. "Concepts are purely differential," he writes, "and defined not by their positive content but negatively by their relations with the other terms of the system" (1966: 117). Or, to put in slightly different terms, the basic attributes of concepts is "in being what the others are not" (1966, 117).

The most important relationship involving concepts is that of opposition, and that may have something to do with the fact that binary oppositions are the fundamental way the mind functions when it deals with concepts. Public space has no meaning without private space, and vice versa, because concepts, being "purely differential" need oppositions.

Saussure provides us with something else that is useful for interpreting or "reading" space—his analysis of the sign. He divides signs, which can be understood as anything that can be used to represent or stand for something else, into signifiers and signifieds. He distinguishes between a *signifier* (which he defines as a sound-image) and a *signified* (which he defines as a concept generated by the signifier). The relationship between the signifier and signified is arbitrary, a matter of convention. It is not natural or in the nature of things. This means we have to learn what signifiers mean. It also suggests that what a signifier means can change over time.

If we think of spaces as being signs, or, more precisely, as "systems of signs," to be read and interpreted, Saussure's insights show their value. We learn how to read spaces and how to distinguish, amongst other things, between public and private spaces. But more on this after we have explored semiotic theory a bit more.

The American philosopher C. S. Peirce is considered, along with Saussure, to be one of the founders of modern semiotic theory. Peirce had a different notion of the sign—one that places more emphasis than Saussure did on someone interpreting a given sign. He suggested that there are three kinds of signs, as the chart below explains.

Peirce on the Three Kinds of Signs

	ICON	INDEX	SYMBOL
Signify by:	resemblance	causality	convention
Example:	photograph	smoke/fire	words, flags
Process:	can see	can figure out	must learn

This chart (adapted from my *Media Analysis Techniques*) shows how people interpret signs. A space might be "iconic" in that it resembles (in its contours) something we are familiar with—a heart, a head, or anything else. Spaces can be read "indexically," also. We can infer certain things about the societies and cultures that are "behind" spaces.

There are three other semiotic concepts to be considered:

Metaphor	Relationship based on Analogy: My love is a red rose
Metonymy	Relationship based on Association: Bowler = English, Rolls Royce = wealthy
Intertextuality	Seeing a text (work) in terms of some other text

These concepts, let me add, can be used to interpret visual phenomena of all kinds, that is, images. We all, it should be added, "read" space semiotically even though we may not be aware of semiotics. Like Moliere's character who didn't realize he spoke prose, we are all semioticians, often in spite of ourselves.

Thus, we interpret some spaces, rugged terrains, metaphorically—as being like moonscapes. We might interpret certain spaces metonymically, and consider Tiananmen Square as standing for or somehow representing the country, and more specifically, the political system in which it is found—China. We do the same in America, when we equate the Pentagon with American military power. We often interpret some spaces intertextually, comparing them with other spaces that we are familiar with. A certain wilderness landscape we come upon may be like one we recall in Kenya. When we do any of these things, we are reading space semiotically.

We use semiotics to read space because we believe that every space is a sign system which reflects, in various ways, a given society's beliefs, values, attitudes and aesthetics. One way to find out about people is to study the way they create and use public and private spaces. Leaving a space untouched is also a sign which can be tied to values and beliefs. That is because, in semiotics, not doing something (no sign) is also a sign. Think, for example, of the famous case of the dog that didn't bark in one of Sherlock Holmes's cases.

On Public and Private Spaces and Other Oppositions

The notion that space can be "private" or "public," is, then, a semiotic one and is tied to the very way we think and use language. There are other oppositions involving space that might also be considered, which relate in varying ways to our central concepts.

Binary Oppositions Relating to Space

PRIVATE	PUBLIC
Profane	Sacred
Personal in Scope	Gigantic in Scope
Individual Rituals	Public Ceremonials
Full	Empty
Closed	Open
Defensible	Attackable
Pedestrian	Vehicular
Inside	Outside
Planned	Accidental
Artificial	Natural
Mainstream	Alternative
Unifunction	Multifunction
Open	Closed

These are some of the more important categories we use when we analyze space. These oppositions help us "frame" space and understand it in a very general way. We get a sense, perhaps, of its purposes and how it came to be the way it is. Space, from this perspective, is not a matter of absence, not a gap between elements in a landscape, not a void. Space exists, as an entity, and can be analyzed and interpreted. Or, to use another term for this kind of activity, *read*.

One way we analyze space is in terms of what might be described, broadly, as aesthetic or perceptual categories:

1. the quality of light in the space.
2. the coloration of the space.
3. the shape of the space (contours).
4. the relation of the space to height and depth (topography).
5. the size of the space.
6. the volume of the space.
7. the textures in the space.
8. the "air" in the space (windy, calm).
9. the relation of the space to a horizon line.

Consider, for example, the quality of light in cathedrals and the way this light contributes (a learned response) to our sense of the sacred. We have learned that cathedrals are sacred and so the light streaming in from windows is seen as being "holy" or something like that.

In the same respect (I almost said light) think about the color of the sky in the desert. Or the sense of insignificance one often feels in the dark, windy, skyscraper-created caverns in Manhattan or Tokyo or in the towering mountains of Tibet. Think also of the difference seeing a horizon line makes, and where the horizon line is, when we can see it. Or the difference between being on a mountain and looking down on a plain and being on a plain and looking up at a mountain.

The size of the spaces we occupy also must be considered, in relation to our notions of privacy. What is the most private space for most people? Probably our bathrooms, where we defecate. (This may be a Eurocentric notion, tied to feelings of shame over bodily functions, which people in other cultures do not share.) What is the most public space we know of? Perhaps Tiananmen Square, in China, the largest man-made or ceremonial space in any city. It is in this space that the Communist Chinese government has held spectacular political rallies, with as many as a million people participating. It is in this square, with the whole world watching on television, that the Chinese Communists crushed a student gathering, an act whose consequences have been inestimable.

Questions to Consider on the Meaning of Space

Our notion of public and private space relates, of course, to people—the way they live, and the way they act and react in a given space. Let me offer some questions and hypotheses that stem from reading space indexically and trying to interpret what it suggests about individuals and societies.

Is There a Relation between Private Space and Democracy?

If we have our "own" living quarters, but are continually monitored by cameras and microphones, are we not in some kind of totalitarian system where there is no really private space? Consider, if you will, how many science fiction dystopias show societies in which there is no privacy, no way of escaping from surveillance. This device was used in the famous series *The Prisoner*. But he used his awareness of his continually being monitored to his advantage at times. Conversely, the notion of public space implies some kind of society that has created this space; you cannot have public space without a public.

When Large Numbers of People Regularly Occupy Public Space, is That a Sign That They Have Inadequate Private Space?

In Hong Kong, for example, the streets are crowded at night. Is this, in part, due to the crowded living conditions in which they live or is it something else in the culture? Is it because people don't have time to shop earlier? Is it because they like being with others?

When Private Space is Adequate for People, Does Spending Time in Public Spaces Become Less Important for Them?

Consider small towns and small villages where living space is plentiful. How do people relate to public spaces? Do they use them only occasionally, for purely utilitarian or socializing purposes? Or do they come to town to assuage feelings of loneliness and separation?

What Do Gigantic Man-Made Public Spaces
Imply about the Society That Creates Them?

Think of the enormous public spaces that have been created—in the Vatican, in Beijing, in Moscow, in various Third World countries. These spaces imply a number of things: a desire to be able to mobilize large numbers of people for religious and political purposes, and perhaps a sense of grandeur (megalomania, in some cases). If one can mobilize huge crowds, does that suggest, in many cases, authoritarian control of a country?

What about the opposite—wilderness areas? The notion of wilderness implies its opposite, civilized areas. Is the passion people have for the wilderness tied to a need they have, from time to time, to escape from civilization, to a sense of the wilderness as "sacred" and to fears people have about phenomena such as the Greenhouse effect? (In this respect, consider the outrage many people feel, all over the world, about the destruction of the rain forests in Brazil and other countries.)

Does Modernization Lead to Increasing Specialization
in the Creation and Use of Space?

In this respect, think, for example, of shopping malls. In these malls what used to be a linear "Main Street" full of little stores in small towns is changed into a circle or rectangle and often placed inside a huge building to allow for air conditioning. Malls are connected to the development of suburbs and the need for parking spaces for automobiles. But these malls often have a coldness and sterility about them (people often use the term "plastic") that you don't find in urban shopping areas, where a variety of different architectural styles exist. What does the development of malls in Third World countries suggest? And what does the development of warehouse stores in the United States and other countries mean?

Can One Connect Public and Private Spaces to
Elements of the Human Psyche?

Freud has suggested that the psyche can be divided into three components: the id (impulse and desire), the ego (reality testing, balancing id and super-ego) and the super-ego (conscience). Does it make any sense to read spaces in terms of these notions?

Spaces and the Human Psyche

ID SPACES	EGO SPACES	SUPER-EGO SPACES
Private	Social	Public
Self dominates	Reason	Group dominates
Bedroom	Classroom	Cathedral

Is there a kind of space that is neither private nor public (social?) where "ego" functions prevail? Is it possible, also, that one of the reasons Americans feel so upset (in varying ways) about the homeless, is that the homeless violate their conventions about public and private space? They live, they take drugs, they defecate and fornicate "in public," so to speak. Is homelessness a concept that is only applicable where there is a tradition of "private" homes for nuclear families?

Is the Distinction between Public Space and
Private Space Held by All People?

The argument now comes full circle. Is it possible that there are cultures which, somehow, do not distinguish between the public and private existence and hence public and private space?

Is it possible that when we differentiate between public and private space we are victims of our languages and a Eurocentric value system? Or is the difference between the public and the private natural and universal? From a semiotic perspective, we must recognize that the relationship between a word and the concept it stands for is arbitrary and based on convention. This reinforces what Durkheim argues—that we always read space in terms of socially determined categories. Attitudes toward space may be commonly held within a given society, but they vary from society to society, which shows they are not natural. As he writes in *The Elementary Forms of The Religious Life* (1967, 24):

> To dispose things spatially there must be a possibility of placing them differently, of putting some at the right, others at the left, these above, those below, at the north of or at the south of, east or west of, etc. etc.

Notice how binary oppositions inform Durkheim's thought. He then makes the point that society shapes spatial consciousness:

> Thus the social organization has been the model for the spatial organization and a reproduction of it. It is thus even up to the distinction between right and left which, far from being inherent in the nature of man in general, is very probably the product of representations which are religious and therefore collective. (1967, 25)

The way we relate to space, then, is not natural but is something that is socially conditioned.

A Final Note

This chapter deals with some of the basic principles of semiotics and with some of the questions raised by applying semiotics to public and private spaces. Semiotics is an imperialistic science that is extremely complicated; it has a long history and an enormous literature. It claims to cover all subjects in which meaning is of consequence, which means it covers everything, since the universe is "perfused with signs," as Peirce put it. Our attitudes toward space are, I would suggest, cultural—deeply imbedded in us and central to the way we live, as individuals and members of society. Reading space as a system of signs, interpreting space semiotically, is a fascinating and necessary activity that all of us do, all the time. I would hope this discussion of applied semiotics contributes to a more knowledgeable and more conscious means of doing so in the future.

16

What Teva Means: Technological
Warfare among Everyday Products

A number of my friends, who used to wear Birkenstocks sandals, have switched to Tevas (and imitations thereof). What might that mean? Let me offer a suggestion or two, in an effort to give us a glimpse of what might be described as the silent (and in some cases not so silent) "warfare" that goes on among companies that produce everyday products, as new technologies evolve and generate products that compete with previously established ones.

Electronic Devices in a Typical House

What relevance does all this have to our everyday lives? A good deal, I would argue. We have a tendency to underestimate or forget about all the stuff we have in our homes. As an example let me list the electrical and electronic devices I have in my house and point out, in passing, that I have always thought of myself as someone who "travels light," who only buys essentials.

Electronic Devices in Typical Household

1. Microwave
2. Hand blender
3. Blender
4. Food Processor
5. Refrigerator
6. Radios (9)

16. Telephone
17. Phone Answering Device
18. Computer (3)
19. Printers (2)
20. Waffle Maker
21. Hot Pot

7.	Toaster	22.	Coffee Grinder
8.	Washing Machine	23.	Saw
9.	Dishwasher	24.	Drill
10.	Stereo Receiver	25.	Portable radiators
11.	Tape Deck	26.	Surge Supressors
12.	CD Player	27.	Sander
13.	Speakers	28.	Vacuum Cleaners (3)
14.	Clocks	29.	Hair Dryers (3)
15.	TV sets (3)	30.	Calculator

We seldom think about the amount of stuff we accumulate, because we do so incrementally, over the years. We become so accustomed to our possessions, electronic and mechanical, that they become almost invisible and we end up taking them for granted.

The Problem of Choice

But every purchase involves a decision on our part, to purchase something that, we believe, will make our lives better, will save us time, save money, make things easier for us. A friend of mine whose wife is a confirmed Luddite (she refuses to have a microwave because she doesn't "need" one) drew the line when their answering machine broke down. Although she proclaimed she could easily "live without" an answering machine, she insisted that her husband buy a new one immediately; and one with more functions than the one they had before.

So most of us find ourselves having to make decisions about which products we should buy and which "models" or "brands" to get. It's at this point that we have to define ourselves as traditionalists or modernist/futurists, relatively speaking. Do we opt for old technologies or new ones?

Old Technologies and New Technologies

The chart below lists a number of "battles" being waged—for our souls and our credit cards—by manufacturers of old and new products and technologies.

Old and New Technologies

OLD TECHNOLOGY	NEW TECHNOLOGY
Leather Sandals	Rubber Sandals
Print Encyclopedias	CD ROM Encyclopedias
Canned Soup	Ramen or microwaveable soups
Gas/Electric Stoves	Microwaves
Drip/Percolator Coffee Pots	Espresso Makers
Snail Mail	Electronic Mail
Zippers	Velcro
Typewriters	Computers and Word Processors
Dot Matrix Printers	Laser and Ink Jet Printers
Fountain Pens	Ball Point Pens (and variations)
Phones with cords	Cordless and Cellular Phones
Rotary Phones	Push Button Phones
Telephone Operators	Voice Mail
Oral Thermometers	Instant Ear Thermometers
Cast Iron Pots	Calophon Aluminum Pots
Steel Wool	Fiber Scrubbers
Paint Brushes	Rollers and Sprayers
Cloth Diapers	Paper Diapers
Vinyl Records	Compact Disks
Thin Wheeled Bikes	Mountain Bikes
Station Wagons	Vans and Sports Vehicles
Penile enlargements	Virtual Sex

This list is much too long for me to cover everything, but I will discuss a number of the items on it. What the list does is provide a picture of the remarkable changes that have taken place in our everyday lives in recent years in a number of different areas. There is so much change that we tend to become blind to the extent and speed of this change, especially since some products that are introduced as luxuries rapidly become, or so we feel, "necessities" and part of our everyday lives.

Let me begin my analysis with Teva sandals. It was while having an Espresso with a friend (at a trendy restaurant called Il Fornaio in Corte Madera) and watching a number of people wearing these sandals (and remembering how many people wore them in Playa del Carmen, where

I had been on vacation a few days earlier in the Summer) that I started thinking about the whole matter of new products and new technologies.

Teva Sandals and Birkenstocks

The Teva rubber sandal, invented and manufactured in America, spawned a host of imitation sandals that now seem to be displacing Birkenstocks, with large numbers of people, as the "hot" sandal of the day. Tevas were invented by Mark Thatcher, a Colorado River boatman who wanted sandals that were tough and would also float, so they wouldn't get lost. (Do we hear echoes of Ivory soap here?) Teva now makes leather sandals, so it would not surprise me to see Birkenstock start making rubber ones, to compete with Teva.

In a sense, a Teva sandal is a glorified zori, but Tevas have a unique strap system that uses velcro (another new technology) and are much more substantial than zoris. This strapping allows the wearer much more control than the buckle-and-strap-with-holes technology found in Birkenstocks and most leather sandals. The top layer of the "All Terrain" model is made of closed cell rubber and the sole of a strong, light-weight crepe rubber.

Some Tevas have thongs, but most of the ones I've seen people wear-ing have straps, so you can wear socks with Tevas, though the genius of the "sports" sandal is that you can wear it without socks. This matter of control, the soft cushiony feel of the sole, and their identity as a kind of sports sandal (just perfect for yuppies in their "all terrain" sports ve-hicles) combine to make Tevas the sandal of choice—for the moment.

CD-ROM Encyclopedias and Reference Works

There are a number of other areas where technological changes have led to new products or ones that replace traditional ones. Consider, for example, the CD-ROM encyclopedia. It is possible now to buy a CD-ROM with an encyclopedia on it, with many color photographs, charts, and video seg-ments, for less than fifty dollars. In the San Francisco area, these encyclope-dias often sell for around twenty-five dollars, as a matter of fact.

These encyclopedias have put the printed encyclopedias into a diffi-cult situation. Of course, a printed encyclopedia can sell its own CD ROM, but it loses a great deal of money by doing this—unless it makes the money up by volume, and by updating itself every year.

The same applies to all printed reference works, such as dictionaries and medical works. CD-ROMS, which only cost a dollar or two to reproduce from a master, can do a faster job of accessing material than humans can do when thumbing through a dictionary or an encyclopedia, looking something up. And some CD-ROMS actually can have the computer read textual material to you. We probably won't be replacing doctors with medical CD-ROMS, but it wouldn't surprise me if they ended up doing a good deal of the work that doctors do now.

Canned Soups and Ramen

Ramen, quick cooking noodles with packets of flavoring, have created a new market and stolen some of the market from the canned soup industry. Now Ramen and other similar products come in styrofoam containers and "cook" in a few minutes, after you add boiling water (or can be zapped in a microwave, after some water has been added). Some of these new microwaveable soups are low in salt, also, and are popular with people who are interested in "light" or "healthy" eating.

The traditional canned soups have fought back with their own low salt products, but they still require a person to either add a can of water or heat them up in a container without any additional water. They can be microwaved, but there are extra steps involved in using canned soups and many people don't want to be bothered taking these extra steps.

Gas and Electric Stoves and Microwaves

Most people do not use microwaves for cooking meat or chicken, but microwaves are very useful for cooking fish, vegetables, and a number of other foods, and for heating left-overs up, as well. Also, microwaves are used to zap various "meals" one can purchase at a market—pizzas, TV-dinners, and the likes. The microwave oven thus complements, rather than replacing, the gas or electric stove.

But microwaves are most useful in the war that is being waged by supermarkets and grocery stores of all kinds against fast food restaurants. Even though microwaveable meals tend to be more expensive than ones cooked from scratch, they are still less expensive than going out to McDonald's or KFC (KFC being Kentucky Fried Foods mode of semantic obfuscation, trying to avoid the term "fried" which is anathema to health-conscious Americans nowadays.)

Microwaves are also used in families where there are no family dinners, where members of a family use the house as a base of operations and zap meals for themselves at odd hours. Thus they play an important role in the phenomenon I have described as "motelization."

Snail-Mail and Electronic Mail

The computer has given us—that is, made it possible to use—not only the CD-ROM, but also the Internet and, in particular, Electronic Mail or, as it is commonly called, E-Mail. With E-Mail it is possible to communicate, almost instantaneously, with people all over the world—as long as they have an address on the Internet. I correspond with people by E-Mail in Great Britain, Japan, Denmark, and various cities in the United States. All you need, as far as technology is concerned, is a computer and a modem that you can hook up to your phone line. And, of course, you have to be connected to the Internet and have an address, but this is relatively easy to do nowadays.

It is difficult to assess what impact E-Mail will have on the postal service, but I've discovered that people who ordinarily never write regular letters (perhaps they don't want to have to bother addressing an envelope and licking a stamp) often are very good E-Mail correspondents. When you get an E-Mail message, all you have to do (with the software I use) to reply is hit an "R" and type a message. You send it, instantaneously, by hitting a couple more keys. And, of course, if you correspond with people in foreign countries, you don't have to wait for a week or two for your letter to get delivered.

Drip and Percolator Coffee Pots and Espresso Makers

In recent years, Espresso coffee—and variations of it, such as cappuccinos—has become increasingly popular. It always was popular, I think, with people who have traveled in Italy, and other countries where Espresso is common, and learned how delicious Espressos can be. But now Espresso seems to be gaining popularity with the general public—especially in cities like Seattle and San Francisco.

There are many coffee houses and one even sees Espresso carts in gasoline stations and small malls. Large malls might have several coffee houses, which are multiplying rapidly. Espresso coffee is made, in essence, by forcing steam through very dark, finely ground, high quality coffee beans. What comes out is a relatively small amount of very flavorful, rich coffee. When foamed steamed milk is added, one has a cappuccino.

The machines that are used make these coffees in coffee houses are relatively expensive, costing many thousands of dollars. (And so are the espressos and cappuccinos one orders.) But now, in department stores and other kinds of stores, smaller espresso makers, that approximate what the big machines do, are available.

A really good, small espresso maker, with a pump that generates crema (a thin layer of foam on black espresso coffee), can be had for a few hundred dollars and other machines that do a tolerably decent job of making espresso can be purchased for as little as fifteen or twenty dollars (fancier ones cost sixty or seventy dollars). One must use a good quality coffee bean to make espresso; Italian roasts or Espresso roasts generally cost in the area of six to eight dollars a pound.

What does the spread of Espresso in America mean, one might ask? The popularity of Espresso might suggest that Italian culture, in particular, and European culture, in general, are having an impact on American society. We are, in a sense, becoming more "Europeanized."

It also might mean that something has changed as far as our sensibilities are concerned. The traditional drip or percolator coffee is relatively weak and bland, and some coffee lovers drink as many as five or ten cups of coffee a day. One could have as much as one wanted because it was cheap and, relatively speaking, not very strong. (In one of the coffee houses where I go, so-called "American blend" coffee is served in gigantic cups and you can have as much of it as you want. That doesn't apply to espresso and cappuccinos.)

Espresso coffee takes all it can from the coffee grounds, forces them to extremities and yields a scant amount of powerful, liqueur-like beverage. American coffee does not ravage the bean, which is more or less sampled. American coffee often is, one might say, more form than substance, more quantity than quality, more idea than reality.

The Mountain Bike: An American Success Story

The mountain bike was invented in Mill Valley, where I live. What it does is blend the ruggedness of the thick-wheeled American bike and the gear-shifting ability and other technological aspects of the thin-wheeled European bike into a composite that is good on rugged terrain yet can go up hills relatively easily. Mountain bikes also have straight handlebars, which make them more comfortable to steer, and a number of other technological features that have to do with gear shifting and riding on rough terrain.

Along with the mountain bike has come a considerable amount of gear: helmets, biking shirts and shorts, shoes, and other products as well. Mountain bikers now have a "look," and mountain biking, due to its costuming, confers on people a kind of identity—as an athlete and one interested in exercise, good health and the good life. Twenty years ago, when people went riding they wore a pair of old pants and some sneakers. Now a group of mountain bikers resemble what you see in a European bike race.

The introduction of the mountain bike to America has led to a considerable amount of conflict between mountain bikers and mountain hikers—people who like to walk on trails in the woods. Now, governmental agencies have started restricting certain trails to hikers—but many mountain bikers do not obey the restrictions, leading to everything from accidents (in which mountain bikers bump into hikers) to fines (when police catch mountain bikers breaking the law) to lawsuits.

Some people still prefer the ten-speed (or higher) narrow tire bicycle, but this bicycle has been eclipsed, in America, at least, by the mountain bike. It appeals to our heroic sense of ourselves: we believe that we can go anywhere and do anything. All it takes is some muscle power and between $350 and $1000 for the bike (and three dollars for a cappuccino, in some Starbucks or other coffee house, along the way).

Penile Enlargements and Virtual Sex

In *The San Francisco Chronicle*, which is the paper I read every day (along, of course, with *The New York Times*), there are often advertisements which read: "For Men Only." They are for penile enlargements— ways of making men's penises "bigger." But sticking devices in men's penises is, though quite remarkable, really an old technology.

Why bother with operations on one's penis when one can have virtual sex via the magic of virtual reality? Through the use of computers one can now simulate a virtual sex partner and simulate a larger virtual penis to use with virtual partner in simulated sex.

A couple recently had a virtual reality wedding (the first one in America as far as I know) in one of the virtual reality emporia in San Francisco. They were projected into a virtual space, and so, I believe, was the minister who married them. Whether they will content themselves with virtual sex is another matter; the report of their wedding did not go into details on that subject.

The problem with virtual sex is similar to the problem faced by people who have virtual meals—after you've had a virtual reality feast, of virtual wine and virtual steak or virtual lobster or virtual whatever, the fact of the matter is that you are still hungry. But I assume the electronics wizards who brought us virtual reality and the possibility of virtual sex are working on that and will soon have an answer.

Conclusions

The list I created shows that there is constant change in American culture. In some cases the changes are quite minor, though corporations may rise and fall on something as trivial as the invention of velcro or the development of new kinds of aluminum frying pans. But in other cases, such as the invention of the chip that makes computers possible, and the development of CD-ROMs and Modems, vast industries arise (think of Microsoft, for example) and changes of considerable magnitude in people's lifestyles often occur.

In some cases, technological changes end up being counter productive. Recently Toyota announced that it is going back to using more workers in some of its assembly plants because it cost too much to purchase and maintain all the robots it had been using. The secret of dealing with the new technologies, I would suggest, is for individuals to use those new technologies that they find beneficial—and to avoid falling victim to technological eroticism and the feeling that you need to have the newest model of the latest technology in all areas: whether it be fiber pot scrubbers or audio systems.

People can find a way to avoid the extremes of being use-nothing-electronic-or-mechanical Luddites and use-nothing-human or simple technophiles. But it takes a certain amount of discipline and restraint. We haven't found a technological device to instill that in people yet, but we don't need to, because we have an old-fashioned way of dealing with this problem: use a bit of common sense. (Unlike the technophiles who buy devices one after the other, I really *need* all the thirty electronic gadgets and devices I listed above. Or, at the very least, six or eight of them!)

Ironically, though many of the devices we've developed help us save time, sociologists have discovered that in America, at least, we now have less free time than in earlier decades. We are cooking faster, sending mail faster on more powerful and faster computers and doing a lot of other things faster, too, but we're losing ground, so it seems, when it comes to have free time.

We are paying another price, too, for despite our new products and new technologies, there is an element of sterility, of frustration, of alienation, of the lack of a human warmth that has crept into our lives—as anyone who has had to deal with the alienating experience of voice mail can tell you. What do we gain if we can "dial" faster (or not even have to bother dialing, in some cases, since the phones do the dialing for us), with pushbutton phones, but have to navigate our way through torturous voice-mail systems and when we get our parties, wait longer?

VIII
Comparative Perspectives: Introduction

I conclude my book with a discussion of popular culture from a comparative perspective. Saussure said that concepts only have meaning differentially. We can take that insight and use it in doing research. When we wish to make sense of something, we can look at it from a historical perspective (then versus now) or from a comparative perspective (here versus there). To state Saussure's principle in an extreme manner, nothing means anything by itself.

For example, it has been estimated that there were approximately 40,000 people killed by guns in America in 1994. What significance does that figure have? We can look at it historically and see how many were killed in 1984, 1974, 1964, and so on, relative to our population at those times, and get some kind of a trend line. Or we can look at the figure for America, a country with approximately 250 million people, and derive a figure of gun fatalities per million people or thousand people. We can compare ourselves with other countries and see whether the figure of 40,000 killings is a high number or not. It is only when we compare ourselves with ourselves in earlier times or with other societies for 1994 that we get any sense of the significance of the 40,000 gun killings figure.

In the same manner, it makes sense to adopt a cross-cultural perspective in dealing with popular culture. In my discussion of "Texts in Contexts," I offer a number of suggestions for how one might analyze television from a cross-cultural perspective and offer a case study of *Dallas*, which has been the subject of a number of analyses by social scientists and other scholars. I also point out that reception theory, which argues that everyone "creates" his or her own interpretation and, thus, his or her own "text" from television programs and other kinds of mass media would give reason to question the validity of the cultural imperialism hypothesis.

In chapter 18, on Thailand, I return to the cultural imperialism hypothesis and discuss it in terms of a trip I took to Thailand in 1991. I concluded that although there was quite obviously an American and western influence in Thailand, especially in Bangkok, I didn't see anything that would make me feel the Thais were become Americanized or that Thai culture was becoming homogenized, or whatever it is that is supposed to happen to third-world cultures when they are exposed to the mass media. Societies are always changing and Thailand was, so I had been told, quite different from what it had been in the Sixties. It was much cheaper, simpler, more primitive. The same, of course, could be said for America. As anyone who has ever traveled knows, when you go abroad and wander around in different countries, you see your own country and culture in a new light. That is because you have a means of comparing the American way of life with other ways of life.

There is no question in my mind that our films, our television shows, our comic books, and other aspects of our popular culture do have some kind of an influence on other countries. How much influence they have is difficult to assess. But influence moves in two directions. We drink Espresso coffee and walk around in Birkenstocks (unless we've switched to Tevas), eat in Chinese and Thai and Italian and French restaurants, and our children play games on their Nintendo machines. So one might argue that Coca-colonization is being countered by Espresso-ization and Nintendo-ization. The comparative method, then, is a valuable resource to understand the significance of popular culture in our society and other societies and the way societies and cultures affect one another.

17

Texts in Contexts: Analyzing Media and Popular Culture from a Cross-Cultural Perspective

I've spent most of my academic career interpreting and analyzing American popular culture. I was trained in American Studies at the University of Minnesota and, unlike many of my colleagues in graduate school, I was interested in popular culture, not "elite" culture. The very notion of popular culture depends upon there being something different, that is unpopular or "elite" culture. In the same way, the notion that there is such a thing as American culture only has meaning because there are other cultures, non-American (and in many cases un-American and anti-American) which we can compare and contrast ourselves with.

What de Saussure said about concepts not having meaning in themselves but gaining it by being in a system in which their oppositional relationships generated the meaning (and I'm simplifying things a bit here) can also be applied to cultures and subcultures. I say this because although there may be some generalizations we can make about American culture and society, and perhaps about so-called American national character, we recognize, as I suggested earlier, that there are actually numerous Americas—different regions (the East coast, the "arcadian" Pacific Northwest, the "Bible-belt" midwest, the "deep" South and so on) and within each of these regions, there are great varieties of lifestyles, belief structures, attitudes, values, and so on.

Let me put this matter of national, regional, and local cultures and subcultures in perspective by offering a chart showing some of the possibilities that exist for comparative analyses.

CATEGORY	EXAMPLE
UNIVERSAL	Humanity
CONTINENTAL	Asian, European, South American
MACRO-REGIONAL	Western Europe, North American
NATIONAL	U.S.A., Canada, Japan, France, etc.
REGIONAL	East Coast, Pacific Northwest
SUB-REGIONAL	California
URBAN	San Francisco
URBAN DISTRICT	Pacific Heights, Mission
STREET	Castro Street

This is our universe of possibilities and when we analyze the media and popular culture we select areas to compare and contrast within this universe. Obviously, the larger the area, the more "glittering" the generalities we have to make about them.

Even within California, for example, there are great differences between Northern California and Southern California and between San Francisco (and the Bay area) and the Los Angeles area. I was once asked to participate in a conference on the two cities (which never came off). We were to meet once in San Francisco and once in Los Angeles. I wrote the following poem, which reflected my notion of the difference between the two cities:

> San Francisco, which I adore,
> Is a place where less is more.
> Whereas poor Los Angeles
> Is a place where more is less.

If it is dangerous, then, to offer generalizations about American culture or any culture, it is even more perilous to compare and contrast cultures. Yet we must, if we are to make sense of ourselves and of others. I have made comparative studies of similar kinds of comics in Italy and America and of the Italian and American weekly magazine press. I've also analyzed aspects of American and British popular culture (in general) among other things. There are advantages for the culture analyst in being a "stranger" in a strange land, and disadvantages, as well. Recognizing, then, that all generalizations are questionable (perhaps even this one), let me proceed.

Why Analyze Media and Popular Culture?

We study the mass media and popular culture (which tends to be mass-mediated, but isn't always, since popular culture also includes fads, fashions, material culture, etc.) because we assume that the media and popular culture will tell us something about the society being studied. We assume that the texts carried on the media reflect interesting things about the society (and country) in which they are created.

We also assume that these texts affect their societies. (When I use the term *media* I really mean the programs or texts carried on the media, as contrasted with the technical aspects of the media or the patterns of ownership and control of the media, though I will have something to say about these matters, too.)

Those of us who look at things from an international perspective (or cross-national or cross-cultural or trans-national) are interested also in how the media and popular culture from one country may be impacting upon people in other countries. Much media and popular culture is now international. Films, television programs, rock groups, folkdance groups, and folksinging groups now travel the world, and it isn't unusual for any good-sized city to have English rock groups, Bulgarian choirs, Tibetan singers, French films, Russian ballet groups, Brazilian bands, Jamaican Reggae musicians, Chinese acrobats, German orchestras, and the like performing at the same time. Many of these groups have records, appear frequently on television and the radio, and so cross whatever line exists (and some people believe that line is very faint) between popular culture and elite culture.

Television and the Problem of Cultural Domination

Let me focus attention now on the medium of television, which is the medium that has been the subject of most of the controversy between critics of the left and right (and some in the middle). For although there is an international cast to cultural and popular cultural flow, when it comes to television, things are quite different.

Television programs from America and Western European countries are much cheaper for Third World countries to buy than produce, and some critics are worried that American and Western European cultural, social, and political values and ideologies will drive out supposedly less hardy and more fragile native cultural values. (American television programs are popular even in "First World" countries like France, which, in order to maintain its cultural identity, has limited the amount of American television that can be shown.)

This thesis is known as "Cultural Imperialism" or, in its American manifestation, "Coca-Colonization." Some critics, who tend to be Marxists or Critical Theorists, believe that American media (and we can include American films, here, too) will destroy regional and local cultures and lead to ideological domination by American "bourgeois" values and to a loss of cultural identity by people in other cultures. Mixing metaphors and food products, we might say that Coca-Colonization will lead to cultural homogenization. This is not looked upon with favor, let me add, by those who seem to believe that in society (as in bottles of milk) the cream should rise to the top.

The Case of *Dallas* in Germany

Dallas is (or was, at one time) broadcast in approximately ninety different countries and has been studied extensively by scholars. About ten years ago, Herta Herzog Massing made a study of the way *Dallas* was viewed in Germany and America and came up with some interesting findings. As she wrote in an article in *Society* (Nov./Dec. 1986: 74):

> Critics of popular culture, and of things American in particular, have concerned themselves with the question of whether the worldwide diffusion of programs such as "Dallas" made possible by the growth of the new media technologies may eventually result in worldwide cultural assimilation at the expense of indigenous diversity.

As the result of her pilot study, she came to the conclusion that viewers in America decoded *Dallas* differently from viewers in Germany. Her conclusion to the article sums things up thusly:

> The answer to my initial question—do viewers in different countries read popular culture differently?—must be answered affirmatively. (1986: 77)

Dallas was not popular in countries such as Brazil, which have their own telenovelas, and various Asian countries. In many countries it got very low ratings.

The notion that everyone decodes, interprets, gets the same things out of a text is very close to being a throwback to the old "hypodermic needle" hypothesis of media effects. The development of semiotics has shown that not only do people in different cultures and societies interpret texts differently, so do people in the same society.

As Umberto Eco has argued in "Towards a Semiotic Inquiry into the Television Message":

> Codes and subcodes are applied to the message [text] in the light of a general framework of cultural references, which constitutes the receiver's patrimony of knowledge: his ideological, ethical, religious standpoints, his psychological attitudes, his tastes, his value systems, etc. (1972, 115)

What we can expect from the mass media, Eco says, is "aberrant decoding." We, as individuals and as members of subcultures and cultures, read texts through the prisms of our knowledge and understanding of the world.

The situation in Eastern Europe, where countries were subjected to forty years of propaganda by state-controlled radio and television stations (and the press) and tossed out the regimes with hardly a second thought (once they realized the Red Army would not invade) suggests that the power of the media is limited. The regimes in Eastern Europe could not cope with the desire of people for consumer goods and political freedom, both of which were connected, in part, with the access people had to television programs from Western Europe showing what life was like in bourgeois societies.

Analyzing Television from a Cross-Cultural Perspective

Let me suggest a number of things one might consider in making an analysis of a televised text (and films, as well) from a cross-cultural perspective. The very notion of cross-cultural analysis implies some kind of a comparison is being made between texts which are similar in nature, most usually in terms of genres. In all of the matters listed below, there is an implicit notion that comparisons between similar kinds of texts (for example, soap operas in America and Brazil) in different countries are to be carried out. With that as a given, let us consider what we might focus our attention on:

1. *Values of the characters.* What values are espoused and what values are attacked, downplayed, or neglected? Values are understood as general notions about what is good and what is bad, what is desirable and what is undesirable.

2. *Socioeconomic class and characteristics of characters.* Although it is difficult to be precise in many cases, we must ask ourselves, What is the socioeconomic class of the various characters and how does this impact upon their roles and their values? Is class membership an important consideration? If there are class differences, how are they shown?

3. *Roles of the characters with particular attention to gender.* What roles do the characters play? What roles do women play and what is suggested as normal and natural for women? Are certain socioeconomic classes (and attendant occupations), sexes, ages, races, and ethnic-types over-represented or under-represented?

4. *How are the plots constructed?* Is there, for example, a difference in the kinds of resolutions of plots that are found in texts from the countries being analyzed? Some critics have suggested that America is a "happy ending" nation. Is that correct? If so, how do you explain it?

5. *What are the heroes and heroines, villains and villainesses like?* What are the characteristics of the protagonists? What do they look like? How do they act? What are their values? What are their qualities and characteristics? How do they function in the text? Are the characters rounded, three-dimensional, and believable, or do they tend to be two-dimensional? Do they have a symbolic significance?

6. *What are the dominant themes found in the texts?* Do texts that are similar in genre and plot have different themes? If so, what does that suggest? If not, what does that suggest?

7. *What are the main stereotypes (if any) found in the text?* If there are stereotypes in the text, what are they and what function do they have? How are the stereotypes shown? What are the common stereotypes of people from countries such as France, Germany, Italy, England and the United States?

8. *Is there an ideological dimension you can find in the text?* Is there some kind of an ideological (which I define as a logically coherent sociopolitical set of beliefs) that is found in the text? If so, what is it? How effective do you think the ideological message is? Is the ideological message overt or is it hidden, somehow, in the text?

9. *Use of language, quality of dialogue.* How would you characterize the language, the dialogue, in the text? What role does language play in the text, as far as indicating class, identity, values, and how does it affect the behavior of the various characters? What is it that makes dialogue "good"?

10. *What is the visual style of the text like?* What is the camera work like? What kinds of shots are dominant? What is the lighting like? How is sound used? How is music used? What editing techniques are used? How "sophisticated" is the text from a technical point of view?

11. *If the text has humorous elements, what techniques of humor are dominant?* Humor, we know, varies considerably from country to country. One way it varies is in terms of the techniques used to generate the humor, and these should be elicited and analyzed. It also varies in terms of who (which occupations, ethnic groups, sexes, kinds of people) is the "butt" of the humor…and how people use humor as a means of resistance against domination by those elements which control society.

Comparing Mass Media Findings with Studies by Other Kinds of Scholars

It is useful to see what sociologists, cultural anthropologists, political scientists, and other scholars have to say about the countries, societies, and cultures being studied. Do your findings correlate with those by others who have investigated other aspects of the country being studied? We must always make sure that we are comparing texts (or anything) that are similar in nature. Otherwise, the comparison doesn't mean anything. As the folk saying goes, "You can't compare apples and oranges."

In 1963, when I made my study of Italian and American comics that were similar in terms of the kinds of main characters they had and when they were published, I found that they differed considerably in terms of attitudes toward authority. I also made use of research by Italian sociologists who argued that the Italian family was a relatively authoritarian one.

In recent years, cultural anthropologists have become interested in the mass media and popular culture and have done some extremely interesting work. An example of this is Conrad Kottak's recent study of television in Brazil, *Prime-Time Society,* a work that makes a number of important methodological advances (and has a cross-cultural perspective). In studying the media and popular culture, we should make use of work by those in other disciplines as much as possible. (Some argue that communications isn't a discipline but an area where scholars trained in a number of different disciplines congregate, a crossroads where, as Wilbur Schramm put it, "few tarry.")

The goal of cross-national studies is to gain insights into such matters as national (and regional) character, social and political values, attitudes and belief systems, and related concerns. It is assumed that the mass media and popular culture help reinforce certain dominant values by championing them and by neglecting other competing values. Every country is involved, I would suggest, in a dialogue with itself, as groups with different perspectives, ideologies, belief systems, and attitudes contend for power and control of things. In our analyses of the media and popular culture, we should pay attention to both sides of this dialogue.

We should also consider how the media and popular culture help people gain and consolidate a sense of identity. In particular we should investigate how nationality ("I am French"), gender ("I am a French woman"), class ("I am a working-class French woman") and ideological ("I am a working-class French woman and am a member of the Communist party") identities are created.

How do we explain the creation and persistence of subcultures in societies where the media are designed to reflect some kind of a national sense of things or are controlled by a relatively small group of people? Or where the state runs the media and uses it as an instrument of propaganda? And how do resistant subcultures make use of media in these various societies?

Between Scylla and Charybdis

Somehow we must find a way to negotiate between hypergeneralizations and hyperspecificity. When talking about the effects of the media, for instance, some scholars suggest that all we can say with any certainty is that "in some cases some people are affected in some ways." On the other side of this polarity are those who make seemingly definitive statements about "the English" or "the French" based on studying the mass media and other things in these countries.

The solution, I believe, is to be humble. We must learn to recognize how complex cultures and societies are, so that we exercise caution in our generalizations. As I write this, a number of countries are experiencing difficulties holding themselves together. In Canada, for example, there is still talk of the French-speaking province of Quebec leaving Canada and becoming a nation. Here language (and culture connected to that language) is the issue. The Soviet Union has collapsed and various territories and other regions have set themselves up as autonomous states. Here, it is language, religion, ethnicity, and race (and combinations of these factors) that are the major factors. The same applies to other countries, as well, where bloody civil wars rage—in what used to be Yugoslavia and in various African nations.

One thing seems to be certain. The mass media in these nations has not "homogenized" the people and the various ethnic, religious and linguistic groups or subcultures have kept hold of their identities. It is increasingly difficult, then, to make generalizations about "the Russians" that are useful. Even generalizations about the Soviet Russians, the people of great Russia, are fraught with danger, as anyone who has read Geoffrey Gorer's remarkable book, *The People of Great Russia*, knows.

Yet, we are social animals and are affected, in profound ways, by the societies in which we live and the cultures in which we grow up. As Durkheim has written in *The Elementary Forms of Religious Life*:

> Collective representations are the result of an immense co-operation, which stretches out not only into space but into time as well; to make them, a multitude of minds have associated, united and combined their ideas and sentiments; for them, long generations have accumulated their experience and their knowledge. A special intellectual activity is therefore concentrated in them which is infinitely richer and complexer than that of the individual. From that one can understand how the reason has been able to go beyond the limits of empirical knowledge. It does not owe this to any vague, mysterious virtue but simply to the fact that according to the well-known formula, man is double. There are two beings in him: an individual being which has its foundation in the organism and the circle of whose activities is therefore strictly limited, and a social being which represents the highest reality in the intellectual and moral order that we can know by observation—I mean society. This duality of our nature has as its consequence in the practical order, the irreducibility of a moral ideal to a utilitarian motive, and in the order of thought, the irreducibility of reason to individual experience. In so far as he belongs to society, the individual transcends himself, both when he thinks and when he acts.

Somehow, in dealing with the mass media from a comparative cultural perspective, we must find a way to negotiate between the conception of the oversocialized, "robotlike" individual and the opposite view of the undersocialized, "anarchic" individual. We have to find a way to navigate between too simplistic notions of what individuals (and societies) are like without being too simplistic ourselves. It is a very dangerous calling—but think how exciting it is when we succeed.

18

Is Thailand Going Western?

A week before I left for Thailand I happened to meet one of my former students. We chatted for a while and then she said, "Are you doing anything exciting this Summer?" "Yes," I replied. "I'm going to Thailand for a few weeks." Her eyes immediately glazed over and her face lit up. "You are so lucky. I'm crazy about the place," she said. Then she told me, speaking rapturously, about a trip she had made to Thailand and India a few years earlier.

A Traveller with Ulterior Motives

I went to Thailand to take a vacation and play the tourist, but I had "ulterior motives." I was interested in finding out about the impact Western culture (in particular, American pop culture) and tourism was having on Thai culture. I might add that riots in Thailand had occurred just a few weeks before I was scheduled to leave and there was some question about whether I'd be able to go. I had made arrangements to do some lecturing at Chulalonkorn University in Bangkok and wanted to go, but I was uneasy and apprehensive about what I'd find in Bangkok. Was it a dangerous place to go? The riots took place on May 18th and my flight was scheduled for May 31st.

My anxieties were eased when I saw the photograph of General Suchinda Kraprayoon, head of the Thai army and the person most responsible for the bloodletting, kneeling in front of the king of Thailand, along with Chamlong Srimuang, the former governor of Bangkok. I was confident, then, that the situation was under control and that the military was going to be contained. Suchinda had led a coup himself, in February of 1991. He overthrew an elected government, it is true, but he got rid of a very corrupt government and had been seen then, ironically, as something of a reformer. He put in an honest and esteemed person as prime minister, Anand Panyarachun.

But when General Suchinda, breaking his promises, "allowed himself" to be nominated for prime minister, there was a tremendous sense of outrage felt by the Thai people, especially the middle classes and students, who promptly demonstrated. Figures vary, but it has been estimated that as many as 600 people were killed by the military during the riots; nobody really knows. But the suppression by the military was bloody and brutal, and it was captured on video, for all to see. Anand eventually was named interim prime minister, elections were scheduled for 13 September, and things quickly settled down.

But the shock was enormous. Thailand's economy was booming and it was, before the riots scared people away, one of the premier tourist destinations; I would describe it, on the basis of three weeks spent traveling all over the country, as one of the last inexpensive paradises. It hosts about five million tourists a year, and the loss of revenues threatened by the decline of tourism and the impact on the economic system, in general, led to quick action.

The military was put back in its box (for how long one wonders) and life returned to a semblance of normalcy. Thailand has seen close to twenty coups in the past forty years, so coups are nothing new to the Thais. The military also is deeply involved in the economy of Thailand; military figures are on the boards or run a number of large industries in Thailand. So controlling the military is not easy to do. On the other hand, Thailand is, in many respects, a very modern country. In Bangkok, for example, a large number of middle-class and professional people carry cellular phones with them and can be seen making calls in restaurants, while walking on the streets, and all kinds of other places. (The rioters used cellular phones and fax machines to coordinate their plans, as a matter of fact.)

One reason for this reliance on cellular phones is that Bangkok can be described, I would suggest, somewhat facetiously, as a traffic jam surrounded by buildings. It can take an hour or two just to go a few miles in Bangkok, because of the congestion. Traffic seems to alternate between long periods when nobody moves and brief moments when there are explosions of traffic, when all kinds of vehicles—automobiles, trucks, buses, motorcycles, and tuk-tuks—go racing down the streets and avenues. That's why cellular phones are so important; it's hard to go anyplace, so business people rely on their telephones.

Someone was kind enough to give me a couple of humorous faxes when I was in Thailand, paste-ups that showed General Suchinda in an unflattering light. In one of the paste-ups his head was attached to the body of a woman in a bathing suit, and in the other, to the body of a scantily clad prostitute. General Suchinda had been feminized and turned into a comic figure, a figure of ridicule, less than a month after the Bangkok riots. This would suggest that people were trying to deal with their anxiety about him and the generals this way or that he and his colleagues were no longer taken seriously and considered an important factor in Thai politics.

The Coca-Colonization, Cultural-Imperialism Question

The cultural imperialism hypothesis argues that First World countries (such as the United States, Western Europe, Japan and, perhaps, a few other countries) overwhelm Third World countries and destroy their native cultures and subcultures. The First World countries, it is suggested, supply films, television programs, and spread their popular culture, which subtly indoctrinates Third World peoples with western values.

Let's assume that America, the source of a great deal of television programming and films and popular culture, is the main culprit. Coca-Colonization, another term for cultural imperialism, is the result of the spread of American popular culture, and is connected to our mass media and, in addition, some would add, American tourists. When you see fast food restaurants such as McDonald's and Kentucky Fried Chicken in Bangkok, you see evidence that American popular culture (in the form of fast food joints) has taken root in Thailand.

The argument is that our media and popular culture reflect (subliminally, so to speak) bourgeois values, in general, and capitalist ideology, in particular. Thus when Third World peoples watch our films and television programs and read our comics, they are (without recognizing it) being colonized on the cultural level.

Let me quote from a book that makes this argument, Ariel Dorfman and Armand Mattelart's book *How to Read Donald Duck: Imperialist Ideology in the Disney Comic*. Dorfman and Mattelart are Chilean Marxists, who use Marx's concepts to explain how cultural imperialism works. They ask why Disney is such a threat and answer as follows:

Our countries are exporters of raw materials, and importers of super-structural and cultural goods. To service our "monoproduct" economies and provide urban paraphernalia, we send copper, and they send machines to extract copper, and, of course, Coca Cola. Behind the Coca Cola stands a whole structure of expectations and models of behavior, and with it, a particular kind of present and future society, and an interpretation of the past. (1971, 97)

Disney, they suggest, without necessarily being aware of the ideological content of his work, shapes the consciousness of his readers in ways that are useful to those who dominate Latin American and other Third World countries.

How to Read Donald Duck was written in 1971, when a rather doctrinaire interpretation of Marx was popular, but many scholars and critics who are not Marxists, still believe that our popular culture and mass media are wreaking havoc on Third World cultures (and on our own culture, as well, in many cases).

This notion assumes two things: first, the media and popular culture are very powerful, smashing "fragile" folk cultures, native traditions and everything else that gets in the way; and second, that everyone interprets a given film or television show or comic book the same way, that everyone "gets the message." There is good reason to argue that Third World cultures are not fragile and easily destroyed.

The notion that all the members of an audience interpret a movie or television show the same way has been cast aside. We now realize that each person interprets or makes sense of a specific film or television show or comic book based on his or her knowledge base, educational level and interests, among other things. We don't automatically get any messages from the media and our ability to misconstrue, misunderstand and misinterpret what we see and hear (compared to the messages those who make films and television shows think they are sending) is awesome.

If the cultural imperialism hypothesis is true, Thailand, a country full of American, Western European and Japanese tourists, should be an excellent case study of a country that has experienced and continues to be Coca-Colonized.

What I Found in Thailand

I travelled north as far as Chiang Mai and south as far as the border with Malaysia, and though I saw a goodly number of tourists and though Bangkok has a number of American fast food joints, I didn't get the sense that the Thais were, somehow, losing their Thai identity and becoming more Americanized.

Thailand is a country that is undergoing rapid modernization; it is shifting from an agricultural country to one that also has manufacturing and heavy industry, so, naturally, there have been considerable changes in Thailand over the past few decades. Thailand has undergone a process that I call "motorcyclization." It is full of motorcycles of every size and description, most of which are made by Japanese companies.

This is the level countries reach before most people can afford automobiles, though there are plenty of autos in Thailand. Too many, I'd say. One day it took me about ten minutes to cross the street in front of the Royal Hotel in Bangkok. That's the area where many of the demonstrations took place and a number of the buildings there showed signs of having been burned. When I was there workmen were putting fences around the buildings and had started working on them.

At Lamai Beach, on Koh (the term means island) Samui, all the restaurants showed videos at dinner and most of the diners, who were westerners, had their eye glued to them. The restaurants all posted signs that indicated which videos they'd be playing that evening with dinner. I did notice, also, that many Thai offices had television sets. The hotel clerks in a number of the hotels I stayed at watched television when they weren't busy with guests. So television does pervade Thailand, but it seems to be something that washes over the Thais and doesn't sink very deep into them.

We should also keep in mind that in Thailand, as in most countries, there are considerable cultural and economic differences between urban dwellers and country dwellers. Bangkok has about six million people and Chiang Mai, the second largest city in Thailand, has about 350,000 people. So, except for a small number of medium size cities, Thailand is a country full of relatively small towns and villages. In Thailand, you still have large numbers of peasants in the countryside, who probably don't live much differently from the way their parents and grandparents lived. In the countryside the temples play an important role.

Thailand is, we must remember, about 96 percent Buddhist, and religion is still very much part of people's lives. Every morning all through Thailand you can see the orange robed monks walking around with their begging bowls and you can see people giving them food. The Thais also show great reverence for the king, which suggests that some traditions are still very powerful in Thailand. Every morning and every evening a brief film clip, showing scenes of the king and the royal family, and a soundtrack of the national anthem, is shown on television in Thailand. Insulting the king is, so the guidebooks suggest, a criminal offense.

The Other Side of the Cultural Imperialism Argument

It can be argued that tourism actually functions as an enhancer of cultural identity. Tourists, as a rule, don't come to Thailand to eat at McDonald's or immerse themselves in the westernized aspects of Thai culture and society. Tourists come to "see the sights," which means that the Thais have a stake in restoring their monuments, keeping traditional crafts alive and maintaining their distinctive culture, so tourists will experience what they seek—something different.

There are, of course, a number of tourists attractions in all countries that are not authentic, that cater to fantasies and stereotypes tourists have. And there is the moral question to be considered relative to the intrusion of tourists into native people's lives, as is the case in northern Thailand where people go trekking and visit hill tribes.

But my point is that it is in the interest of the Thais to maintain their culture. Take food, for example. It is possible to eat Western style breakfasts in many restaurants in Thailand, but Thai cuisine shows no sign of being destroyed by Western tastes. The Thais do hold down the spices in some of their dishes for "farangs" (foreigners) but this is done to shield westerners from the mouth blistering heat of certain Thai dishes. Ironically, Thai restaurants are now extremely popular in America. I live in Mill Valley, which is in Marin county, just over the Golden Gate Bridge from San Francisco. Thai restaurants can be said to be "colonizing" this area. We now have a large number of Thai restaurants in Marin county and new ones are opening up all the time.

The Thais have their own kind of fast food. In Chiang Mai I can remember a wonderful lunch at the Galare Center. You buy coupons from an attendant, and then use them to purchase various dishes from a dozen concessionaires who are all grouped together in a central area. The dishes are all cooked up for you, as you wait—wonderful spicy Thai soups, noodle dishes, charcoal grilled chicken on skewers, and so on. And for those who want to try something different, you can also get hamburgers and french fries. Just as Americans find Thai food exotic, so do Thais find American fast food (the only kind commonly available) exotic.

Tourism is now, along with entertainment, one of the world's mega-industries. People travel, in part, because they wish to spend their money "experientially," doing things that enhance their sense of well being—instead of, for example, spending their money on material goods. Of course, tourists do spend money buying things, and some tourists go to places like Hong Kong primarily to buy things. But there is an element of cultural anthropology to tourism, a sense people have that there are things to see, places to go, adventures to be had, by traveling to distant lands, and that these experiences enhance us and enrich us spiritually.

It is unlikely, I would surmise, that First World or Western media and popular culture have, either by accident or by plan, spread bourgeois values to unsuspecting people in Thailand, making it easy for them, so the cultural imperialism argument goes, to be more cruelly exploited by the Thai capitalist elites. Thai culture is being affected by modernization, and like all cultures, is continually evolving. But I had the sense that Western media, pop culture and tourists were not radically altering Thai culture and changing Thai identity. The economy in Thailand has been booming in recent years, and Bangkok is full of new skyscrapers and other buildings that are being built. You get a sense that Thailand doesn't need to take lessons from America about bourgeois values. And the Thais, led by Chinese Thais who seem to be the major entrepreneurs, might be able to give us lessons about how to create a vibrant economic scene.

Thailand does suffer from a terrible AIDS problem. There are many prostitutes in Thailand and a large percentage of them have the disease. For a long time the Thai authorities refused to acknowledge that AIDS was a problem, but in recent years they have admitted there is a problem--too late for the thousands of women who are already infected and for their customers. But AIDS is not unique to Thailand.

A Personal Memoir

One morning in Chiang Mai I got up early, around six o'clock, and went off to the market to get some fruit. It had rained the night before and the air was warm and perfumed. As I walked along the streets, various food sellers were getting prepared for the day. They were starting their charcoal fires or already cooking things over gas stoves. In many of the Thai towns, there are many vendors selling food on the street— roast birds, cakes, tea, noodles with meat, and roasted corn—the variety is incredible. The Thais love to eat and Thailand is bursting with food, including some wonderful tropical fruits that are not sold in America.

There is a kind of sweetness to the Thais, a friendliness and honesty that is very appealing. The streets were spotless and the legions of mad motorcyclists had not begun to make their presence known. The May riots seemed never to have existed. You didn't get a sense that anyone was tense and anxiety ridden about what the generals might be doing. People were going about their business as they usually did, while governments might rise and fall in Bangkok. In Bangkok, when I was out walking, I was often approached by individuals wanting to make some kind of a deal—change money, get me tickets to a girlie show, whatever. In Chiang Mai, I sensed that the basic elements of Thai everyday life were pretty much intact and that the Thais faced little danger from being Coca-colonized or having their culture destroyed by western (and American, in particular) mass media and popular culture.

Bibliography

Abelove, Henry, Michele A. Barale, and David Halperin, eds. *The Lesbian and Gay Studies Reader*. New York: Routledge, 1993.

Adorno, Theodor W. *Prisms*. Trans. Samuel and Shierry Weber. Cambridge: MIT Press, 1991.

———. The Culture Industry: Selected Essays on Mass Culture. London: Routledge, 1991.

Aitken, Stuart C., and Leo E. Zonn. *Place, Power, Situation and Spectacle: A Geography of Film*. Lanham, Md.: Rowman & Littlefield, 1994.

Armstrong, Nancy. *Desire and Domestic Fiction: A Political History of the Novel*. New York: Oxford University Press, 1987.

Aronowitz, Stanley. *The Politics of Identity*. New York: Routledge, 1992.

———. *Dead Artists, Live Theories and Other Cultural Problems*. New York: Routledge, 1993.

Atkin, Charles, and Lawrence Wallack. *Mass Communication and Public Health*. Thousand Oaks: Sage Publications, 1992.

Bakhtin, M. M. *The Dialogic Imagination*. Trans. Caryl Emerson and Michael Holquist. Michael Holmquist, ed. Austin: University of Texas Press, 1981.

Bakhtin, Mikail. *Rabelais and His World*. Trans. Helene Iswolsky. Bloomington: Indiana University Press, 1984.

Bal, Mieke. *Narratology: Introduction to the Theory of Narrative*. Toronto: University of Toronto Press, 1985.

Barker, Martin, and Ann Beezer. *Reading into Cultural Studies*. London: Routledge, 1992.

Barthes, Roland. *Writing Degree Zero & Elements of Semiology*. Trans. Annette Lavers and Colin Smith. Boston: Beacon Press, 1970.

———. *Mythologies*. Trans. Annette Lavers. New York: Hill and Wang, 1972.

———. *S/Z*. Trans. Richard Miller. New York: Hill & Wang, 1974.

———. *The Pleasure of the Text*. Trans. Richard Miller. New York: Hill & Wang, 1975.

———. *Roland Barthes by Roland Barthes*. Trans. Richard Howard. New York: Hill & Wang, 1975.

———. *A Lover's Discourse*. Trans. Richard Howard. New York: Hill & Wang, 1978.

———. *Empire of Signs*. Trans. Richard Howard. New York: Hill & Wang, 1982.

———. *The Semiotic Challenge*. Trans. Richard Howard. New York: Hill & Wang, 1988.

Bateson, Gregory. *Steps to an Ecology of Mind*. New York: Ballantine Books, 1972.

Baudrillard, Jean. *Simulations*. Trans. Paul Foss, et al. New York: Semiotext(e), 1983.

———. *Symbolic Exchange and Death*. Trans. Ian Grant. Thousand Oaks: Sage Publications, 1994.

Beilharz, Peter, Gillian Robinson, and John Rundell. *Between Totalitarianism and Postmodernity: A Thesis Eleven Reader*. Cambridge, Mass.: MIT Press, 1992.

Bennett, Tony, and Janet Woollacott. *Bond and Beyond: The Political Career of a Popular Hero*. New York: Methuen, 1987.

Berger, Arthur Asa. "Authority in the Comics." *TransACTION* (Dec. 1966).

———. *The Comic-Stripped American*. New York: Walker & Co., 1973.

———. "Anatomy of the Joke." *Journal of Communication* 26, no. 3 (Summer, 1976).

———. *Television as an Instrument of Terror: Essays on Media, Popular Culture and Everyday Life*. New Brunswick, N.J.: Transaction Publishers, 1980.

———. *Media Analysis Techniques*. Newbury Park, Calif.: Sage Publications, 1982.

———. *Signs in Contemporary Culture: An Introduction to Semiotics*. New York: Annenberg-Longman, 1984.

———, ed. "Introduction" to "Humor, the Psyche and Society." *American Behavioral Scientist* 3, no. 3 (January/February 1987).

———, ed. *Television in Society*. New Brunswick, N.J.: Transaction Publishers, 1987.

———, ed. *Visual Sociology and Semiotics*. Aachen, Germany: Edition Herodot, 1987.

———. "Humor and Behavior: Therapeutic Aspects of Comedic Techniques and Other Considerations." In Brent D. Ruben, ed. *Information and Behavior* 2. Transaction Publishers, 1988.

———. *Political Culture and Public Opinion*. New Brunswick, N.J.: Transaction Publishers, 1989.

———. *Seeing is Believing: An Introduction to Visual Communication*. Mountain View, Calif.: Mayfield Publishing Co., 1989.

———. *Agitpop: Political Culture and Communication Theory*. New Brunswick, N.J.: Transaction Publishers, 1990.

————. "Comics and Popular Culture: Not Just Kid's Stuff." *The World & I* (July, 1990).

————. *An Anatomy of Humor.* New Brunswick, N.J.: Transaction Publishers, 1993.

————. *Blind Men and Elephants: Perspectives on Humor.* New Brunswick, N.J.: Transaction, 1995.

————. *Essentials of Mass Communication Theory.* Thousand Oaks, Calif.: Sage Publications, 1995.

Berman, Marshall. *All That is Solid Melts Into Air: The Experience of Modernity.* New York: Touchstone Books, 1982.

Bernstein, Richard J. *The New Constellation: The Ethical-Political Horizons of Modernity/Postmodernity.* Cambridge, Mass.: MIT Press, 1992.

Best, Steven, and Douglas Kellner. *Postmodern Theory.* New York: Guilford, 1991.

Bettelheim, Bruno. *The Uses of Enchantment.* New York: Knopf, 1976.

Bird, John, et al. *Mapping the Futures: Local Cultures, Global Change.* London: Routledge, 1993.

Bhabha, Homi. *Location of Culture.* New York: Routledge, 1993.

Blau, Herbert. *To All Appearances: Ideology and Performance.* London: Routledge, 1992.

Bloom, Clive, ed. *Creepers: British Horror and Fantasy in the Twentieth Century. Boulder, Colo.: Westview, 1993.*

Bogart, Leo. *Polls and the Awareness of Public Opinion.* New Brunswick, N.J.: Transaction Publishers, 1985.

Borges, Jorge Luis. *A Universal History of Infamy.* New York: Dutton, 1972.

Bourdieu, Pierre. *Sociology in Question.* Trans. Richard Nice. Thousand Oaks: Sage Publications, 1994.

Bourdieu, Pierre and Jean-Claude Passeron. *Reproduction in Education, Society and Culture.* Newbury Park, Calif.: Sage Publications, 1990.

Bowlby, Rachel. *Shopping with Freud: Items on Consumerism, Feminism and Psychoanalysis.* London: Routledge, 1993.

Branigan, Edward. *Narrative Comprehension and Film.* New York: Routledge, 1992.

Brenkman, John. *Straight Male Modern: A Cultural Critique of Psychoanalysis.* New York: Routledge, 1993.

Brenner, Charles. *An Elementary Textbook of Psychoanalysis.* Garden City, N.Y.: Anchor Books, 1974.

Brody, Michael. "The Wonderful World of Disney—Its Psychological Appeal." Unpublished paper, 1975.

Brown, Mary Ellen, ed. *Television and Women's Culture: The Politics of the Popular.* Newbury Park, Calif.: Sage Publications, 1990.

Brown, Mary Ellen. *Soap Opera and Woman's Talk: The Pleasure of Resistance*. Thousand Oaks, Calif.: Sage Publications, 1994.

Buck-Morss, Susan. *The Dialectics of Seeing: Walter Benjamin and the Arcades Project*. Minneapolis, Minn.: University of Minnesota Press, 1989.

Butler, Judith. *Bodies That Matter*. New York: Routledge, 1993.

Cantor, Muriel G. *The Hollywood TV Producer*. New Brunswick, N.J.: Transaction, 1988.

Cantor, Muriel G. and Joel M. Cantor. *Prime-Time Television: Content and Control*. Thousand Oaks, Calif.: Sage Publications, 1991.

Carey, James, ed. *Media, Myths and Narratives: Television and the Press*. Newbury Park, Calif.: Sage Publications, 1988.

Certeau, Michel de. *The Practice of Everyday Life*. Trans. Steven Rendall. Berkeley, Calif.: University of California Press, 1984.

Certeau, Michel de. *Heterologies: Discourse on the Other*. Trans. Brian Massumi. Minneapolis, Minn.: University of Minnesota Press, 1986.

Clark, Katerina & Michael Holmquist. *Mikhail Bakhtin*. Cambridge, Mass.: Harvard University Press, 1984.

Clarke, John. *New Times and Old Enemies: Essays on Cultural Studies and America*. London: Routledge, 1992.

Collins, Jim, Hillary Radner, and Ava Preacher Collins, eds. *Film Theory goes to the Movies: Cultural Analysis of Contemporary Film*. New York: Routledge, 1992.

Collins, Richard, James Curran, Nicholas Garnham, and Paddy Scannell, eds. *Media, Culture & Society*. Newbury Park, Calif.: Sage Publications, 1986.

Corliss, Richard. "It's Already the TV Movie." *Time* (18 July), 1994.

Cottom, Daniel. *Text and Culture: The Politics of Interpretation*. Minneapolis, Minn.: University of Minnesota Press, 1989.

Coward, Rosalind and John Ellis. *Language and Materialism: Developments in Semiology and the Theory of the Subject*. London: Routledge & Kegan Paul, 1977.

Crane, Diane. *The Production of Culture: Media and the Urban Arts*. Newbury Park, Calif.: Sage Publications, 1992.

Creed, Barbara. *The Monstrous-Feminine: Film, Feminism, Psychoanalysis*. London: Routledge, 1993.

Crimp, Douglas, ed. *AIDS: Cultural Analysis/ Cultural Activism*. Cambridge, Mass.: MIT Press, 1988.

Crook, Stephen, Jan Pakulski, and Malcolm Waters, ed. *Postmodernization: Change in Advanced Society*. London: Sage Publications, 1992.

Cross, Gary. *Time and Money: The Making of a Consumer Culture*. London: Routledge, 1993.

Culler, Jonathan. *Structuralist Poetics: Structuralism, Linguistics and the Study of Literature*. Ithaca, N.Y.: Cornell University Press, 1975.

——. *Ferdinand de Saussure*. New York: Penguin Books, 1977.

——. *The Pursuit of Signs*. Ithaca, N.Y.: Cornell University Press, 1981.

——. *On Deconstruction*. Ithaca, N.Y.: Cornell University Press, 1982.

Danesi, Marcel. *Messages and Meanings: An Introduction to Semiotics*. Toronto: Canadian Scholars Press, 1994.

Danesi, Marcel, and Donato Santeramo, eds. *Introducing Semiotics: An Anthology of Readings*. Toronto: Canadian Scholars Press, 1992.

Davis, Robert Con, and Ronald Schleifer. *Criticism & Culture*. London: Longman, 1991.

Dayan, Daniel, and Elihu Katz. "Television Ceremonial Events." In Arthur Asa Berger, ed., *Television in Society*. New Brunswick, N.J.: Transaction Publishers, 1987.

De Fleur, Melvin L., and Otto N. Larsen. *The Flow of Information: An Experiment in Mass Communication*. New Brunswick, N.J.: Transaction Publishers, 1987.

Denney, Reuel. *The Astonished Muse*. New Brunswick, N.J.: Transaction, 1989.

Denzin, Norman K. *Images of Postmodern Society: Social Theory and Contemporary Cinema*. London: Sage Publications, 1991.

Derrida, Jacques. *Of Grammatology*. Trans. Gayatri Chakravorty Spivak. Baltimore, Md.: Johns Hopkins University Press, 1967.

——. *Positions*. Trans. Alan Bass. Chicago, Ill.: University of Chicago Press, 1981.

Doane, Mary Ann. *The Desire to Desire: The Woman's Film of the 1940s*. Bloomington: Indiana University Press, 1987.

——. *Femmes Fatales*. New York: Routledge, 1991.

Donald, James, and Stuart Hall, eds. *Politics and Ideology*. Bristol, Pa.: Taylor & Francis, 1985.

Douglas, Mary. *Implicit Meanings: Essays in Anthropology*. London: Routledge & Kegan Paul, 1975.

——. *Risk and Blame: Essays in Cultural Theory*. London: Routledge, 1992.

Duncan, Hugh Dalziel. *Communication and The Social Order*. New Brunswick, N.J.: Transaction Publishers, 1985.

Dundes, Alan. *Cracking Jokes: Studies in Sick Humor Cycles and Stereotypes*. Berkeley, Calif.: Ten Speed Press, 1987.

Durkheim, Emile. *The Elementary Forms of the Religious Life*. New York: The Free Press, 1967.

Dworkin, Dennis L., and Leslie G. Roman. *Views Beyond the Border Country: Raymond Williams and Cultural Politics*. New York: Routledge, 1992.

Dyer, Richard. *The Matter of Images: Essays on Representations*. London: Routledge, 1993.

Eagleton, Terry. *Marxism and Literary Criticism*. Berkeley, Calif.: University of California Press, 1976.

————. *Literary Theory: An Introduction.* Minneapolis, Minn.: University of Minnesota Press, 1983.

Easthope, Antony. *Literary into Cultural Studies.* London: Routledge, 1991.

Eco, Umberto. "Towards a Semiotic Inquiry into the Television Message." *Working Papers in Cultural Studies.* Centre for Contemporary Cultural Studies, University of Birmingham (Autumn, 1972).

————. *A Theory of Semiotics.* Bloomington, Ind.: Indiana University Press, 1976.

————. *The Role of the Reader.* Bloomington, Ind.: Indiana University Press, 1984.

Ehrmann, Jacques, ed. *Structuralism.* Garden City, N.Y.: Anchor Books, 1970.

Elam, Keir. *The Semiotics of Theatre and Drama.* London: Methuen, 1980.

Eliade, Mircea. *The Sacred and The Profane.* New York: Harcourt, Brace & World, Inc., 1959.

Enzenberger, Hans Magnus. *The Consciousness Industry: On Literature, Politics and the Media.* New York: Seabury, 1974.

Ettema, James S. and D. Charles Whitney, eds. *Audiencemaking: How the Media Create the Audience.* Thousand Oaks, Calif.: SAGE Publications, 1994.

Ewen, Stuart. *Captains of Consciousness.* New York: McGraw-Hill, 1976.

Ewen, Stuart, and Elizabeth Ewen. *Channels of Desire: Mass Images and the Shaping of American Consciousness.* New York: McGraw-Hill, 1982.

Featherstone, Mike, ed. *Postmodernism: Theory, Culture & Society* 5, nos. 2-3. London: Sage Publications (June, 1988).

————. *Consumer Culture & Postmodernism.* London: Sage Publications, 1991.

Ferguson, Russel, Marcha Gever, Trimh T. Minh-ha, and Cornel West, eds. *Out There: Marginalization and Contemporary Cultures.* Cambridge, Mass.: MIT Press, 1990.

Fiske, John, and John Hartley. *Reading Television.* London: Methuen & Co., 1978.

Fiske, John. *Reading the Popular.* London: Routledge, 1989.

————. *Understanding Popular Culture.* London: Routledge, 1989.

Fjellman, Stephen M. *Vinyl Leaves: Walt Disney World and America.* Boulder, Colo.: Westview, 1992.

Franklin, Sarah, Celia Lury, and Jackie Stacey. *Off-Centre: Feminism and Cultural Studies.* London: Routledge, 1992.

Freud, Sigmund. *A General Introduction to Psychoanalysis.* Trans. Joan Riviere. New York: Washington Square Press, 1960.

————. *Jokes and Their Relation to the Unconscious.* Trans. James Strachey. New York: W.W. Norton, 1963.

———. *The Interpretation of Dreams*. Trans. James Strachey. New York: Avon, 1965.

Fry, William F. *Sweet Madness: A Study of Humor*. Palo Alto, Calif: Pacific Books, 1968.

———. "Using Humor to Save Lives." Address given to the Annual Convention of the American Orthopsychiatric Association, Washington D.C., 1979.

Frye, Northrop. *Anatomy of Criticism*. Princeton, N.J.: Princeton University Press, 1957.

Gandelman, Claude. *Reading Pictures, Viewing Texts*. Bloomington: Indiana University Press, 1991.

Garber, Marjorie. *Vested Interests: Cross-Dressing and Cultural Anxiety*. New York: HarperPerennial, 1993.

Garber, Marjorie, Jann Matlock, and Rebecca Walkowtiz, eds. *Media Spectacles*. New York: Routledge, 1993.

Garber, Marjorie, Pratibha Parmar, and John Greyson, eds. *Queer Looks: Perspectives on Lesbian and Gay Film and Video*. New York: Routledge, 1993.

Gitlin, Todd. *Inside Prime Time*. New York: Pantheon, 1985.

———. "Postmodernism Defined, at Last!" In *Utne Reader* (July/August, 1989).

Glaskow University Media Group. *Bad News*. London: Routledge & Kegan Paul, 1976.

———. *More Bad News*. London: Routledge & Kegan Paul, 1980.

Goldstein, Ann, Mary Jane Jacob, Anne Rorimer, and Howard Singerman. *A Forest of Signs: Art in the Crisis of Representation*. Cambridge, Mass.: MIT Press, 1989.

Greenblatt, Stephen J. *Learning to Curse: Essays in Early Modern Culture*. New York: Routledge, 1992.

Gronbeck, Bruce, Thomas J. Farrell, and Paul A. Soukup, eds. *Media, Consciousness and Culture: Explorations of Walter Ong's Thought*. Newbury Park, Calif.: Sage Publications, 1991.

Grossberg, Lawrence. *We Gotta Get Out of This Place: Popular Conservatism and Postmodern Culture*. New York: Routledge, 1992.

Grossberg, Lawrence, Cary Nelson, and Paula Treicher. *Cultural Studies*. New York: Routledge, 1991.

Grotjahn, Martin. *Beyond Laughter: Humor and the Subconscious*. New York: McGraw-Hill, 1966.

Guiraud, Pierre. *Semiology*. London: Routledge & Kegan Paul, 1975.

Gumbrecht, Hansl Ulrich. Trans. Glen Burns. *Making Sense in Life and Literature*. Minneapolis: University of Minnesota Press, 1992.

Habermas, Jurgen. *Communication and the Evolution of Society*. Trans. Thomas McCarthy. Boston: Beacon Press, 1979.

————. Trans. Frederick G. Lawrence. *The Philosophical Discourse of Modernity: Twelve Lectures.* Minneapolis: University of Minnesota Press, 1987.

————. Trans. Shierry Weber Nicholsen. *The New Conservatism: Cultural Criticism and the Historians' Debate.* Minneapolis: University of Minnesota Press, 1989.

Hall, Stuart. *The Hard Road to Renewal.* London: Verso, 1988.

————. *New Times: The Changing Face of Politics in the 1990s.* London: Routledge, 1991.

Hall, Stuart, and Paddy Whannel. *The Popular Arts: A Critical Guide to the Mass Media.* Boston, Mass.: Beacon Press, 1967.

Hall, Stuart, and Tony Jefferson, eds. *Resistance Through Rituals: Youth Subcultures in Postwar Britain.* London: Routledge, 1990. (This was originally published as *Working Papers in Cultural Studies 7/8,* from the Centre for Contemporary Cultural Studies at the University of Birmingham. For an in-depth study of Stuart Hall's work, see *Journal of Communication Inquiry* [Summer, 1986], which is devoted to him.)

Hartley, John. *The Politics of Pictures: The Creation of the Public in the Age of Popular Media.* London: Routledge, 1992.

————. *Tele-ology: Studies in Television.* London: Routledge, 1992.

Haug, W. F. *Critique of Commodity Aesthetics: Appearance, Sexuality and Advertising in Capitalist Society.* Trans. Robert Bock. Minneapolis: University of Minnesota Press, 1971.

————. *Commodity Aesthetics, Ideology & Culture.* New York: International General, 1987.

Hoggart, Richard. *The Uses of Literacy.* New Brunswick, N.J.: Transaction Publishers, 1992.

Holland, Norman. *Five Readers Reading.* New Haven, Conn.: Yale University Press, 1975.

Hoover, Stewart M. *Mass Media Religion: The Social Sources of the Electronic Church.* Newbury Park, Calif.: Sage Publications, 1988.

Huizinga, Johan. *The Waning of the Middle Ages.* Garden City, N.Y.: Anchor Books.

Hutcheon, Linda. *The Politics of Postmodernism.* London: Routledge, 1989.

Jacobs, Norman, ed. *Mass Media in Modern Society.* New Brunswick, N.J.: Transaction Publishers, 1992.

Jakobson, Roman. *Verbal Art, Verbal Sign, Verbal Time.* Krystyna Pomorska, and Stephen Rudy, eds. Minneapolis: University of Minnesota Press, 1985.

Jally, Sut, and Justin Lewis. *Enlightened Racism: The Cosby Show, Audiences and the Myth of the American Dream.* Boulder, Colo.: Westview, 1992.

Jameson, Frederic. *Marxism and Form: Twentieth Century Dialectical Theories of Literature.* Princeton, N.J.: Princeton University Press, 1971.

———. *The Political Unconscious*. Ithaca, N.Y.: Cornell University Press, 1981.

———. *The Geopolitical Aesthetic: Cinema and Space in the World System*. Bloomington: Indiana University Press, 1992.

———. *Signatures of the Visible*. New York: Routledge, 1992.

Jauss, Hans Robert. *Aesthetic Experience and Literary Hermeneutics*. Trans. Michael Shaw. Minneapolis: University of Minnesota Press, 1982.

———. *Toward an Aesthetic of Reception*. Trans. Timothy Bahti. Minneapolis: University of Minnesota Press, 1982.

Jensen, Joli. *Redeeming Modernity: Contradictions in Media Criticism*. Newbury Park, Calif.: Sage Publications, 1990.

Jones, Ernest. *Hamlet and Oedipus*. New York: Norton, 1949.

Jones, Steve. *Rock Formation: Music, Technology and Mass Communication*. Thousand Oaks, Calif.: Sage Publications, 1992.

Jones, Steven G., ed. *Cybersociety: Computer-Mediated Communication and Community*. Thousand Oaks, Calif.: Sage Publications, 1994.

Jowett, Garth, and James M. Linton. *Movies as Mass Communication*. Newbury Park: Sage Publications, 1989.

Jowett, Garth S., and Victoria O'Donnell. *Propaganda and Persuasion*, 2nd. ed. Thousand Oaks, Calif.: Sage Publications, 1992.

Jung, Carl G., ed. *Man and His Symbols*. New York: Dell, 1968.

Kaplan, E. Ann. *Motherhood and Representation*. London: Routledge, 1982.

Kellner, Douglas. *The Persian Gulf TV War*. Boulder, Colo.: Westview, 1992.

Korzenny, Felix, and Stella Ting-Toomey, eds. *Mass Media Effects Across Cultures*. Newbury Park, Calif.: Sage Publications, 1992.

Kottak, Conrad Phillip. *Prime-Time Society: An Anthropological Analysis of Television and Culture*. Belmont, Calif.: Wadsworth, 1990.

Lacan, Jacques. *Ecrits: A Selection*. Trans. Alan Sheridan. New York: Norton, 1966.

Larsen, Neil. *Modernism and Hegemony: A Materialist Critique of Aesthetic Agencies*. Minneapolis: University of Minnesota Press, 1989.

Laurentis, Teresa de. *Alice Doesn't: Feminism, Semiotics, Cinema*. Bloomington: Indiana University Press, 1984.

———. *Technologies of Gender: Essays on Theory, Film and Fiction*. Bloomington: Indiana University Press, 1987.

Lavers, Annette. *Roland Barthes: Structuralism and After*. Cambridge, Mass.: Harvard University Press, 1982.

Le Bon, Gustav. *The Crowd: A Study of the Popular Mind*. New York: The Viking Press, 1960. (Originally published in 1895.)

Lefebvre, Haari. *Everyday Life in the Modern World*. Trans. Sacha Rabinovitch. New Brunswick, N.J.: Transaction Publishers, 1984.

Lévi-Strauss, Claude. *Structural Anthropology*. Garden City, N.Y.: Doubleday, 1967.

Levy, Mark R., and Michael Gurevitch, eds. *Defining Media Studies: Reflections on the Future of the Field*. New York: Oxford University Press, 1994.

Lipsitz, George. *Time Passages: Collective Memory and American Popular Culture*. Minneapolis: University of Minnesota Press, 1989.

Lotman, Yuri M. *Semiotics of Cinema*. Ann Arbor: Michigan Slavic Contributions, 1976.

———. *The Structure of the Artistic Text*. Ann Arbor: Michigan Slavic Contributions, 1977.

———. *Universe of the Mind: A Semiotic Theory of Culture*. Bloomington: Indiana University Press, 1991.

Lull, James. *Popular Music and Communication*. Thousand Oaks, Calif.: Sage Publications, 1991.

Lyotard, Jean-Francois. *The Postmodern Condition: A Report on Knowledge*. Minneapolis: University of Minnesota Press, 1984.

MacCabe, Colin. *Tracking the Signifier: Theoretical Essays on Film, Linguistics, and Literature*. Minneapolis: University of Minnesota Press, 1985.

MacCannell, Dean. *The Tourist: A New Theory of the Leisure Classy*. New York: Schocken Books, 1976.

MacCannell, Dean, and Juliet Flower MacCannell. *The Time of the Sign: A Semiotic Interpretation of Modern Culture*. Bloomington: Indiana University Press, 1982.

MacDonald, J. Fred. *One Nation Under Television*. Chicago: Nelson-Hall, 1994.

Mandel, Ernest. *Delightful Murder: A Social History of the Crime Story*. Minneapolis: University of Minnesota Press, 1985.

Martin-Barbero, Jesus. *Communication, Culture, and Hegemony: From the Media to Mediations*. Thousand Oaks, Calif.: Sage Publications, 1993.

Massing, Herta Herzog. "Decoding *Dallas*." *Society* (November/December 1986).

Massumi, Brian. *A User's Guide to Capitalism and Schizophrenia: Deviations from Deleuze and Guattari*. Cambridge, Mass.: MIT Press, 1992.

Mattelart, Armand and Michele Mattelart. *Rethinking Media Theory*. Trans. James A. Cohen, and Marina Urquidi. Minneapolis: University of Minnesota Press, 1992.

McCarthy, Thomas. *Ideals and Illusions: On Reconstruction and Deconstruction in Contemporary Critical Theory*. Cambridge, Mass.: MIT Press, 1991.

McClue, Greg. *Dark Knights: The New Comics in Context*. Boulder, Colo.: Westview, 1993.

McLuhan, Marshall. *Understanding Media: The Extensions of Man*. New York: McGraw-Hill, 1965.

———. *Culture is Our Business*. New York: McGraw-Hill, 1970.

McLuhan, Marshall, and Quentin Fiore. *The Medium is the Massage*. New York: Bantam Books, 1967.

McQuail, Denis. *Media Performance: Mass Communication and the Public Interest*. Thousand Oaks, Calif.: Sage Publications, 1992.

———. *Mass Communication Theory: An Introduction*. Thousand Oaks, Calif.: Sage Publications, 1994.

Mellencamp, Patricia. *Indiscretions: Avant-Garde Film, Video and Feminism*. Bloomington: Indiana University Press, 1990.

———. *Logics of Television: Essays in Cultural Criticism*. Bloomington: Indiana University Press, 1990.

Metz, Christian. *The Imaginary Signifier: Psychoanalysis and the Cinema*. Trans. Celia Britton, et al. Bloomington: Indiana University Press, 1982.

Mindess, Harvey. *Laughter and Liberation*. Los Angeles: Nash Publishing, 1971.

Modleski, Tania. *Loving with a Vengeance: Mass-Produced Fantasies for Women*. New York: Routledge, 1984.

———, ed. *Studies in Entertainment: Critical Approaches to Mass Culture*. Bloomington: Indiana University Press, 1986.

———. *The Women Who Knew Too Much: Hitchcock and Feminist Theory*. New York: Routledge, 1988.

Morley, David. *Family Television: Cultural Power and Domestic Leisure*. London: Routledge, 1988.

———. *Television Audiences and Cultural Studies*. London: Routledge, 1993.

Mulvey, Laura. *Visual and Other Pleasures*. Bloomington: Indiana University Press, 1989.

Naremore, James, and Patrick Brantlinger, eds. *Modernity and Mass Culture*. Bloomington: Indiana University Press, 1991.

Nash, Christopher, ed. *Narrative in Culture*. London: Routledge, 1990.

Navarro, Desiderio, ed. "Postmodernism: Center and Periphery." *The South Atlantic Quarterly*. Durham, N.C.: Duke University Press (Summer, 1993).

Newman, Oscar. *Defensible Space*. New York: Collier Books, 1973.

Nichols, Bill. *Ideology and the Image: Social Representation in the Cinema and Other Media*. Bloomington: Indiana University Press, 1981.

———. *Representing Reality: Issues and Concepts in Documentary*. Bloomington: Indiana University Press, 1992.

Penley, Constance. *The Future of An Illusion: Film, Feminism and Psychoanalysis*. Minneapolis: University of Minnesota Press, 1989.

Phelan, James, ed. *Reading Narrative: Form, Ethics, Ideology*. Columbus: Ohio State University Press, 1989.

Piddington, Ralph. *The Psychology of Laughter*. New York: Gamut Press, 1963.

Powell, Chris, and George E. C. Paton, eds. *Humour in Society: Resistance and Control*. New York: St. Martin's Press, 1988.

Prindle, David. F. *Risky Business: The Political Economy of Hollywood*. Boulder, Colo.: Westview, 1993.

Propp, Vladimir. *Morphology of the Folk Tale*, 2nd. ed. Austin: University of Texas Press, 1973.

———. *Theory and History of Folklore*. Trans. Ariadna Y. Martin, and Richard P. Martin. Minneapolis: University of Minnesota Press, 1984.

Ramet, Sabrina Petra, ed. *Rocking the State: Rock Music and Politics in Eastern Europe and the Soviet Union*. Boulder, Colo.: Westview, 1993.

Real, Michael R. *Supermedia: A Cultural Studies Approach*. Newbury Park, Calif.: Sage Publications, 1989.

Reinelt, Janelle G., and Joseph R. Roach, eds. *Critical Theory and Performance*. Ann Arbor: University of Michigan Press, 1993.

Richter, Mischa, and Harald Bakken. *The Cartoonist's Muse: A Guide to Generating and Developing Creative Ideas*. Chicago: Contemporary Books, 1992.

Rieff, Philip, ed. *Freud: Character and Culture*. New York: Collier Books, 1963.

Rosenberg, Bernard, and David Manning White. *Mass Culture: The Popular Arts in America*. New York: The Free Press, 1957.

Rouch, Irmengard, and Gerald F. Carr, eds. *The Semiotic Bridge: Trends from California*. Berlin: Mouton de Gruyter, 1989.

Ryan, Michael, and Douglas Kellner. *Camera Politica: The Politics and Ideology of Contemporary Hollywood Film*. Bloomington: Indiana University Press, 1988.

Sabin, Roger. *Adult Comics: An Introduction*. London: Routledge, 1993.

Said, Edward. *The World, the Text, and the Critic*. Cambridge, Mass.: Harvard University Press, 1983.

Saint-Martin, Fernande. *Semiotics of Visual Language*. Bloomington: Indiana University Press, 1990.

Saussure, Ferdinand de. *Course in General Linguistics*. Trans. Wade Baskin. New York: McGraw-Hill, 1966.

Schechner, Richard. *The Future of Ritual: Writings on Culture and Performance*. London: Routledge, 1993.

Schneider, Cynthia, and Brian Wallis, eds. *Global Television*. Cambridge, Mass.: MIT Press, 1989.

Schostak, John. *Dirty Marks: The Education of Self, Media and Popular Culture*. Boulder, Colo.: Westview, 1993.

Schwichtenberg, Cathy, ed. *The Madonna Collection*. Boulder, Colo.: Westview, 1992.

Sebeok, Thomas, ed. *A Perfusion of Signs*. Bloomington: Indiana University Press, 1977.

————, ed. *Sight, Sound and Sense*. Bloomington: Indiana University Press, 1978.

Seldes, Gilbert. *The Seven Lively Arts*. New York: Sagamore Press, 1924.

————. *The Public Arts*. New York: Simon and Schuster, 1956.

Shukman, Ann. *Literature and Semiotics: A Study of the Writings of Yuri M. Lotman*. Amsterdam: North-Holland Publishing, 1977.

Silverman, Kaja. *The Subject of Semiotics*. New York: Oxford University Press, 1983.

Smith, Gary, ed. *On Walter Benjamin: Critical Essays and Recollections*. Cambridge, Mass.: MIT Press, 1988.

Smith, Paul. *Discerning the Subject*. Minneapolis: University of Minnesota Press, 1988.

Spivak, Gayatri Chakravorty. *Outside in the Teaching Machine*. New York: Routledge, 1993.

Staake, Bob. *The Complete Book of Caricature*. Cincinnati, Ohio: North Light Books, 1991.

Steidman, Steven. *Romantic Longings: Love in America 1830-1980*. New York: Routledge, 1993.

Stephenson, William. *The Play Theory of Mass Communication*. New Brunswick, N.J.: Transaction Publishers, 1988.

Szondi, Peter. *On Textual Understanding*. Trans. Harvey Mendelsohn. Minneapolis: University of Minnesota Press, 1986.

Todorov, Tzvetan. *The Fantastic: A Structural Approach to a Literary Genre*. Trans. Richard Howard. Ithaca, N.Y.: Cornell University Press, 1975.

————. *Introduction to Poetics*. Trans. Richard Howard. Minneapolis: University of Minnesota Press, 1981.

————. *Mikhail Bakhtin: The Dialogical Principle*. Minneapolis: University of Minnesota Press, 1984.

Traube, Elizabeth G. *Dreaming Identities: Class, Gender, and Generation in the 1980s Hollywood Movies*. Boulder, Colo.: Westview, *1982*.

Turner, Bryan S. *Theories of Modernity and Postmodernity*. London: Sage Publications, 1990.

Villela-Minnerly, Lucia, and Richard Morkin. "Star Wars as Myth: A Fourth Hope." *Psychoanalytic Review* 74, 3 (Fall, 1987.)

Volosinov, V.N. *Freudianism: A Critical Sketch*. Trans. I. R. Titunik. Bloomington: Indiana University Press, 1987.

Weibel, Kathryn. *Mirror Mirror: Images of Women Reflected in Popular Culture*. Garden City, N.Y.: Anchor Books, 1977.

Wernick, Andrew. *Promotional Culture: Advertising, Ideology and Symbolic Expression*. London: Sage Publications, 1991.

Willemen, Paul. *Looks and Frictions: Essays in Cultural Studies and Film Theory*. Bloomington: Indiana University Press, 1993.

Williams, Raymond. *Culture and Society: 1780–1950*. New York: Columbia University Press, 1958.

———. *Keywords*. New York: Oxford University Press, 1976.

———. *Marxism and Literature*. New York: Oxford University Press, 1977.

Williams, Rosalind. *Notes on the Underground: An Essay on Technology, Society and the Imagination*. Cambridge, Mass.: MIT Press, 1990.

Williamson, Judith. *Decoding Advertisements: Ideology and Meaning in Advertising*. London: Marion Boyars, 1978.

Willis, Paul. *Common Culture: Symbolic Work at Play in the Everyday Cultures of the Young*. Boulder, Colo.: Westview, 1990.

Winick, Charles. *Desexualization in American Life: The New People*. New Brunswick, N.J.: Transaction Publishers, 1994.

Wollen, Peter. *Signs and Meaning in the Cinema*. Bloomington: Indiana University Press, 1972.

———. *Raiding the Icebox: Reflections on Twentieth-Century Culture*. Bloomington: Indiana University Press, 1993.

Wright, Will. *Sixguns and Society: A Structural Study of the Western*. Berkeley, Calif.: University of California Press, 1975.

Zizek, Slavoi. *Looking Awry: An Introduction to Jacques Lacan through Popular Culture*. Cambridge, Mass.: MIT Press, 1991.

Name Index

Subject Index